THE
FOOTBALL
ENCYCLOPEDIA

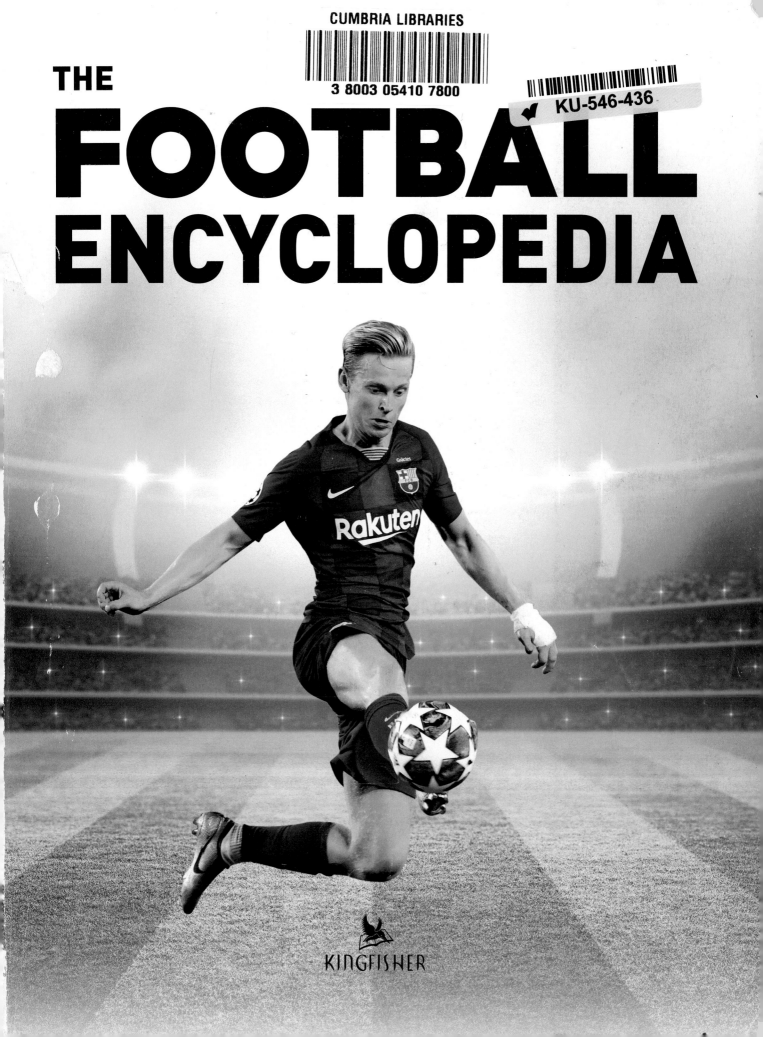

KINGFISHER

KINGFISHER

First published in 2022 by Kingfisher
An imprint of Macmillan Children's Books
The Smithson, 6 Briset Street, London, EC1M 5NR
Associated companies throughout the world
www.panmacmillan.com

Copyright © Macmillan Publishers International Ltd 2022

Author: Clive Gifford
Consultants: Simon Mugford and Anthony Hobbs
Illustrations: Peter Liddiard, Sudden Impact Media
Design: Darren Jordan, RockJaw Creative
Cover design: Jake Da'Costa

ISBN 978-0-7534-4784-0

9 8 7 6 5 4 3 2 1
1TR/0622/WKT/RV/128MA

Printed in China

A CIP catalogue record for this book is available from
the British Library.

EU representative: 1st Floor, The Liffey Trust Centre,
117-126 Sheriff Street Upper, Dublin 1 D01 YC43

FSC
www.fsc.org

MIX
Paper from
responsible sources
FSC® C116313

CONTENTS

THE BEAUTIFUL GAME

Football's dynamic action, breathtaking skills and heartstopping drama are all crammed into 90 minutes of play. It is sport as drama, making heroes and villains out of its players, managers and officials. Clubs and national teams inspire passion and loyalty in fans, and major competitions are watched avidly worldwide. From humble beginnings in the 19th century, football has grown to become a major industry that provides great moments of excitement, celebration and despair. No other sport has quite the same power to unite and divide.

A CHANGING SPORT

As football has grown, dozens of changes have occurred. Some have involved the laws of the game – from the two-handed throw-in, introduced in 1883, to the backpass law for goalkeepers that was adopted 99 years later. Other changes – such as the arrival of promotion and relegation up and down a league – have shaped the competitions of which matches are a part.

Football's adaptability has been one of its strengths. Another great part of its appeal is that people of all ages and skill levels can play the game. At its most basic, football is a simple sport that can be enjoyed without expensive equipment and played almost anywhere – from a sandy beach to an office or hallway with a crumpled ball of paper.

The simplicity of football is a big selling point with new fans. The finer details of rules and tactics may pass them by at first, but the basics of the game and the skills of star players – their pace, ball control, passing, shooting and tackling – can be admired by almost anyone.

◀ Wendie Renard of France and Brazil's Cristiane at the 2019 FIFA Women's World Cup. Over 993 million people watched some of the tournament on TV, a record for the women's game.

◥ France's Kylian Mbappé battles for the ball with Bernardo Silva of Portugal at EURO 2020. Incredibly, Mbappé won the FIFA World Cup, the UEFA Nations League, four Ligue 1 titles and three Coupes de France before the age of 23.

▲ Football is a sport that generates intensely strong bonds between supporters and their teams. This fan, dressed in the national colours of Mali, celebrates during the 2021 African Nations Championship semi-final against Guinea.

▼ Football can be played practically anywhere, in almost any conditions. These Brazilian schoolchildren are enjoying a casual game just days before their country hosted the 2014 World Cup.

THE NUMBERS GAME

In its full version, football is a game in which two teams of 11 people play two halves of 45 minutes. Today, more than 50 million footballers around the world play in official competitions. Many millions more play the game on a regular basis – a survey by world football's governing body, the *Fédération Internationale de Football Association* (FIFA), estimates that figure to be more than 265 million. Top leagues, such as Serie A in Italy, Spain's La Liga and Germany's Bundesliga, attract millions of viewers. In 2021, English Premier League games or highlights were broadcast to more than 190 countries. The final of the 2018 FIFA World Cup between France and Croatia, held in Russia, was watched by a staggering 1.12 billion people – a seventh of the entire human population

FOOTBALL'S ORIGINS

An alehouse in Victorian England seems an unlikely place to launch a sport that would become the world's biggest and most popular. Yet that is precisely what occurred in 1863 at the Freemason's Tavern in London, England. There, representatives of 12 clubs met to form the Football Association (FA) and draw up a single set of rules for the game.

HISTORY MYSTERY

No one knows where or when the first ever forerunner of football was played. Many nations claim early ball games as their own, from the ancient Greeks with *episkyros* to the Roman game of *harpastum*.

The ancient Chinese game of *tsu chu* (or *cuju*) was played more than 2,000 years ago and was even used as military training during the Ch'in dynasty (255-206 BCE). Players tried to propel a ball made of animal skin stuffed with hair through bamboo posts or a circular hole in netting. Equally ancient is the mysterious Mesoamerican ball game played with a solid rubber ball in a stone court by the ancient peoples of Central America over 2,500 years ago.

In medieval Europe, games of mob football were so unruly and violent that the leaders of several countries, including Charles V in France and Oliver Cromwell in England, attempted to ban the sport. In contrast to mob football, the Italian game of *calcio* was first played in the 16th century by aristocrats and religious leaders, including three popes. Each team was made up of 27 players, and goals were scored by kicking or throwing the ball over a certain spot on the edge of the field.

▲ Illustrations from the first ever international match, in 1872. Despite England fielding eight forwards and Scotland six, the game ended in a 0-0 draw.

◀ The Japanese game of *kemari* is at least 1,500 years old. Players had to stop the ball from touching the ground by juggling and passing it with their feet.

GETTING ORGANIZED

By the late 18th and early 19th centuries, a kicking-and-rushing ball game was played in public schools and universities across Britain, but rules varied from place to place. In 1848, players at Cambridge University drew up football's first set of rules. This attempt to bring order into the game had only limited success, and so in 1863 representatives of 12 clubs (including the Crusaders, No Names of Kilburn and Crystal Palace) met in London. They formed the FA, developed the laws of the game and, eight years later, set up the world's oldest surviving cup competition, the FA Cup. The first ever international, between England and Scotland, was played in 1872, and in 1888 the first football league was founded in England.

THE WOMEN'S GAME

Women's football struggled from the beginning against male prejudice that it was 'unladylike' for females to play the game. Interest in women's football reached its first peak after World War I thanks to the exploits of the Dick, Kerr Ladies side (see page 79). The women's game was then stifled for almost half a century following the introduction of a ban on women playing at the grounds of FA member clubs. Between 1969 and 1972, bans were lifted in a number of countries and women's football slowly began to expand. The first European Championships for women were held in 1984, while an Olympic competition was launched in 1996. More than 60 nations entered the qualifying competition for the first Women's World Cup in 1991.

(see page 79)

WHAT'S IN A NAME?

Around the world, many teams have taken their names from European clubs. Here are just a few:

Arsenal Lesotho
Lesotho Cup winners 1989, 1991, 1998

Liverpool
Uruguay, Supercopa Uruguaya winners 2020

Barcelona
Ecuador, league champions '95, '97, 2012, 2016

Benfica de Macao
Macao, league champions 2018

Juventus
Belize, league champions 1999, 2005

Berekum Chelsea
Ghana, league champions 2011

◀ US striker Alex Morgan leaps over Dutch keeper Sari van Veenendaal during the Tokyo 2020 Olympic quarter-final. The USA won on penalties, on their way to a bronze medal.

FOOTBALL EXPORTS

Football spread rapidly around the globe in the late 19th century. The game was exported first by British players and then by converts from other European nations, particularly to their colonies. Football was introduced to Russia in 1887 by two English mill owners, the Charnock brothers, while resident Englishmen founded Italy's oldest league club, Genoa, six years later.

In 1885, Canada defeated the USA 1-0 in the first international match to be played in the Americas. In Argentina, British and Italian residents encouraged the formation of South America's first club, Buenos Aires, in 1865. The first league in South America was set up 28 years later.

In 1904, FIFA was founded in Paris, with seven members: Belgium, Denmark, France, Holland, Spain (represented by Madrid FC), Sweden and Switzerland. Over time, FIFA became the dominant organization in world football. In 1930, it had 45 member nations; in 1960, that figure stood at 95. In 2016, FIFA welcomed Gibraltar and Kosovo as its 210th and 211th members.

◀ W. R. Moon of Corinthians, an English amateur team, in his kit. Corinthians helped to spread football by touring the world. Their 1910 trip to South America inspired the formation of the famous Brazilian side Corinthians Paulista.

THEN AND NOW

Going back in time 150 years, a modern football fan would be surprised to find no referees, corners or pitch markings at a game. Players wore coats and even top hats; they handled the ball in the air and wrestled with each other on the ground. Over time, football has evolved into the game that we know today.

▼ The referee's whistle was first blown at a football match in 1878. British firm Acme Whistles, astonishingly, has sold over 200 million Acme Thunderer whistles, which have been heard at World Cups and in top leagues around the globe.

PITCHING UP

Unlike in most sports, the pitch in football can vary in size. Most are around 100m long and 65–70m wide. Back in the 1860s, a pitch could be as long as 180m. The first markings arrived in 1891, including a centre circle and a line running the width of the pitch, 10.98m in front of the goal line. A penalty could be taken from any point along that line. It was another 11 years before the pitch markings we know today were introduced. Since then, only two additions have been made – the penalty arc at the front of the penalty area (in 1937) and the corner quadrants (in 1938).

GOALS

To score a goal, a team has to propel the whole of the ball over the goal line, between two posts that are set 7.32m apart. On many occasions, controversy has raged over whether the ball crossed the line – from the 1966 World Cup final between England and West Germany to the DFB-Pokal Cup final in 2014 between Borussia Dortmund and Bayern Munich.

Early goals consisted of just two posts. Following arguments over the height of a shot, a white tape was fitted to the posts, 2.44m above the ground. Wooden crossbars began to replace tape in the 1870s. Goal nets came later, invented by an engineer from Liverpool, John Alexander Brodie. They were first given a trial in January 1891, when Everton's Fred Geary became the first footballer to put the ball in the back of the net. Incidentally, that game was refereed by Sam Widdowson, who had invented shinpads 17 years earlier.

THE MEN AND WOMEN IN BLACK

Referees did not feature in early games of football because the sport's founders believed that gentlemen would never intentionally foul or cheat. Instead, each side had an umpire to whom they could appeal. By 1891, games were controlled by a referee in order to cut down on controversial decisions and long stoppages for debate, and the two umpires became linesmen. (Since 1996, linesmen have been known as assistants.) Despite often being described as the 'men in black', referees have played in all sorts of colours. Early referees tried to keep up with play dressed in the popular fashions of the time – trousers, a blazer and even a bow tie.

▲ Referee Anna-Marie Keighley tests the goal line technology before a 2019 Women's World Cup match. Fourteen 3D cameras track the ball to determine whether it crosses the goal line or not.

▶ Hugo Guillamón of Valencia receives the first red card of the 2021-22 La Liga season after just three minutes of a match against Getafe. Red and yellow cards were first used at the 1970 World Cup.

BOOTS AND BALLS

No game is complete without a football, up to 60 million of which are sold every year. Early balls were made from the inflated bladder of a pig or sheep, covered in a shell of stitched pieces of brown leather held in place by laces. Brazilian club Santos pioneered the use of a more visible white ball, while today's balls – made from leather and synthetic materials – are often bright and colourful. A referee has to check that the match ball and spares are the correct size, weight and air pressure before a game begins.

Early football boots were heavy, above-ankle work boots often with metal toecaps and metal or leather studs nailed into the sole. Modern boots are lightweight and flexible, enabling players to feel the ball on their foot. Their soles come in a variety of customizable studs, blades or dimples which players select depending on the condition of the pitch.

▲ Arsenal's Alex James tries out a muscle-enhancing machine in the 1930s. Today's players undergo carefully planned exercise regimes and eat a diet that is scientifically monitored by their clubs.

▼ A vintage ball and pair of boots at Barcelona's Camp Nou museum.

▲ Brazilian players show off their multi-coloured boots in training ahead of the 2018 World Cup.

KITTED OUT

Today's lightweight football kits are the result of years of research and development. During the first ever international fixture, in 1872, the Scotland and England teams wore knickerbockers (long trousers), long shirts and bobble hats or caps. Gradually, football kit developed to give players more freedom of movement, although shorts remained almost knee length until the 1960s. Numbers appeared on shirts regularly for the first time in the 1930s, but player names did not arrive until the late 1980s. In 1924, the English Football Association (FA) began to insist that teams have a second strip (known as an away strip) that could be worn in the event of a colour clash. Today, kit manufacture is a highly profitable business. Teams often have two or even three away strips; they update their kit design every season and sell many thousands of replica shirts to fans.

FACTFILE
The Belgian referee at the 1930 World Cup final, Jean Langenus, wore a dinner jacket, golfing plus-four trousers and a red striped tie.

◀ High-profile transfers can send fans into a shirt-buying frenzy. When Lionel Messi's move to Paris Saint-Germain was confirmed in August 2021, the club website sold out of 150,000 'Messi 30' shirts within 30 minutes.

THE GLOBAL GAME

FIFA is in control of world football, while the sport is organized regionally by six continental confederations. South America and Europe have been the traditional powerhouses, but the men's and women's game has boomed globally and talented players now emerge from all over the world.

BALANCE OF POWER

Great advances have been made by the federations and national teams of regions outside Europe and South America. More and more national football teams have become truly competitive on the world stage, thanks to the emergence of dozens of high-quality footballers in Africa, Asia, Oceania and North and Central America. Australia's 2018 World Cup appearance was their fourth in a row. Before 2006, they had last qualified in 1974. New Zealand was the only team at the 2010 World Cup not to lose a game. African nations have featured in three of the last six Olympic men's football finals, winning two golds and one silver. In December 2021, the continent had 11 men's teams ranked in FIFA's top 60. There have also been strong showings by Japan, Costa Rica and the USA at recent international tournaments. As a reflection of this, African and Asian nations have been chosen to host many tournaments, including the World Cups of 2002 (South Korea and Japan), 2010 (South Africa), 2022 (Qatar) and the Women's World Cup of 2007 (China). Additionally, Africa and Asia now enjoy more automatic places at the World Cup than ever before.

▲ Steve Mokone was the first black South African to play professionally in Europe. From the 1950s, he starred for Coventry City, Dutch side Heracles, Spain's Valencia, Marseille in France and Italy's Torino. Mokone later played in Australia and Canada.

CONCACAF
CONFEDERATION OF NORTH, CENTRAL AMERICAN AND CARIBBEAN ASSOCIATION FOOTBALL

FOUNDED: 1961 · MEMBERS: 41

Mexico and the USA – traditionally the strongest CONCACAF nations – have hosted three World Cups, while smaller nations such as Costa Rica have reached the tournament. CONCACAF teams have often been invited to play in South America's Copa América competition, and the federation actually includes two South American nations, Guyana and Suriname.

▶ The Copa América is South America's top international tournament. In 2021, Argentina beat Brazil to win their 15th title.

CONMEBOL
CONFEDERACIÓN SUDAMERICANA DE FÚTBOL

FOUNDED: 1916 · MEMBERS: 10

CONMEBOL teams have won nine men's World Cup finals, while the Brazilian women's national team were World Cup runners-up in 2007. Argentina won the 2004 and 2008 Olympic men's finals and are rarely out of the top five of FIFA's world rankings. Domestic leagues, however, are suffering with clubs in debt and most of the continent's top players heading for Europe and elsewhere to play.

OFC
OCEANIA FOOTBALL CONFEDERATION

FOUNDED: 1966 · MEMBERS: 11

Football has struggled for support in Oceania. In the larger countries, it has to compete with more popular sports, while smaller nations suffer from a lack of finance, facilities and players. Australia, the OFC's biggest and most successful nation, became frustrated by the lack of an automatic World Cup place for the confederation. In January 2006 it left the OFC to join the Asian Football Confederation.

FACTFILE
Australia was the first OFC side to reach a World Cup, in 1974.

UEFA
UNION OF EUROPEAN FOOTBALL ASSOCIATIONS

FOUNDED: 1954 · MEMBERS: 55

As the most powerful confederation, UEFA was awarded 13 of the 32 places at the 2022 World Cup. It runs the two largest competitions after the World Cup – the UEFA European Championships and the UEFA Champions League. Thousands of foreign footballers play in Europe, but UEFA clubs may soon be forced to include a minimum number of home-grown players in their squads.

► Chelsea celebrate their 2021 UEFA Champions League triumph over Premier League rivals Manchester City.

HAVE BOOTS, WILL TRAVEL

Professional footballers travel the world. Thousands of South American and African footballers, in particular, move continents, seeking out clubs that will employ them. The richest clubs are mostly found in Europe, partly due to the huge sums some receive from television rights, advertising and prize money for appearing in competitions such as the UEFA Champions League. This revenue enables European clubs to pluck the very best talents from around the globe, even if it leaves another country's league bereft of its best players. None of the 23-man Algerian squad that won the 2019 African Cup of Nations, for example, played for Algerian clubs. Other nations also recruit large numbers of foreign footballers. Each MLS club in the US is allowed up to eight international players, while the Chinese Super League has twice broken the £50-million barrier to bring Brazilian players into its competition (Hulk and Oscar).

AFC
ASIAN FOOTBALL CONFEDERATION

FOUNDED: 1954 · MEMBERS: 47

Asian football is booming. The highly successful Asian Champions League was set up in 2002, and national leagues are now well supported. Many foreign footballers play in Asia – 63 Brazilians played in Japan's J.League in 2020-21, for example. Australia joined the AFC in 2006, but all eyes are now turning to China, which has the world's largest pool of potential players and supporters.

► Kawasaki Frontale's Leandro Damião celebrates with the J1 League trophy in 2021, his club's fourth league title.

CAF
CONFÉDÉRATION AFRICAINE DE FOOTBALL

FOUNDED: 1957 · MEMBERS: 54

Africa was not awarded an automatic World Cup place until 1970, but the CAF sent six teams to the 2010 World Cup including the host nation, South Africa. While national sides continue to improve, the domestic game struggles because of a lack of finance and the movement of its best players out of Africa. In 2021, for example, more than 500 African footballers were playing in 11 of the top leagues in Europe.

Barcelona's Alexia Putellas challenges defender Ivana Sanz of Real Madrid during the UEFA Women's Champions League quarter-final in March 2022 that smashed the world attendance record for a women's club match. Barça's historic 5-2 win gave them an 8-3 victory on aggregate.

SNAPSHOT
A RECORD CROWD

On 17 March 2019, a 99-year-old record was smashed. A world-beating 60,739 fans packed into the Wanda Metropolitano stadium, home of Atlético Madrid, to watch a women's club match between Atlético and Barcelona. The previous women's record attendance of 53,000 occurred on Boxing Day 1920, when women's team Dick, Kerr Ladies (see page 79) beat St Helens 4-0 at Goodison Park, the home of Everton.

The two teams were competing in the Primera División de la Liga de Fútbol Femenino – Spain's top women's football league, founded in 1988. Barcelona won this historic encounter 2-0, but it would be Atlético's fans that enjoyed their third league title in a row at the end of the season.

Just over three years later, an even larger crowd of 91,553 fans poured into the Camp Nou stadium to watch the Barcelona women's side come from 2-1 down to secure a glorious 5-2 victory over fierce rivals Real Madrid. World Footballer of the Year Alexia Putellas was amongst Barça's scorers in the first game that the women's team had played at the Camp Nou in front of fans. The match shattered a ten-year-old UEFA Women's Champions League attendance record – set in the 2012 final between Lyon and Frankfurt – by more than 40,000.

BASIC SKILLS

In the words of former Liverpool manager Bill Shankly, 'Football is a simple game based on the giving and taking of passes, on controlling the ball and on making yourself available to receive a pass.' Shankly's words highlight the most fundamental skills in football.

BALL CONTROL

The world's top players, such as Cristiano Ronaldo and Lionel Messi, appear to control the ball effortlessly. Their easy command and movement of the ball masks thousands of hours of practice and training, often from a very early age. As children, many great footballers spent long hours playing games with a tennis ball, crumpled ball of paper or a battered piece of fruit.

Players can control the ball with any part of their body except for their hands and arms. Cushioning is a technique in which a player uses a part of the body to slow down a moving ball and then bring it under control with his or her feet. High balls can be cushioned using the chest, thigh or a gentle header to kill the ball's speed and bring it down. For a low, incoming ball, the foot is preferred – either the inside of the boot or its instep (where the laces are). A ball that is rolling across the pitch can be stopped with the sole of the foot – a technique known as trapping.

◀ Achraf Hakimi uses the side of his foot to push the ball forwards for Paris Saint-Germain in a 2021 Ligue 1 match.

◀ Liverpool right-back Trent Alexander-Arnold leans back to bring the ball under control with a chest cushion.

▼ An instep cushion is used to control a ball arriving front-on. Here, the player meets the ball with the laces of his boot and instantly pulls back his foot, killing the pace of the ball.

SHIELDING AND OBSTRUCTION

When footballers have the ball at their feet, they are said to be in possession and have a number of options. These include: running with the ball; dribbling with the ball close to the feet; passing; shooting; and shielding the ball. Shielding or screening involves a player putting his or her body between the ball and an opponent to prevent the other player from gaining possession. This gives the shielding player crucial time to decide on the next move, which may be a pass backwards to a team-mate or a sharp turn and an attempt to play the ball round the opponent. Shielding players have to be careful not to hold, push or back into the other player. They must also keep the ball close by and under control, otherwise the referee may award an indirect free kick for obstruction (in which a player unfairly blocks an opponent's path to the ball). An obstruction usually occurs when a player steps into the path of an opponent when the ball is several metres away.

▲ Venezuela's Salomón Rondón shields the ball from Uruguayan defender Diego Godin during a Copa América game.

◀ Crystal Dunn (left) of the USA challenges Australia's Hayley Raso for the ball during the Olympic bronze-medal match in 2021.

PASS MASTERS

Passes can be made with a thrust of the chest or with a carefully directed header. Usually, however, they are made with one of three parts of the boot – the outside, the instep or the inside. The inside or sidefoot pass is the most common and accurate pass, allowing players to stroke the ball around with a high level of precision. Some players attempt as many as 60 or 70 passes in a game, most of which are sidefoot passes. Italian midfielder Manuel Locatelli completed 2,749 passes in the 2020-21 Serie A season.

For longer passes, players tend to use the instep. This allows them to propel the ball with force. The instep can also be used for lofted drives that send the ball into the air as a cross or a clearance, as well as to stab down on the back of the ball. This makes the ball rise up at a steep angle, known as a chip. A pass's weight – the strength with which it is hit – is as important as accuracy for the pass to be successfully completed. At EURO 2020, strong passers such as Aymeric Laporte, Pedri, Jorginho and Pau Torres made hundreds of passes with over 90 per cent success.

▼ Voted 2018 world footballer of the year, Luka Modric of Croatia hits a long instep drive pass.

▶ Pedri González plays an accurate sidefoot pass. At EURO 2020 he won the young player of the tournament award and successfully completed 429 passes in just six games. Aged 18, he was the youngest Spaniard to ever play at a EURO.

MOVEMENT AND SPACE

Football is a dynamic, fast-moving sport. Throughout a game, pockets of space open and close rapidly all over the pitch. Players who have great awareness of where space is or shortly will be, and who have the ability to pass or move into it, are a real asset to their team.

◄ PSG defender Paulina Dudek strikes a sidefoot pass. Top footballers play with their heads up, looking for team-mates' moves and runs.

FACTFILE
At the 2018 World Cup, England completed 3,336 passes – more than any other team.

SPOTTING AND CREATING SPACE

The ball can zip around a pitch far more quickly than even the fastest of players. Good footballers make the ball do the work, moving it around with quick, accurate passes. Vision is the priceless ability to spot a pass, space or goalscoring opportunity that other players do not see, or before they do. Players with good vision look to move into space, timing their run to give a team-mate who has the ball a chance of making a pass that cannot be intercepted by an opponent. Once the ball has left the passer's control, he or she often moves into a position to receive a return pass. All players, not just midfielders and attackers, must be capable of passing well and moving into space to receive passes in return.

Players can create space for themselves or for team-mates through quick, agile movement and the use of feints or dummies, with which they attempt to fool a nearby opponent into thinking they are moving one way, before sprinting off in another direction.

▼ A wall pass (also known as a one-two pass) is a classic way to cut out an opposition player. It involves two passes that must be hit quickly and accurately, with the first passer running on to collect the return ball.

▲ Making space can be crucial to winning the ball at a throw-in. Here, one player makes a decoy run towards the thrower, dragging a defender with him and creating space in which a team-mate can collect the ball.

► Manchester City's Raheem Sterling attempts to drive round the outside of Tottenham defender Japhet Tanganga.

OFFSIDE

Players have to stay aware of Law 11, the offside law, throughout a game. This law causes controversy and has been altered throughout the sport's history. Today, a player is offside if, at the moment the ball is played, he or she is in the opposition half and is nearer the opponent's goal line than both the ball and the second-from-last opponent. That opponent can be an outfield player or the goalkeeper. Players cannot be offside in their own half or if they receive the ball directly from a goal kick, throw-in or corner.

Being in an offside position is not always an offence. Referees must judge whether the player in an offside position is involved in active play, moves towards the ball or does anything to make it harder for an opponent to play the ball. This tests an official's judgement to the limit. Is a player offside but a long way from the ball involved in 'active play'? Perhaps he or she is drawing defenders out as markers. If a referee does stop the game, an indirect free kick is awarded to the opposing team where the player was judged to be offside.

▲ French striker Djibril Cissé looks ruefully at the referee's assistant after being signalled offside in a French league match.

▶ Portugal defeated Argentina 2-1 to win the 2021 FIFA Futsal World Cup, their first title. Brazil top the list of winners, with five titles.

▲ Here, the player at the top left of the picture is in an offside position when the ball is struck. The referee decides that he is not interfering with play, however, and awards the goal.

▶ You cannot be offside if you are behind the ball when it is played. This scorer receives the ball from a team-mate who is ahead of him, so he is onside and the goal is given.

SMALL-SIDED GAMES

In many countries, children under the age of 11 play matches that feature six, seven or eight players per team. These small-sided games give young footballers an invaluable chance to see more of the ball and improve their control, passing and movement. Futsal is FIFA's official five-a-side game. A match lasts for 40 minutes (two halves of 20 minutes) and is played on a pitch the size of a basketball court, without surrounding boards or walls.

Futsal was devised by a Uruguayan, Juan Carlos Ceriani, in 1930. The game has flourished since then, with continental competitions for clubs and national sides, including a UEFA Futsal Champions League and a 24-team men's World Cup. Kazakhstan side AFC Kairat have won the Champions League twice, while Sporting Lisbon won the title in 2021.

THE OFFICIALS

Frequently abused by players, managers and supporters, referees are football's guardians and the enforcers of its laws. Their job is to impose order on a match and prevent intimidation, injury and cheating.

THE REFEREE'S ROLE

Referees perform a surprisingly large number of tasks before and after a match. These include checking the goals, nets and balls and deciding whether the pitch and weather conditions are suitable for the game to go ahead. Afterwards, they write a report containing details of disciplinary actions and other important incidents. On the pitch, the referee runs the game. His or her duties range from adding on time because of injuries, other stoppages and time-wasting, to deciding whether the ball is in or out of play or has crossed the goal line. If a player commits a foul or breaks a law, referees must stop play and order a restart, such as a drop ball or a free kick. They can caution players and team officials, and even abandon a match if weather, crowd trouble or another factor makes the game unplayable. Referees have to follow the laws of the game, but they have a certain amount of freedom to interpret aspects of the rules as they wish. For example, if a player is fouled when his or her side is in a promising position, a referee may let the match continue, playing the advantage rule to keep the game flowing.

ASSISTANTS AND THE FOURTH OFFICIAL

A referee relies on his or her assistants as extra pairs of eyes. Referee's assistants indicate when the ball goes out of play and whether a goal kick, corner or throw-in should be awarded. They also use flag signals to point out that a substitution has been requested, a player is offside or whether an offence has taken place out of the view of the referee. A referee can consult with an assistant if he or she was closer to the action, but it is up to the referee to make the final decision. Fourth officials have duties before and after a match, as well as helping with substitutions and displaying the amount of time added on at the end of each half for injuries and other stoppages.

◀ A fourth official uses a digital board to signal the time added on to the first half of the Germany v France EURO 2020 match in 2021.

▼ Roma's head coach, Paulo Fonseca, receives a red card for arguing with the referee.

▲ Early in a game, a good referee talks to players to calm them down or issues verbal warnings rather than cards. Here, Nicole Petignat soothes AIK Solna's Krister Nordin in the first UEFA Cup game to be refereed by a woman, in 2003.

FACTFILE

In 1998, English referee Martin Sylvester sent himself off after punching a player during a match in the Andover and District Sunday League.

TOP-FLIGHT PRESSURES

Thousands of amateur referees give up their weekends and evenings for free, purely to give something back to the game they adore. Top referees have their performances assessed, attend training seminars, undergo regular medical checks and are tested for fitness. A referee may run between 9.5 and 11.5km during a match (even further if extra time occurs) and often has to sprint to keep up with play. Referees work in a harsh, unforgiving climate, in which footage from multiple cameras and slow-motion television replays are broadcast over and over again, highlighting each poor decision. However, the very technology that puts referees under pressure is now coming to their aid. Goal-line technology removes doubt about whether a goal has been scored by sensing if the whole of the ball has crossed the goal line.

◀ Referee Daniele Orsato brandishes the 26th red card of Spanish defender Sergio Ramos' career during a 2020 UEFA Champions League match. Although a record in Europe, other players elsewhere have more – Colombia's Gerardo Múnera received 46 during his career (1995-2015).

CAUTION!

A player is shown a yellow card if he or she:
- is guilty of unsporting behaviour, such as simulation;
- shows dissent by word or action;
- persistently breaks the rules, by making repeated foul tackles for example;
- delays the restart of play;
- fails to stand at the required distance at a corner kick or free kick;
- enters or leaves the field of play without the referee's permission.

A player is sent off if he or she receives two yellow cards or one red card. Red-card offences include a very dangerous tackle, spitting and stopping a goal with a deliberate handball.

VAR

In 2018, FIFA introduced the Video Assistant Referee (VAR) to the elite game. The VAR studies TV footage of contentious penalties, goals, straight red card decisions and cases of mistaken identity, and alerts the onfield referee. The referee can make a rectangle signal, race to the sideline and review a moment of the game on a monitor to aid their decision.

VAR features in more and more league and cup competitions. It is designed to stop major mistakes in matches, but a referee must still stay alert for the many fouls and infringements that occur in a fast-moving game. Spotting contact in a crowded penalty area is a particularly difficult task, especially when some players fall to the ground with the slightest of contact or with no contact at all – a bookable offence known as simulation.

RED-CARD RECORDS

Fastest in a top league
Ten seconds – Giuseppe Lorenzo, Serie A, Bologna v Parma, 1990

Fastest in the World Cup
55 seconds – José Batista, Uruguay v Scotland, 1986

Most in one match
36 – Claypole v Victoriano Arenas (Argentina), 2011

▼ Chile's Daniela Zamora is fouled by Pitsamai Sornsai of Thailand at the 2019 Women's World Cup.

▶ Referee Chris Beath reviews VAR footage before awarding Brazil a penalty in the Tokyo 2020 Olympic men's final.

DEFENDING

Compared to strikers or creative midfielders, defenders are rarely praised as match-winners. Yet the foundation of every successful team is a composed, secure defence. Defending consists of a range of individual skills allied to good teamwork and understanding between players so that they defend as a unit. Defenders require strength and excellent heading and tackling skills, along with intense concentration, quick reactions and bravery. But, in truth, all players must defend if their side is to remain competitive in a match.

▲ French defender Raphael Varane shows expert timing to rob Turkey's Cenk Tosun of the ball. Tough, accurate tackling that wins possession is a crucial part of the game.

TRACKING AND TACKLING

The two keys to defending well are denying the opposition the chance to score and winning the ball back. As soon as an opponent gets the ball, defenders try to get between the ball and their goal and close down space. Defenders spend much of a game tracking opponents as they make runs and closing down the player with the ball to delay his or her progress. This is called jockeying. The aim is to slow down an attack until the defending side is in a stronger position. The defender tries to shepherd the attacker into a weaker position, such as near the sideline where there is little support. When a defender has cover from nearby team-mates, he or she may make a tackle. The defender should stay on his or her feet in order to gain possession.

◄ This attacker has spotted a weak pass by an opponent and reacts quickly to make an interception. Sometimes, attackers drop back to help their team defend.

▲ Philadelphia Union's Jakob Glesnes stretches to block a shot by América's Roger Martínez during a 2021 CONCACAF Champions League match.

FALLING FOUL OF THE LAW

Many of football's laws, such as obstruction, apply to defenders. A jockeying defender must be careful not to commit a foul, such as pushing, holding or shirt-pulling. A poorly timed tackle may result in a foul. Tackles from behind are especially risky, often leading to a yellow or red card if the defender makes contact with the attacker. A professional foul is a deliberate foul made to deny an attacking side a clear goalscoring chance. Two of the most common types are using the hands or arms to stop a goalbound ball and bringing down an attacker with the ball when he or she has a clear path to goal. Both should result in a sending off.

DEFENSIVE FORTRESS

During periods of open play, defending teams mark opponents man-to-man or with a zonal system (see page 60). At corners and free kicks from a wide position, they tend to mark man-to-man. A team may also try to catch out attackers by playing an offside trap (see page 61). Communication between defenders is crucial to prevent attackers getting free and into space to score. Certain teams equipped with highly skilled defenders who work well together have been able to squeeze the life out of opposition attacks. Czech side Slavia Prague went through the entire 2020-21 league season unbeaten, drawing eight of 34 games. The Juventus women's team did even better, winning all 22 games and conceding just ten goals in their march to the Serie A title.

◀ Virgil van Dijk (right) jockeys for the ball with Everton's Richarlison during a 2020 Premier League match. Van Dijk looks to secure possession of the ball or clear it away from danger.

◀ Australia's Alanna Kennedy rises high to head the ball clear and away from US attacker Carli Lloyd during the Tokyo 2020 Olympic bronze-medal match in 2021.

CLEAN SHEETS

Goalkeepers and defenders are especially proud of a clean sheet – a game in which their side does not concede a goal. Clean sheets are usually credited to goalkeepers, but in truth they depend on a solid defence as well as midfielders and strikers who are willing to chase, harry, track and tackle. In 2021, Italy played 1,168 minutes without conceding a single goal, marshalled by their central defender Giorgio Chiellini and young goalkeeper Gianluigi Donnarumma. The record run was ended by a goal from Austria in the EURO 2020 Round of 16. The longest run without conceding in club football occurred in Brazil in 1977-78 when the Vasco da Gama keeper, Mazarópi, went 1,816 minutes unbeaten – that's more than 20 matches.

LONGEST UNBEATEN LEAGUE RUNS (IN GAMES)

108	ASEC Abidjan (Ivory Coast), 1989-94
104	Steaua Bucharest (Romania), 1986-89
88	Lincoln FC (Gibraltar), 2009-14
85	Esperance (Tunisia), 1997-2001
71	Al-Ahly (Egypt), 2004-07
63	Sheriff Tiraspol (Moldova), 2006-08
62	Celtic (Scotland), 1915-17
61	Levadia Tallinn (Estonia), 2008-09
60	Al-Hilal (Sudan), 2016-18
	Union Saint-Gilloise (Belgium), 1933-35
59	Boca Juniors (Argentina), 1924-27
	Pyunik Yerevan (Armenia), 2002-04
58	AC Milan (Italy), 1991-93
	Olympiakos (Greece), 1972-74
	Skonto Riga (Latvia), 1993-96

FACT FILE

Rangers went unbeaten during the 38-game 2020-21 Scottish Premiership season, conceding just 13 goals.

GOALKEEPING

Goalkeepers are different. Their role is unique. They are the only players allowed to handle the ball and must wear different shirts from their team-mates. They act as the crucial last line of defence and can be match-winners thanks to their saves, decision-making, agility, bravery and presence in goal.

◄ Antonio Mirante of Roma makes a brave save at the feet of Udinese forward Rodrigo de Paul.

▲ Atlético Madrid's Jan Oblak stretches to make a diving save against Red Bull Salzburg.

KEEPING CONTROL

Goalkeepers can use their arms or hands to control the ball inside their own penalty area but otherwise they must obey all the same rules as outfield players. They cannot handle the ball:

- after releasing it and without it touching another player;
- after receiving the ball directly from a throw-in;
- if it has been deliberately kicked to them by a team-mate.

▲ Celta Vigo's Ruben Blanco punches away a dangerous ball.

This last rule, known as the backpass rule, came into effect in the 1990s to reduce time-wasting from goalkeepers and their defenders passing the ball back and forth to each other. If a keeper handles the ball in the above situations, the opposition is awarded an indirect free kick at the point where the offence occurred. This can be dangerously close to goal.

In the past, goalkeepers could be barged into but today they are well protected. Even so, they must be brave to contest a ball in a crowded penalty area or to dive at an opponent's feet. If a keeper fouls or brings down the attacker, they may give away a penalty and be sent off.

A KEEPER'S SKILLS

To achieve a clean sheet, goalkeepers need more than supreme agility and the talent to make diving saves. Top keepers train hard to improve their handling skills, learning to take the ball at different heights and from different angles. They must be able to stay alert for the entire game. Many minutes can go by before, suddenly, they are called into action. Keepers need good decision-making skills too, as a cross or shot may call for them to choose whether to try to hold the ball in a save, punch it away or tip it over the bar or round a post. Goalkeepers are in a unique position to see opposition attacks developing, and they must communicate instructions to their team-mates. They line up walls at free kicks and command their goal area, urging defenders to pick up unmarked opponents. A defence and keeper that communicate well can be a formidable unit.

▶ VfL Wolfsburg's Katarzyna Kiedrzynek instructs her defenders, hoping to snuff out an opposition attack as early as possible.

DEFENCE INTO ATTACK

With the ball in their possession, keepers can distribute it either with their hands or feet. Keepers have three types of throw (underarm, overarm and the javelin throw from the shoulder) with which to direct the ball to a team-mate. A quick, accurate throw can release a wing back or midfielder to start an attack. Alternatively, a keeper with the ball in hand can kick the ball on the volley or half-volley to send it long upfield. Manuel Neuer, Marc-André ter Stegen, Ederson and Alisson are examples of modern-day sweeper keepers. These players are extremely comfortable with the ball at their feet and may adopt a high position out of their goal area to act as an extra outfield player.

▶ Washington Spirit's Aubrey Bledsoe, NWSL Goalkeeper of the Year in 2019 and 2021, pulls off a spectacular full-stretch save.

▲ Barcelona's Marc-André ter Stegen prepares to bowl out the ball underarm.

FACTFILE

The world's first black professional footballer was a goalkeeper. Born in the Gold Coast (now Ghana), Arthur Wharton turned out in 1889 for Rotherham United in the English league.

GOALSCORING KEEPERS

While goalkeepers strive to prevent goals, they occasionally score them as well. Some are scored from long goal kicks that have caught out the opposing goalkeeper through their flight path or a deceptive bounce. Others have been scored by a keeper running into the opposition penalty area in the dying seconds of a game to try to force an equaliser or winning goal. This was the case in 2021, when Liverpool's Alisson Becker scored the winner in a Premier League game against West Bromwich Albion. A handful of goalkeepers have made a reputation for scoring from free kicks and penalties, such as Germany's Hans-Jörg Butt who scored 30 goals during his career. None can compare to Brazilian keeper Rogério Ceni, however, who scored an incredible 131 goals for São Paulo.

◀ In a one-on-one situation, many keepers come off their line to narrow the angle – reducing how much of the goal the attacker can see. They stay upright for as long as possible to increase the chance of the shot striking them.

◥ Liverpool keeper Alisson shows his skill with the ball at his feet, launching an attack with an accurate long kick.

ATTACKING

As soon as a team gains possession of the ball, with time and in space, its players' thoughts turn to attack. There are many ways in which a team can launch an attack, from a fast drive into space by a player who is sprinting forwards and pushing the ball ahead, to a slow, probing attack in which many players keep the ball securely in possession and look for an opening.

▼ Paul Pogba plays a diagonal pass behind Liverpool defender Andrew Robertson to set up an attack for Manchester United. Accurate, sharp passing can often open up an opposition defence.

▶ Olivia Moultrie dribbles past Paige Nielsen in a 2021 match between the Portland Thorns and the Washington Spirit. Moultrie is the youngest player to start a regular-season National Women's Soccer League game, aged 15.

TEAM ATTACKS

Many attacks rely on two or more team-mates working together to create a promising position. The wall pass (see page 16), for example, is a good way of propelling the ball past a defender with two quick movements. Attacking players also make decoy runs that draw defenders in one direction, creating space for another attacker to run into. Using the full width of the pitch can be vital to the success of an attack. Full-backs, wing-backs or wingers who are in space near the sideline may join an attack and make an overlapping run down the line. Receiving the ball, they may be able to head further forwards to put in a cross or cut infield and move towards goal. An overload is a situation in which the attacking side has more players in the attacking third of the pitch than the defending team. Classic ways of creating an overload are through a counter-attack – in which one side's attack breaks down and the opposition launches a rapid, direct attack – and an accurate long pass that is received by an attacker who is supported by team-mates, with only an isolated defender to beat.

BEATING OFFSIDE TRAPS

Some teams play an offside trap (see page 61), in which defenders move up in a straight line to catch opponents offside. Beating an offside trap takes cunning, skill and awareness. A perfectly weighted through pass can unlock the trap if the ball is collected by a player who stays onside until the moment the ball moves ahead of him or her. A long diagonal pass that switches play forwards and across the pitch may also work. The receiver makes a run from a deep position, staying onside until the ball moves ahead, then collects the ball behind the defence. Individual brilliance – such as dribbling or playing a short 'push and go' pass – can also beat some offside traps.

▶ Dutch winger Lieke Martens whips a cross into Australia's penalty area for a team-mate to attack during a 2021 friendly. She was part of the Barcelona Femení team that in 2021 won a league-cup-UEFA Champions League treble.

Schollen

Ibrahimovic 4

Mendes da Silva 3

Mendes da Silva 2

Ibrahimovic 2

Mendes da Silva 1

Stam

Ibrahimovic 3

Zonneveld

Ibrahimovic 1

MATCH ACTION

In a 2004 game against NAC Breda, Ajax's Zlatan Ibrahimovic scored a legendary solo goal. After receiving a pass with his back to goal, Ibrahimovic won a tackle with Mike Zonneveld, twisted past David Mendes da Silva and headed goalwards. Weaving his way to the edge of the penalty area, Ibrahimovic's options looked limited with four defenders around him. Yet with supreme balance and a series of feints and turns, he avoided the lunging tackle of Ronnie Stam. At the very last moment, when a shot with his right foot looked likely, Ibrahimovic switched the ball to his left foot to slide a shot past goalkeeper Davy Schollen.

▼ New England Revolution's Antonio Delamea Mlinar (no.19) out-jumps the Houston Dynamo defence to score with a header from a whipped-in corner kick.

SET PIECES

Set pieces are often planned in training. They are attacking moves made from a restart such as a free kick, corner or throw-in. If a team has a player who can throw the ball a long way, it may treat a throw-in that is level with the penalty area as if it were a corner. Often, a target player just inside the penalty area will attempt to flick the throw into the goal area. Mostly, set pieces are planned from corners and attacking free kicks (see page 28). At a corner, a team's tallest players or its best headers of the ball move up, usually from defence, to join strikers and attacking midfielders in the penalty area. Corners are sometimes played short to catch the defending team off guard, but usually they are whipped into the goal area. The attacking side looks for a header or shot on goal or a flick-on to a team-mate.

◄ An unexpected piece of brilliance – such as this acrobatic volley by Neymar – can open up a defence or result in a goal.

MATCH MAGICIANS

Some attacks are inspired by a piece of individual skill, trickery or brilliance. A player may break free of a defence with a sudden change of pace and direction or a trick move such as a Cruyff turn or a dragback. Some players, like Kylian Mbappé and Romelu Lukaku, can simply outpace or outmuscle a defence, bursting through to score. Dribbling – jinking and moving with the ball under control – is an exciting way to beat defenders. Top dribblers such as Cristiano Ronaldo, Marta, Lionel Messi and Neymar can open up games by themselves. They strike fear into defenders who know that one false move or a poorly timed challenge may allow the dribbler to go past or win their team a free kick or penalty.

GOALSCORING

Players who score goals regularly are the most valuable of all footballers. But scoring is not just reserved for the strikers in a side. A successful team needs its midfielders to contribute a number of goals each season, while tall defenders who are experts at heading often score five or six goals per season from set pieces. For out-and-out strikers, goals are what they play for and are judged on. As Argentinian striker Gabriel Batistuta once said, 'Goals are like bread. I need them to live.'

OWN GOALS

An own goal is technically any goal in which the last person to touch the ball before it crossed the line was a player on the defending team. In practice, however, an own goal is awarded not only when the ball has been deflected, but also when a defending player has made a genuine error or caused a major change in the course of the ball. The history of professional football is littered with outrageous own goals. Among the most common are goalkeeping errors, skewed defensive clearances that are sliced into the net, and misdirected headers. In 2021, Portugal became the first team to score two own goals in a major championship game as they lost 4-2 to Germany in a EURO 2020 Group F game.

THE GOALSCORER'S ART

Pace, power, accuracy, confidence and a deadly eye for a chance are just some of the qualities required to be a top goalscorer. Some skills can be honed in training – close ball control or swerving a shot, for example. Other qualities, such as confidence and vision, are harder to master. Football has got quicker at the highest level and most strikers need great pace to break past increasingly mobile defenders or into space to receive the ball before anyone else. Strength to hold off a challenge can be an asset, too. Some strikers, however, rely more on wits, fast reactions and ball skills to dribble through a crowded penalty area. Others are taller, stronger players who can score with towering headers or blasted shots. Most crucially of all, strikers have to be able to spot a goal chance and take it well. They need to react instinctively, using their vision to time runs into a scoring position. Once on the ball, they rarely have long to shoot. In an instant, strikers have to weigh up their options, know where the goal, defenders and keeper are, and hit a shot with enough pace, bend or accuracy to beat the goalkeeper.

◀ Canada's Christine Sinclair holds the world record for the most international goals, with 188 scored from 308 games.

FACTFILE

Seventeen women players have scored 100 or more goals for their national team. Seven of these are US footballers.

◥ Tottenham's Harry Kane, one of the deadliest strikers in the world, has won three Premier League Golden Boots as well as the 2018 World Cup Golden Boot.

▶ France's Kylian Mbappé uses his strength and athleticism to score an acrobatic volleyed goal against Wales in 2021.

GOALSCORING RECORDS

All-time leading goalscorers
Artur Friedenreich (Brazil) – 1,329 goals (1909-39)

Pelé (Brazil) – 1,281 goals (1956-77)

Most international goals (men)
115 – Cristiano Ronaldo (Portugal), 2004-

Most international goals (women)
188 – Christine Sinclair (Canada) 2000-

Most goals in one international match
13 – Archie Thompson (Australia), 2001

Fastest international goal
8.1 seconds – Christian Benteke (Belgium) versus Gibraltar, 2016

Fastest international hat-trick
Inside $3^{1}/_{2}$ minutes – Willie Hall (England), 1938

Most hat-tricks in consecutive matches
4 – Masashi Nakayama for Jubilo Iwata (Japan), 1998

Fastest goal
2 seconds – Vuk Bakic for GSP Polet (Serbia), 2012

Fastest own goal
8 seconds – Pat Kruse for Torquay United (England), 1977

◀ Goalscorers need poise and accuracy to put away a chance. Here, the Netherlands' Vivianne Miedema lifts the ball over Zambia's keeper to score at the Tokyo 2020 Olympics.

FACTFILE
The world record for own goals in one game is a staggering 149! In the last match of the 2002 Madagascan league season, against champions AS Adema, Stade Olympique l'Emryne repeatedly scored own goals from the kick-off in protest at a refereeing decision in their previous game.

GOAL CELEBRATIONS
As fans celebrate a goal, so do players. For many years, celebrations were no more flamboyant than a punch of the air and a hug from a nearby team-mate. That all changed in the 1980s and 1990s, partly thanks to the acrobatic backflips of Mexican striker Hugo Sanchez. Since then, players have rocked imaginary babies, danced the conga and pulled off spectacular gymnastic moves. Icelandic team Stjarnan FC have gained fame for their elaborate team celebrations, which include all the team members pretending to row a boat and reel in a player acting as a fish. This performance clocked up over a million views on YouTube in 2011. Referees can penalize teams for time-wasting or removing shirts during such celebrations.

▼ Players from the Democratic Republic of Congo dance in line to celebrate a goal at the 2017 Africa Cup of Nations.

FREE KICKS AND PENALTIES

▼ Referee Ravshan Irmatov marks out where Morocco's defensive wall can stand from a Spanish free kick at the 2018 World Cup. The spray marks a point 9.1m from the ball, and vanishes in minutes.

Referees award a free kick when a player breaks one of the laws of the game. Common free-kick offences are mistimed tackles, shirt-pulling, obstruction and offside. There are two types of free kick – indirect, which cannot be scored from without a second player touching the ball, and direct, which can be scored from directly and is awarded for more serious fouls. If a direct free-kick offence is committed by the defending team inside its penalty area, the referee may award a penalty.

▶ Max Aarons lies behind the Norwich wall to guard against a low shot in a 2021 Premier League match. This allows the rest of the wall to jump if the free-kick taker aims high.

FREE KICKS

Both types of free kick are taken from where the foul or offence was committed, although a rule change means that in some competitions the referee can move a kick 9m closer to goal if the other team wastes time or shows dissent. Opposition players must move at least 9m away from the ball, giving the team taking the kick valuable possession in space and with time. Some free kicks are taken quickly to get the ball moving in the middle of the field. Wide free kicks are often crossed with pace towards the goal area.

Attacking free kicks engage the two teams in a battle of wits. Players on the defending side mark attackers in the penalty area and form a defensive wall to block a direct shot. The kick taker may pass to a team-mate in space or try to hit a cross or shot past the wall. Some free kick specialists rely on powerful and direct strikes, while others – such as Paulo Dybala, Hakan Calhanoglu and Cristiano Ronaldo – are famous for the extreme bend they put on the ball.

◀ Liverpool's Trent Alexander-Arnold strikes across the back of the ball to make it bend over and around West Bromwich Albion's defensive wall.

PENALTY KICKS

Introduced in 1891, a penalty is an outstanding opportunity to score. The penalty taker is just 11m away from goal with only the keeper to beat. All other players must stay outside the area until the taker has struck the ball, and a referee can order a penalty to be retaken if players encroach. Penalty takers must kick the ball forwards and cannot touch the ball a second time until it has touched another player – a reason why the taker must stay alert in case it strikes the goalkeeper and rebounds. Some penalty takers favour accuracy over power, directing the ball into the corner of the goal. Others prefer a stuttering run to put the keeper off, or blast the ball hard. For the keeper, trying to figure out where the ball will go is a crucial guessing game.

FACTFILE

During qualifying for the 1954 World Cup, Spain and Turkey drew 2-2 in a playoff. A blindfolded boy, Luigi Franco Gemma, drew lots to decide the winner. Spain were knocked out.

▲ Germany's U21 keeper Finn Dahmen dives the right way but cannot reach Gustav Isaksen's perfectly placed penalty.

◥ Stephanie Labbé holds her nerve to save a penalty during Canada's 3-2 shootout win over Sweden in the Tokyo 2020 Olympic final.

SHOOTOUT!

Tense and unpredictable, penalty shootouts bring fans to the edge of their seats. Professional football's first shootout took place in a 1970 English cup competition between Hull City and Manchester United, with United winning 4-3. The 1972 Asian Nations Cup semi-final between Thailand and South Korea was its first appearance at a major tournament. Germany lost the first European Championships shootout to Czechoslovakia in 1976, but defeated France in the first World Cup shootout six years later.

SHOOTOUT RULES

In a shootout, five players per side are chosen to take one penalty each, all at one end of the pitch. A shootout is not considered to be part of the actual match, meaning that a goal is not added to a player's season or career tally. Neither penalty takers nor team-mates are allowed to score from a rebound – each player has just one shot at glory. The keeper knows this and often does his or her best to intimidate a penalty taker. If the scores are level after each team has taken five penalties, the competition goes into sudden death. Teams take one penalty each until one side misses and the other scores.

Some shootouts really go the distance. Ivory Coast and the Democratic Republic of Congo contested a 22-penalty shootout in the 2015 Africa Cup of Nations semi-final, as did Villareal and Manchester United in the 2021 UEFA Europa League final. In that shootout, the first 21 penalties were scored before David de Gea, United's keeper, missed.

FACTFILE

The first ever penalty was given by mistake to Scottish club Airdrieonians in March 1891. The new law did not actually take effect until the following season.

MOST PENALTIES IN A SHOOTOUT

PENS	SHOOTOUT SCORE	COMPETITION
48	KK Palace 17 Civics 16	Namibian Cup, 2005
44	Argentinos Juniors 20 Racing Club 19	Argentinian league, 1988
40	Obernai 15 ASCA Wittelsheim 15	Coupe de France, 1996

Italy's Gianluigi Donnarumma saves England's fifth and final penalty, taken by 19-year-old Bukayo Saka. Donnarumma, Italy's youngest ever goalkeeper, won UEFA's player of the tournament award – the first keeper ever to win the accolade.

SNAPSHOT
SHOOTOUT SUCCESS

It was a dramatic end to a dramatic tournament in which only two of the 51 matches ended goalless. Italy, the favourites for the EURO 2020 crown, faced a resurgent young England team in a penalty shootout after the final ended 1-1 after extra time. Both teams had had their chances in open play but now were pitted against each other in the cauldron of an unbearably tense shootout watched by hundreds of millions on television.

There had been 21 penalty shootouts at European Championships before and Italy had taken part in six, more than any other team. They had suffered defeat on three occasions but had already enjoyed shootout success in this tournament, knocking Spain out at the semi-final stage. They also had their EURO 2012 shootout win over England to bolster them.

England went ahead after Jordan Pickford's save from Andrea Belotti was sandwiched between two strong penalties by Harry Kane and Harry Maguire. England manager Gareth Southgate had brought on two last-gasp attacking substitutes, Jadon Sancho and Marcus Rashford, with the aim of them taking penalties. It was a bold move but it backfired, with both players failing to convert their attempts. A third miss by England handed Italy their second European Championship crown, 53 years after their victory at EURO 1968.

FOOTBALL SUPERSTARS

From France's Zinedine Zidane to Argentina's Lionel Messi, football has been lit up by the talents of thousands of highly committed and skilful players, all of whom have enthralled spectators and inspired their teams to great achievements. Packed into this section are profiles of more than 70 of the finest players to have graced the game.

FACTFILE
Gordon Banks won FIFA's Goalkeeper of the Year award a record six times.

KEY
COUNTRY = international side · CAPS = international games · GOALS = international goals (to April 2022)

GOALKEEPERS

PETER SCHMEICHEL
DENMARK · BORN 1963 · CAPS: 129 · GOALS: 1

After playing for Hvidøvre and then Brøndby, Schmeichel became one of the best keepers of the 1990s after Alex Ferguson took him to Manchester United in 1991 for the modest fee of £550,000. The high point of his international career came with winning the 1992 European Championships, while the silverware poured in at club level. The hugely committed Dane redefined one-on-one goalkeeping, standing menacingly tall and large or bravely sprawling at an attacker's feet. After winning a treble (Premier League, FA Cup and UEFA Champions League) with Manchester United in 1999, he moved to Sporting Lisbon and helped the Portuguese side win its first league title in 17 years. He made a surprise return to the Premier League in 2001, with Aston Villa and then Manchester City, before injury forced him to retire.

◀ Peter Schmeichel won ten league titles in Denmark, England and Portugal.

▶ Iker Casillas organizes his defence during a La Liga match between Real Madrid and Celta Vigo.

IKER CASILLAS
SPAIN · BORN 1981
CAPS: 167 · GOALS: 0

Spain's number one keeper for more than a decade, Casillas played over 700 times for Real Madrid, with whom he won five La Liga titles, before moving to Porto in 2015. In 2000, he became the youngest goalkeeper to play in a UEFA Champions League final, which Real won 3–0. With his razor-sharp reflexes and superb positioning, Casillas was voted keeper of the year five times and captained Spain to two European Championship titles and the 2010 World Cup. He retired in 2020 after suffering a heart attack.

BEST GOALKEEPER AT THE WORLD CUP

Year	Winner
1994	Michel Preud'homme (Belgium)
1998	Fabien Barthez (France)
2002	Oliver Kahn (Germany)
2006	Gianluigi Buffon (Italy)
2010	Iker Casillas (Spain)
2014	Manuel Neuer (Germany)
2018	Thibault Courtois (Belgium)

GORDON BANKS
ENGLAND • 1937–2019
CAPS: 73 • GOALS: 0

'Banks of England' was as secure a keeper as any nation could call upon in the 1960s. During his ten-year international career, he kept 35 clean sheets and was on the losing side just nine times. His professional career began at Chesterfield, before a £7,000 move took him to Leicester City. In 1962, Banks made his debut for England, with whom he won the 1966 World Cup. The following year, he moved to Stoke City, but a car crash in 1972 caused Banks to lose the sight in his right eye. The accident ended his career in Britain, although he did play in the USA for the Fort Lauderdale Strikers in 1977–78.

◀ Gordon Banks in action for Stoke City in 1970. Throughout his career, Banks trained tirelessly on angles and repeat drills to improve his strength and agility.

SARAH BOUHADDI
FRANCE • BORN 1986
CAPS: 149 • GOALS: 0

After spells early in her career with CNFE Clairefontaine, Toulouse and Juvisy, Bouhaddi joined Lyon. There she enjoyed an incredible era of success, playing more than 280 games for the pre-eminent French club and winning 11 league titles, eight Coupes de France Féminine and seven UEFA Women's Champions League crowns. Bouhaddi made her debut for France in 2004 and was still playing for her country in 2020.

◀ Bouhaddi issues instructions at the 2019 Women's World Cup. The following year she won the Best FIFA Goalkeeper award.

◀ Lev Yashin makes a great save at the 1966 World Cup.

JAN OBLAK
SLOVENIA • BORN 1993
CAPS: 46 • GOALS: 0

Oblak has been one of the world's best keepers ever since he was part of Benfica's 2013-14 treble-winning team. He became La Liga's most expensive goalkeeper when Atlético Madrid paid €16 million for his services in 2014, and it has proved a wise investment. Oblak's slick positioning, safe handling and unflappability saw him break a longstanding La Liga record in 2020 – becoming the fastest goalkeeper to reach 100 clean sheets, a feat he managed in 189 matches.

◀ Jan Oblak captained the Slovenian national team for the first time in 2019.

LEV YASHIN
SOVIET UNION • 1929–90
CAPS: 75 • GOALS: 0

In South America, Yashin was called the Black Spider. In Europe he was the Black Panther; but everywhere he was regarded as the finest goalkeeper of his era and, possibly, of all time. Blessed with extraordinary anticipation and agility, Yashin made countless, seemingly impossible saves and stopped as many as 150 penalties during his career, which was spent entirely at Moscow Dynamo. In 1954, he made his debut for the national team. Yashin's bravery, vision and shot-stopping skills helped the Soviets to an Olympic title in 1956, the European Championship crown in 1960 and a semi-final place at the 1966 World Cup. With Moscow Dynamo, Yashin won six league titles and two Soviet Cups. In 1963, he became the first – and still the only – goalkeeper to win the coveted European Player of the Year award.

GIANLUIGI BUFFON
ITALY • BORN 1978
CAPS: 176 • GOALS: 0

Top goalkeepers can have long careers but few can surpass the longevity or continued excellence of this Italian veteran, who spent six years at Parma before his world-record €52-million transfer to Juventus in 2001. A commanding and reassuring presence in goal, Buffon spent an incredible 17 consecutive years at Juve (plus two further seasons later on). There, he won ten Serie A championships, five Coppa Italia and played nearly 700 games for the club. For Italy, he won the World Cup in 2006 and reached the EURO 2012 final. One season at PSG (2018-19) was followed in 2021 by an emotional return to his first club, Parma, now playing in Serie B.

▶ Gianluigi Buffon kisses the Serie A trophy in 2018. It was his seventh league title in a row for Juventus.

HOPE SOLO
USA • BORN 1981 • CAPS: 202 • GOALS: 0

The USA number one keeper from 2005 to 2016, Solo started her professional career with Philadelphia Charge in 2003 before having spells in Sweden and France and returning to the US with a succession of WUSA and WPS teams. In 2013, she joined the Seattle Reign in the newly formed National Women's Soccer League. She has won Olympic gold twice (2008, 2012) and was a member of the USA team that were runners-up at the 2011 World Cup. Solo was voted keeper of the World Cup, a feat she repeated four years later as five clean sheets helped her side become 2015 champions.

FACTFILE

At EURO 2016, Neuer set a record of 557 minutes without conceding a goal in a major tournament.

▶ Manuel Neuer was voted German footballer of the year for the 2014-15 season, a rare accolade for a goalkeeper.

MANUEL NEUER
GERMANY • BORN 1986 • CAPS: 109 • GOALS: 0

A dynamic sweeper-keeper, comfortable on the ball and brilliant in one-on-one situations, Neuer joined Schalke 04 in 1991 and didn't leave until 2011 when he moved for a record fee of 22 million euros to Bayern Munich. He made an instant impact, notching up over 1,000 minutes without conceding a goal in a string of games in his first season, winning three Bundesliga titles and the 2012–13 UEFA Champions League. Debuting internationally in 2009, he only conceded one goal in Germany's EURO 2012 campaign. More was to come in 2014 when he became a World Cup winner and was voted goalkeeper of the tournament.

DEFENDERS

MARCEL DESAILLY
FRANCE • BORN 1968 • CAPS: 116 • GOALS: 3

Marcel Desailly is world famous as one of the French players who won the World Cup and European Championship crowns in 1998 and 2000. He was born in Ghana and came to France as a young child. A skilful and commanding central defender, Desailly began his career with FC Nantes and then Olympique Marseille. In 1993, he won the UEFA Champions League with Marseille, before moving to AC Milan and winning the Champions League again the following year. After a series of outstanding performances at the 1998 World Cup, Desailly moved to Chelsea, where he proved a popular leader. In 2004, Desailly retired from international football and left Chelsea to join Qatar's Al-Ittihad club.

FACTFILE

World Cup winner Marcel Desailly became the third player to be sent off in a World Cup final when he was dismissed against Brazil in 1998 after receiving two yellow cards.

▲ Marcel Desailly was nicknamed 'The Rock' for his strength and consistency. Here, he holds off Marcus Bent of Ipswich while playing for Chelsea in 2002.

▼ Virgil van Dijk steps across Leeds United's Raphinha to seize possession in typically controlled fashion.

LUCY BRONZE
ENGLAND • BORN 1991
CAPS: 86 • GOALS: 9

Starting out in Sunderland's youth team, this tough tackling yet skilful defender made her first-team debut at the age of 16. Moving to the US in 2009, Bronze became the first English player to win the NCAA Cup with the University of North Carolina's Tar Heels side. Spells at Everton, Liverpool and Manchester City followed before she signed for Lyon in 2017, where she won both the French league and the UEFA Women's Champions League in 2018. Arguably the most consistent all-round defender in women's football, her resolute displays and occasional goal threats helped propel England to third place at the 2015 Women's World Cup. In 2020, she returned to Manchester City and won the FIFA Women's Player award – the first defender to do so.

▶ Lucy Bronze hits a pass for Manchester City in the FA Cup. She has won the trophy twice, in 2017 and 2020.

VIRGIL VAN DIJK
NETHERLANDS • BORN 1991
CAPS: 46 • GOALS: 5

A towering yet calm presence in central defence, van Dijk has justified the enormous £75-million transfer fee Liverpool paid Southampton in 2018 for his services. The Saints had purchased him from Scottish club Celtic for £13 million two and a half years earlier. Van Dijk began his senior career at Dutch side Groningen before moving to Scotland in 2013, but it was in England that he truly flourished. Powerful and skilful in the air, van Dijk is equally masterful on the ground where his timing and clean tackling have seen him receive only 11 yellow cards in 186 Premier League appearances. A bad knee injury kept him out of most of the 2020-21 season, but he has returned with his old verve to the relief of his club and the Netherlands, which he has captained since 2018.

WENDIE RENARD
FRANCE • BORN 1990
CAPS: 129 • GOALS: 32

A defensive rock for club and country, Renard has played all her club football for Lyon, with whom she has won a remarkable 14 Division 1 Féminine league titles and seven UEFA Women's Champions Leagues. A strong, fast central defender, she was the tallest player at the 2019 Women's World Cup, at 1.87m. She is extremely adept at snuffing out opposition attacks and driving forwards with the ball to link defence and attack. Renard also presents a serious goalscoring threat herself, especially at set pieces. From 2017-18 onwards, she scored a dozen or more goals a season for four consecutive seasons, an incredible feat for a defender.

◄ Wendie Renard uses her body to cushion the ball and bring it under control.

▼ Bobby Moore played more than 500 games in defence for West Ham between 1958 and 1974.

PAOLO MALDINI
ITALY • BORN 1968 • CAPS: 126 • GOALS: 7

One of the best defenders in world football, Paolo Maldini was a one-club player. He made his first-team debut for AC Milan in 1985 and played over 900 games for the Italian club, mostly at left-back, although he would also play as a central defender or as a sweeper. Maldini was able to read the game extremely well, tackle cleanly and move the ball forwards accurately. He debuted for Italy in 1988 and soon became a regular in the national side. He played in four World Cups and four European Championships, retiring from international football after the 2002 World Cup. Winning seven Serie A titles, Maldini also lifted the UEFA Champions League trophy in 2003 and 2007. He eventually retired just short of his 41st birthday.

▶ Paolo Maldini, Italy's longest-serving defender, clears the ball out of his penalty area during the 1994 World Cup final against Brazil.

BOBBY MOORE
ENGLAND • 1941–93 • CAPS: 108 • GOALS: 2

England's finest ever defender, Moore appeared to lack the pace and the commanding physique to be a great central defender. However, he was blessed with a wonderful eye for the game and always appeared to be one step ahead of opposition attackers. His tackling was clean and surgical, and he was very rarely cautioned. One of football's truly outstanding captains, Moore led England in 90 games – a record shared with Billy Wright – including the 1966 World Cup triumph. He spent most of his career at West Ham, only joining Fulham (alongside George Best) at the age of 32, before finally moving to the USA to play for Seattle Sounders and San Antonio Thunder. His friendship with Pelé was cemented in 1970, when the two men played out an epic struggle for supremacy in England's World Cup game against Brazil. Pelé called Moore the greatest defender he had played against.

DANIEL PASSARELLA
ARGENTINA
BORN 1953
CAPS: 70 • GOALS: 22

Passarella was a gifted central defender who made surging runs into midfield to build attacks. He was exceptionally good in the air despite being of average height, and struck devastating free kicks. In 298 Argentinian league matches, he scored an astonishing 99 goals. Passarella had success with River Plate before a move to Europe in 1982, first to Fiorentina and then to Internazionale. In 1985–86, he scored 11 goals for Fiorentina, a record for a defender that lasted for 15 years. He won the 1978 World Cup, played in the 1982 tournament and was picked for 1986, but was sidelined through injury. After retiring, Passarella became a coach, managing Argentina at the 1998 World Cup.

FRANZ BECKENBAUER
WEST GERMANY • BORN 1945 • CAPS: 103 • GOALS: 14

Der Kaiser made his debut for Bayern Munich in 1964 as an attacking inside-left. Just 27 games later, he was in the national side. At the 1966 World Cup, Beckenbauer played in midfield and scored four goals on the way to the final. By the 1970 tournament, he had moved into defence, where he revolutionized the ultra-defensive role of sweeper with his astonishing vision and silky skills on the ball. Time and again he would turn defence into attack, striding up the pitch to release team-mates or take a chance himself. With his stylish attacking play, it is sometimes forgotten that he was a masterful defender, always cool under pressure. In 1972, Beckenbauer won the European Championships with West Germany and was European Footballer of the Year. Two years later, he won the first of three consecutive European Cups with Bayern Munich and also captained his country to World Cup glory. In 1977, he made a surprise move to the USA, playing in a star-studded New York Cosmos team before returning to Germany in 1980 with Hamburg. He became West Germany's coach in 1984, leading them to two World Cup finals and winning one.

◀ Franz Beckenbauer at the 1974 World Cup. Sixteen years later, he became the second man – after Brazil's Mario Zagalo – to have won the World Cup as both a player and a manager.

THIAGO SILVA
BRAZIL • BORN 1984
CAPS: 105 • GOALS: 7

Tough and skilful, Silva can play in any position across the defence and actually started out as a midfielder in Brazil before moving to Europe in 2004. After spells at Porto and Dynamo Moscow, where he contracted tuberculosis and nearly quit football, Silva joined Fluminense and helped them to win their first ever Copa do Brazil in 2007. AC Milan paid around 10 million euros to bring him back to Europe in 2009, where he won the 2010–11 Serie A before becoming the world's most expensive defender with a move to Paris Saint-Germain. Silva won the 2013 FIFA Confederations Cup and the 2019 Copa América with Brazil, and in 2020 moved to Chelsea.

▼ Thiago Silva strikes a long, accurate crossfield pass during Chelsea's UEFA Champions League game against Zenit St Petersburg.

RUUD KROL
NETHERLANDS • BORN 1949
CAPS: 83 • GOALS: 4

Krol was a vital part of the great Ajax and Dutch 'total football' sides of the late 1960s and 1970s, comfortable playing in almost any defensive position. With Ajax he won six league titles and two European Cups (1972 and 1973). Krol was the last of the Ajax greats to move away, when in 1980 he played for Vancouver Whitecaps in Canada. He returned to Europe the following year to play for Napoli and later for Cannes in the French second division, where injury forced him to retire in 1987. He has since managed in a variety of countries, including Switzerland, Egypt and Belgium.

▶ Ruud Krol evades a sliding tackle from France's Didier Six in a World Cup qualifier in 1981.

LINDA MEDALEN
NORWAY • BORN 1965 • CAPS: 152 • GOALS: 64

Medalen started her career as a striker, making her debut for Norway in 1987 and going on to win the 1988 unofficial Women's World Cup and the 1993 European Championships. At the 1991 World Cup she was her side's top scorer, with six goals, as Norway finished runners-up. As Medalen's career progressed, she moved into defence, where her skill in the air and strong tackling helped Norway to win the 1995 World Cup, conceding just one goal in six games. Medalen played in the 1999 tournament, but a knee injury kept her out of the 2000 Olympics, which Norway won. At club level, she won five league championships and three cup competitions for the Norwegian side Asker SKK.

▲ John Charles (centre) leaps for the ball. Charles' name is still revered by Juventus fans, who nicknamed him *Il Buon Gigante* – the Gentle Giant.

▶ Linda Medalen tackles China's legendary midfielder Sun Wen at the 1999 World Cup.

JOHN CHARLES
WALES • 1931–2004 • CAPS: 38 • GOALS: 21

The gloriously talented Charles was equally skilled as a bustling, powerful centre-forward or as a hugely commanding central defender. In both positions, he was world class. Appearing in attack for Leeds United, he scored a record 42 goals in one season, while playing internationally as a central defender. In the Welsh side, Charles was joined by his brother, Mel, and team-mates Ivor and Len Allchurch – the first time that any national side had included two pairs of brothers. In 1957, the British transfer record was smashed as he moved to Juventus for £67,000. Charles became a genuine legend in Italy for his towering performances, generous behaviour towards fans and his sportsmanship. In a highly defence-minded league, he scored an astonishing 93 goals in 155 matches, helping Juve win three Serie A titles and two Coppa Italia. He later moved back to Leeds, then on to Parma, Cardiff City and Hereford United, before retiring.

GEORGIO CHIELLINI
ITALY • BORN 1984
CAPS: 116 • GOALS: 8

Strong, aggressive and streetwise, Chiellini has been a mainstay of the Juventus defence either at left-back or in central defence since the mid-2000s. He formed a strong defensive partnership with Leonardo Bonucci, with whom he played for club and country through most of the 2010s. During that decade, Chiellini won nine Serie A titles and numerous other trophies. At international level, he was part of Italy's EURO 2012 side that reached the final and captained his country for the first time later that year. Nine years later, he led Italy to EURO 2020 glory.

▶ Georgio Chiellini celebrates Italy's dramatic EURO 2020 final win over England on penalties.

MIDFIELDERS AND WINGERS

KEVIN DE BRUYNE
BELGIUM • BORN 1991 • CAPS: 88 • GOALS: 23

A complete, modern midfielder, de Bruyne is comfortable striding forwards in possession, delivering telling passes and assists, or shooting himself. He started at Genk before he was bought by Chelsea, who moved him on loan to Werder Bremen and then sold him to Vfl Wolfsburg. There, he set a new Bundesliga record with 21 assists in the 2014–15 season. Weeks after assisting for the winning goal that defeated Bayern Munich in the 2015 DFL-Supercup, de Bruyne moved to Manchester City for around £55 million. He has since become the lynchpin of a side that won three league titles between 2018 and 2021 and reached the final of the 2020-21 UEFA Champions League.

◀ Manchester City's Kevin de Bruyne controls the ball with the outside of his boot.

CARLOS VALDERRAMA
COLOMBIA • BORN 1961
CAPS: 110 • GOALS: 10

Famous for his flamboyant play and hairstyle, Carlos Valderrama was an exquisite passer of the ball in midfield, who would often link with the attack to devastating effect. He played for three Colombian teams – Union Magdalena, Millionarios and Deportiva Cali – before moving to France in 1988, where he won the league title with Montpellier. In 1996, he moved to the USA to play for Tampa Bay Mutiny and then Miami Fusion. Valderrama captained Colombia to three World Cup tournaments in a row (1990–98) and retired from international football after the 1998 tournament. Yet, even past his 40th birthday, Valderrama was still one of the biggest stars in the MLS.

◀ Landon Donovan prepares to pick out a team-mate with a pass during an MLS game between LA Galaxy and FC Dallas.

▶ Carlos Valderrama on the ball during Colombia's 1998 World Cup game against England.

LANDON DONOVAN
USA • BORN 1982
CAPS: 157 • GOALS: 57

Donovan came to prominence early when he was voted the best player of the 1999 FIFA Under-17 World Championship and was signed the same year by Bayer Leverkusen. Returning to the USA on loan with the San Jose Earthquakes, Donovan would later have short loan spells with Bayern Munich and Everton, but in 2005 he joined the LA Galaxy. He won five MLS Cups, three with LA Galaxy and two with the San Jose Earthquakes, as well as winning the CONCACAF Gold Cup three times with the US team. Two-footed and capable of devastating attacking bursts from midfield, Donovan's eye for a goal saw him score more than 160 times in the MLS and other US club competitions. His 57 goals make him, far and away, the US national team's most prolific goal scorer.

FACTFILE
Andrés Iniesta's consistency saw him voted into FIFA's World XI nine seasons in a row (2009-19).

DAVID BECKHAM
ENGLAND • BORN 1975
CAPS: 115 • GOALS: 17

David Beckham is one of the most recognizable footballers on the planet. He began his career as a youth-team player at Manchester United, then had a loan spell with Preston North End, before announcing his arrival in English football with a Premiership goal from inside his own half against Wimbledon. At the 1998 World Cup he was heavily criticized for kicking out at Argentina's Diego Simeone and receiving a red card. But Beckham's excellence for club and country, particularly his trademark swerving free kicks, won back public support – notably when he ensured England's qualification for the 2002 World Cup with a last-gasp goal against Greece. He also won 'the treble' of Champions League, Premiership and FA Cup with Manchester United in 1999. When David Beckham joined Paris Saint-Germain, in 2013, he donated his entire salary to a local children's charity. He became the first English player to win the league in four different countries (England, Spain, the USA and France). He is now a co-owner of MLS side Inter Miami CF.

◄ David Beckham salutes the crowd during a 2019 friendly between the treble-winning 1999 Manchester United side and their rivals in the 1999 Champions League final, Bayern Munich.

XAVI HERNÁNDEZ
SPAIN • BORN 1980
CAPS: 133 • GOALS: 12

Rising through the ranks of youth and reserve teams at Barcelona, Xavi made his first-team debut in 1998 and played over 750 games for the Spanish club before moving to Qatar in 2015 to play for Al Sadd. With Barcelona, he won eight La Liga titles and four Champions Leagues and enjoyed EURO 2008 and 2012 and 2010 World Cup glory with Spain. Brilliant at finding space even in the most crowded parts of the pitch, Xavi was a passing maestro – enabling his side to keep possession and attack.

ANDRÉS INIESTA
SPAIN • BORN 1984
CAPS: 131 • GOALS: 13

Quick feet and an even quicker footballing brain enabled this slight midfielder to become one of the most celebrated players in world football. Joining Barcelona as a youth teamer, Iniesta later formed a formidable central midfield partnership with Xavi Hernández for both club and country. With Barcelona, he won nine La Liga titles, four Champions Leagues and six Spanish Super Cups. Internationally, he scored the winning goal in the 2010 World Cup final.

◄ Xavi and Andrés Iniesta celebrate winning the UEFA Champions League in 2015.

HRISTO STOICHKOV
BULGARIA • BORN 1966
CAPS: 83 • GOALS: 37

As an attacking midfielder or a striker, the strong, stocky Stoichkov was surprisingly quick over a short distance and possessed unstoppable power, particularly in his left foot. He emerged as a skilful youngster at CSKA Sofia before moving to Barcelona. Unpredictable and prone to tempers, Stoichkov fell out with Barcelona manager Johan Cruyff when he was asked to play out wide. He later moved to Parma, Japanese side Kashiwa Reysol and the Chicago Fire in the MLS. He arrived at the 1994 World Cup as the star player in an underrated Bulgarian side that sensationally knocked out Germany before losing the semi-final to Italy. Stoichkov finished the tournament as joint top scorer. It was his finest hour as a player.

► At Barcelona, Stoichkov won the European Cup in 1992 and five La Liga titles in just seven seasons.

MICHEL PLATINI
FRANCE • BORN 1955 • CAPS: 72 • GOALS: 41

A truly great attacking midfielder, Platini was the glittering jewel in a French side that suffered semi-final heartbreak at the 1982 World Cup. Two years later, he was top scorer at the European Championships (nine goals) as France won the title. In partnership with Alan Giresse and Jean Tigana, Platini exhibited immense skill and vision. At club level, Platini played for AS Joeuf, Nancy and Saint-Étienne before turning down a transfer to Arsenal in favour of Italian giants Juventus in 1982. He was Serie A's leading marksman three times and was crowned European Footballer of the Year three times in a row (1983–85) – a unique achievement. Retiring in 1987, he went on to manage France and then led his country's bid to host the 1998 World Cup. In 2007, he became president of UEFA.

◀ Michel Platini during France's 4-1 win over Northern Ireland at the 1982 World Cup.

GARRINCHA
BRAZIL • 1933–83
CAPS: 50 • GOALS: 12

Manuel Francisco dos Santos was nicknamed Garrincha – meaning 'little bird' – at a young age. A small player at only 1.69m tall, a childhood illness had left his legs distorted, with one bent inwards and the other 6cm shorter. Yet those who saw Garrincha play remember him as the greatest dribbler in the history of football. He played for Botafogo in Brazil but also for clubs in Colombia, Italy, and in France for Red Star Paris. It was on the international stage, however, that Garrincha became famous. He starred in the 1958 World Cup, which Brazil won, but eclipsed those performances at the 1962 competition. Voted player of the tournament, he was joint leading scorer as he struck two goals to knock out England in the quarter-final, and then two more to beat Chile in the semi-final. Sadly, his life away from football was troubled, and he died of alcohol poisoning at the age of 49.

▶ Garrincha perfected the bending banana kick, which he used to great effect for Brazilian side Botafogo, scoring 232 goals in 581 matches.

DZSENIFER MAROZSÁN
GERMANY • BORN 1992
CAPS: 109 • GOALS: 33

Born in Hungary, Marozsán moved to Germany when she was a child so that her father could play for FC Saarbrücken. She played for the women's team there and in 2007, at the age of 14 years and 7 months, became the youngest player to appear in the women's Bundesliga. In 2009, she moved to FFC Frankfurt, winning the UEFA Women's Champions League in 2014-15. A skilled and relentless passer, Marozsán is unflashy but very effective, and she became a vital cog in a star-studded Lyon side after her transfer in 2016. In 2021, after winning four league titles with Lyon, she went on loan to the OL Reign of the US National Women's Soccer League.

FACTFILE
Garrincha retired in 1966, after Brazil's loss to Hungary in the World Cup. Astonishingly, in his 50 matches it was the only time he was on the losing side for Brazil.

◀ Marozsán has won four Champions Leagues at Lyon and made UEFA's squad of the season five years in a row (2015-19).

ZINEDINE ZIDANE
FRANCE • BORN 1972
CAPS: 108 • GOALS: 31

The son of Algerian immigrants, Zidane grew up in Marseille with posters of his idol, Enzo Francescoli of Uruguay, on his wall. His first club was Cannes, followed by Bordeaux, where he won France's Young Player of the Year award in 1992. On his international debut in 1994, he scored both of France's goals in a 2-2 draw with the Czech Republic. In 1995–96, Zidane played 57 matches – more than any other French player – and he appeared jaded as he underperformed at EURO '96. But a move to Juventus in the same year saw him regain his best form, as he helped the Serie A giants win two league titles. Zidane was a key part of the French side that captured a double of World Cup (1998) and European Championships (2000). As the best midfielder in the world, he won World Player of the Year titles in 1998, 2000 and 2003. Zidane's last tournament, the 2006 World Cup, was memorable as he led France to the final, scoring three goals on the way and being voted FIFA's player of the tournament. He was sent off in the final, however, for a headbutt to the chest of Italy's Marco Materazzi.

◀ Zidane in action during France's 3-1 win over Spain at the 2006 World Cup.

CRISTIANO RONALDO
PORTUGAL • BORN 1985
CAPS: 186 • GOALS: 115

A winger who, in his later years, has played more as a centre-forward, Ronaldo began his career on the Portuguese island of Madeira before joining Sporting Clube de Portugal. After impressing in a pre-season friendly, he joined Manchester United in 2003, where he blossomed into one of the world's greatest attackers, bewildering defenders with tricks and pace, outstanding ball control and masterful free kicks. His club performances helped to propel Manchester United to three successive Premier League titles as well as the Champions League crown in 2008. Ronaldo joined Real Madrid in 2009 for a world-record fee of £80 million and made a huge impact, scoring 450 goals in just 438 games as he won four Champions League and two Spanish league titles with the Spanish giants. He captained Portugal to EURO 2016 and UEFA Nations League 2019 glory, by which time he was freely scoring for Juventus, netting 101 goals in 138 games before returning to Manchester United in 2021.

▶ Cristiano Ronaldo has captained Portugal since 2008 and is his country's most-capped player and leading scorer.

WORLD-RECORD TRANSFERS

PLAYER	FROM	TO	FEE	YEAR
Neymar	Barcelona	Paris Saint-Germain	£198 million	2017
Kylian Mbappé	Monaco	Paris Saint-Germain	£158 million	2018
Philippe Coutinho	Liverpool	Barcelona	£106 million	2018
Ousmane Dembélé	B. Dortmund	Barcelona	£110 million	2017
João Félix	Benfica	Atlético Madrid	£104 million	2019
Antoine Griezmann	Atlético Madrid	Barcelona	£103 million	2019
Jack Grealish	Aston Villa	Manchester City	£100 million	2021
Romelu Lukaku	Inter Milan	Chelsea	£97.5 million	2021
Paul Pogba	Juventus	Manchester United	£89.3 million	2016
Eden Hazard	Chelsea	Real Madrid	£89 million	2019
Cristiano Ronaldo	Real Madrid	Juventus	£88.5 million	2018

PAUL POGBA
FRANCE • BORN 1993
CAPS: 91 • GOALS: 11

This powerhouse central midfielder can play further forwards or wide, where his surging runs open up defences. He joined Manchester United from Le Havre in 2009, but limited opportunities to play saw him move to Juventus on a free transfer in 2012. There, he turned games with bursts of rapid skill, power and audacity as Juve won Serie A in all four seasons he was part of the squad. Transfer rumours swirled near the end of his time in Italy, but it was still a surprise when Manchester United broke their own transfer record to pay £89.3 million to bring him back. At club level, he has both inspired and infuriated team-mates and fans, whilst on the international stage he has a World Cup winners' medal after France's triumph in 2018.

◄ Paul Pogba looks for an opening in attack for France against Wales in 2021.

MICHAEL LAUDRUP
DENMARK • BORN 1964 • CAPS: 104 • GOALS: 37

The peak of Michael Laudrup's international career came in the quarter-finals of the 1998 World Cup, where Denmark lost narrowly to Brazil 3-2 – despite his younger brother, Brian, scoring a goal. Laudrup was much in demand as an attacking midfielder, playing for Lazio and Juventus in Italy and winning five league titles in Spain with Barcelona and Real Madrid. Sadly, he missed out on Denmark's finest hour – their EURO '92 triumph, when he argued about tactics with the coach and was dropped.

FACTFILE
Michael Laudrup is the only player to have appeared for Real Madrid in a 5-0 win over Barcelona and also for Barcelona when they have beaten Real 5-0.

▲ Michael Laudrup drives effortlessly forwards during a 1996 friendly match against Germany.

CARLI LLOYD
USA • BORN 1982 • CAPS: 316 • GOALS: 134

A livewire attacker with stamina, pace and a lethal shot, Lloyd played for W-League team New Jersey Splash whilst still at High School. She made her international debut at age 23 and became a fixture in the US women's team that won two Olympic gold medals and the 2015 World Cup. In that competition, Lloyd was at her peak, scoring six times, including a hat-trick in the final that featured a goal from the halfway line. Lloyd was made player of the tournament and was also voted the world's best female footballer in both 2015 and 2016. Save for a short spell in 2017-18 with Manchester City, Lloyd's club career was spent entirely in the US with teams including Chicago Red Stars and Western New York Flash. In 2021, she announced her retirement, going out with a bang by scoring five goals in a friendly against Paraguay.

► Carli Lloyd celebrates a 4-3 US victory over Australia to win Olympic bronze in 2021.

AMANDINE HENRY
FRANCE • BORN 1989
CAPS: 93 • GOALS: 13

Henry's first season in senior football saw the bustling midfielder score 11 goals in 20 games for Henin-Beaumont – an outstanding return considering she was just 15. After two years at France's female football academy, Clairefontaine, she joined Lyon. Severe injuries blighted her early time there before she got the chance to shine. Henry mostly operates as a central or defensive midfielder, intercepting attacks and setting up her own team's forward play using her expert eye for a pass. She has been a valuable asset for title-winning Lyon and France, with whom she won the Silver Ball as the second-best player at the 2015 Women's World Cup.

►Amandine Henry moves upfield against Brazil at the 2019 World Cup. She scored the extra-time winner.

MOHAMED SALAH

EGYPT • BORN 1992 • CAPS: 84 • GOALS: 47

The 'Egyptian King' is beloved by neutrals and Egypt and Liverpool fans alike for his exuberant play and humble personality. A seemingly slight frame disguises his strength, sudden acceleration and brilliance in dribbling, creating chances for team-mates, or scoring audacious goals. After three seasons in the Egyptian Premier League and a spell in Switzerland with Basel, Salah was signed by Chelsea in 2014 but was given little chance to make an impact, playing just 13 league games before he was loaned out to Fiorentina and then Roma, who signed him permanently. A season later he joined Liverpool for £36.5 million, making an immediate impact with 44 goals in his debut season. He has barely let up since, taking just 151 games to notch 100 league goals.

▶ Salah won the Champions League in 2019 and the Premier League in 2020.

JAIRZINHO

BRAZIL • BORN 1944
CAPS: 82 • GOALS: 34

Jair Ventura Filho, better known as Jairzinho, was an electrifying right-winger in a similar mould to his childhood hero, Garrincha. First capped for Brazil in 1964, he was moved to the left wing to accommodate Garrincha in the 1966 World Cup. At the 1970 tournament Jairzinho was moved back to his favoured right side, where he shone, scoring in each of the six rounds of the competition – a record to this day. At club level, Jairzinho spent most of his career at Brazil's Botafogo, also having short spells with Marseille in France, Portuguesa in Venezuela and the Brazilian side Cruzeiro, with whom he won the Copa América in 1976.

▲ Jairzinho worked as a ball boy at Botafogo before going on to make over 400 appearances for the Rio-based team.

SUN WEN

CHINA • BORN 1973
CAPS: 152 • GOALS: 106

A legend in women's football, Sun Wen won seven regional championships with Chinese side Shanghai TV, before moving to the USA in 2000 to play for Atlanta Beat. Playing in midfield or attack, she became one of the world's leading international goalscorers, thanks to her strong shooting, vision and eye for a goal. Sun Wen won both the Golden Boot (top scorer) and the Golden Ball (top player) awards at the 1999 Women's World Cup, where China were narrowly beaten on penalties in the final by the USA. In 2000, she was named FIFA World Player of the Century alongside the USA's Michelle Akers. After China's surprise World Cup exit at the hands of Canada in 2003, she retired.

LUKA MODRIC

CROATIA • BORN 1983
CAPS: 148 • GOALS: 21

A finalist with Croatia at the 2018 World Cup, where he was voted the tournament's best player, Modric is a skilled playmaker with an eye for the perfect pass. After long spells with Dinamo Zagreb and Tottenham Hotspur, Modric joined Real Madrid in 2012, with whom he has won four UEFA Champions Leagues. In 2018, he won the Ballon D'Or as the world's best footballer.

◀ Luka Modric makes a typically slick and accurate sidefoot pass for Croatia.

STRIKERS

JOHAN CRUYFF
NETHERLANDS • 1947–2016
CAPS: 48 • GOALS: 33

Cruyff was one of the game's finest ever players and a pivotal part of the Dutch 'total football' revolution. Blessed with great vision and remarkable ball skills, he is the only player to have a move named after him – the Cruyff turn. He won three European Cups in a row at Ajax, before following his old boss, Rinus Michels, to Barcelona in 1973 and helping them to win Spanish league and cup titles. Cruyff played as a centre-forward, but would drift around the pitch, creating confusion among defenders. His total of 33 goals for the Netherlands would have been higher were it not for his refusal to play in the 1978 World Cup (see page 110). Cruyff later managed Ajax and Barcelona to success in Europe.

▲ After Barcelona, Cruyff played for two seasons in the USA.

◀ George Best won two First Division titles and the European Cup in 11 seasons at Manchester United.

GEORGE BEST
N. IRELAND
1946–2005
CAPS: 37
GOALS: 9

Best was just 17 when he made his first-team debut for Manchester United. He was the most gifted player to emerge from the British Isles, and its first superstar. Best's goalscoring exploits and his eye for an outrageous pass or move quickly made him a legend. He was also a fearless tackler and great dribbler, and was Manchester United's leading scorer five seasons in a row. Sadly, he was denied the biggest stage of all as Northern Ireland failed to qualify for the World Cup during his career. In 1974, Best sensationally retired from the game. He made a series of comebacks in England, the USA and Australia, where he appeared for the Brisbane Lions in 1983.

ROBERT LEWANDOWSKI
POLAND • BORN 1988 • CAPS: 129 • GOALS: 75

An absolute goal machine, Lewandowski has scored wherever he has played. He started out in Polish lower league sides before two seasons at Lech Poznań earned him a move to Borussia Dortmund. A quiet first season was contrasted by an explosion of goalscoring in the three that followed. His record since joining Bayern Munich in 2014 is outstanding – 333 goals in 361 matches. In 2020-21, he broke Gerd Muller's record of most Bundesliga goals in a season with 41 in just 29 games. In 2021 his talent finally received the recognition it deserves with FIFA's Best Male Player award.

FERENC PUSKAS
HUNGARY • 1927–2006 • CAPS: 84
(4 FOR SPAIN) • GOALS: 83

A star for his club, Kispest (which became Honved), and his country, Puskas was short, stocky and an average header of the ball. But his sublime skills, vision and thunderbolt of a left-foot shot made him a devastating striker. After the Hungarian revolution in 1956, Puskas searched for a club in western Europe for more than a year. In his thirties and overweight, he was eventually signed by Real Madrid in 1958. He repaid Real's faith by heading the Spanish goalscoring table four times, netting four goals in the 1960 European Cup final and a hat-trick in the 1962 final. In 1966, he began a coaching career, which saw him take Greek side Panathinaikos to the 1971 European Cup final.

◀ Poland's Robert Lewandowski lines up a tricky sidefoot volley during a World Cup qualifier against Andorra.

LIONEL MESSI
ARGENTINA • BORN 1987
CAPS: 160 • GOALS: 81

Locals in the Argentinian city of Rosario knew they were seeing a special talent when Messi, not yet in his teens, powered his local children's football team to lose just one game in four years. Moving from Argentina to Spain at the age of 13, Messi was schooled in Barcelona's youth sides before making his official debut for the first team at the age of 17. He won ten La Liga, seven Copa del Rey and four UEFA Champions League titles with the Spanish giants as well as 2008 Olympic gold with Argentina. His close control, vision and flair is almost unparalleled in the modern game. The 2009–10 season saw Messi score 47 goals, and the following season he upped this to a staggering 73 goals in all competitions. By 2021, Messi had scored 30-plus goals every season for 13 seasons in a row. In that year, he failed to agree a deal with Barcelona and moved to Paris Saint-Germain.

▶ Lionel Messi surges forward for Argentina, perfectly balanced, looking for an opening to attack.

FACTFILE
A 2021 hat-trick versus Bolivia made Lionel Messi South America's leading international goalscorer, beating Pelé's record.

▶ Dennis Bergkamp made more than 400 appearances for Arsenal, scoring 120 goals.

DENNIS BERGKAMP
NETHERLANDS • BORN 1969
CAPS: 79 • GOALS: 37

Named after the Scottish striker Denis Law, Bergkamp was a product of the famous Ajax youth academy. He played in the Dutch league for the first time in 1986. The most technically gifted Dutch footballer since Johan Cruyff, Bergkamp often played in the space between midfield and attack, where he used his eye for an unexpected pass, plus world-class technique, to create as many goals as he scored. After an unsuccessful spell at Internazionale, Bergkamp moved to Arsenal for £7.5 million in 1995. In his 11 years at the club, he won three Premier League titles and scored or set up more than 280 goals. He retired in May 2006 after the final of the Champions League against Barcelona.

MATCH ACTION
Dennis Bergkamp broke the deadlock in a tense 1998 World Cup quarter-final against Argentina with a sensational goal. On the stroke of 90 minutes, Frank de Boer hit a 50-metre pass into the penalty area. Controlling the ball with one delicate touch of his right boot, Bergkamp took a second touch to turn Argentinian defender Roberto Ayala, before shooting powerfully past keeper Carlos Roa. The goal saw Bergkamp become the Netherlands' leading international scorer.

Roa

Ayala 2

Bergkamp 1

Bergkamp 2

Ayala 1

ANDRIY SHEVCHENKO
UKRAINE • BORN 1976 CAPS: 111 • GOALS: 48

Shevchenko scored just one goal in 16 games in his first season at Dynamo Kyiv, but his perfect blend of pace and power propelled Kyiv to five Ukrainian league titles and strong showings in the Champions League. A multi-million-pound transfer to AC Milan followed in 1999. On three occasions Shevchenko scored 24 goals per season in the ultra-tough Italian league. In 2004, Shevchenko was voted European Footballer of the Year. Two years later he moved to Chelsea for more than £30 million, but returned to Milan on loan for the 2008–09 season. He then returned to Kyiv, where he made more than 80 appearances before retiring in 2012.

◀ Shevchenko on the move for Ukraine in a World Cup qualifier in 2005.

▶ Spain's Raúl was the top scorer in qualifying for EURO 2000, with ten goals from eight games. Here, he evades a tackle during EURO 2004.

RAÚL
SPAIN • BORN 1977
CAPS: 102
GOALS: 44

Raúl González Blanco made his debut for the Real Madrid first team at 17 – their youngest ever player – and went on to score six times in his first 11 games. In the years that followed, Raúl became the biggest star in Spanish football and the country's all-time leading goalscorer. At club level, he won two Spanish league titles and three Champions Leagues with Real Madrid. Top scorer in the Spanish league twice, Raúl's goals in the 2003–04 Champions League campaign saw him become the first player to net more than 40 times in the competition.

GERD MÜLLER
WEST GERMANY • 1945–2021
CAPS: 62 • GOALS: 68

The Bomber, as Gerd Müller was nicknamed, holds a series of goalscoring records. From 1963, he scored a club record 365 goals in 427 league matches for Bayern Munich. During 16 years with Bayern, he won four Bundesliga titles, four German Cups and three European Cups. For his country, Müller held one of the greatest international striking records, scoring more than a goal every game. His two strikes against the Soviet Union helped West Germany win the 1972 European Championships. Müller's tally of 14 World Cup goals remained a record until 2006, while his final international goal won West Germany the 1974 World Cup on home soil.

▶ Gerd Müller (right) battles Konrad Weise of East Germany in 1974.

ROBERTO BAGGIO
ITALY • BORN 1967 • CAPS: 57 • GOALS: 27

Blessed with great skill and vision, Roberto Baggio made his professional debut with Vicenza, in the Italian third division, at just 15 years of age. He broke into Italy's Serie A with Fiorentina in 1985, and when Baggio was transferred to Juventus in 1990, three days of rioting by Fiorentina fans ensued. The fee of £7.7 million made him the world's most expensive player at that time. Crowned World Footballer of the Year in 1993, Baggio scored spectacular goals for his country and his clubs, AC Milan, Bologna, Inter Milan and Brescia. In 2004, while playing for Brescia, he scored his 200th Serie A goal. He appeared in three World Cups and scored five out of Italy's eight goals in the 1994 competition. However, Baggio will always be remembered for his costly penalty miss in the final of the tournament. The striker was given an emotional send-off in 2004 when he played for Italy for the first time in five years, in a friendly against Spain.

ERLING HAALAND
NORWAY
BORN 2000
CAPS: 17 • GOALS: 15

The son of Alf-Inge Håland, who played for Leeds United, Manchester City and Norway, Haaland began at his father's home club, Bryne. He moved to Molde under the management of Ole Gunnar Solskjær and in 2019 to Red Bull Salzburg. There, he scored three hat-tricks within months of arriving and a further three goals on his UEFA Champions League debut. Haaland is an explosive, lethal striker, fully exploiting his height (1.94m), mobility, aggression and incredible finishing skills. A big-money move to Borussia Dortmund did not stem his flow of goals. In his first two-and-a-half seasons, he averaged over a goal a game, making him one of the hottest properties in world football.

BOBBY CHARLTON
ENGLAND • BORN 1937 • CAPS: 106 • GOALS: 49

Apart from a final season with Preston North End, Charlton was a one-club player with Manchester United, for whom he made his debut in 1956. Known around the globe for his trophy-winning exploits in both the World Cup and the European Cup, Charlton was one of the few survivors of the devastating Munich air crash, which claimed the lives of many of his Manchester United team-mates. As a player he showed great sportsmanship and dedication – in training, he even wore a slipper on his right foot to encourage him to pass and shoot with his weaker left foot. Operating as a deep-lying centre-forward with a phenomenal shot from either foot, Charlton scored 245 goals from 751 appearances for United. He was knighted in 1994.

▶ Bobby Charlton's 1970 World Cup campaign was his fourth in a row as part of the England squad.

◀ Erling Haaland hunts down the ball for Norway. At the 2019 U-20 World Cup, he scored nine goals in one match.

▶ Sam Kerr keeps her eyes on the ball as she brings it down with the inside of her foot.

SAM KERR
AUSTRALIA • BORN 1993
CAPS: 108 • GOALS: 56

Astonishingly, Sam Kerr made both her W-League debut for Perth Glory and her national team debut at the age of 15. A prodigious talent, Kerr has developed into a reliable goalscorer who does her best work in and around the opponent's penalty area. Most of her goals are followed by her trademark backflip celebration. Much in demand, Kerr played for Sydney FC and three US clubs – Western New York Flash, Sky Blue FC and Chicago Red Stars – before moving to Chelsea in 2019. Internationally, Kerr has appeared at three Women's World Cups and in 2019 became the first Australian, male or female, to score a World Cup hat-trick.

DIEGO MARADONA
ARGENTINA • 1960–2020
CAPS: 91 • GOALS: 34

Diego Armando Maradona was a phenomenal footballer. Stocky and with a low centre of gravity, he conjured mesmeric, weaving runs through the tightest defences, lightning turns that left opposition players kicking at thin air, and sublime shots, chips and flicks. Maradona debuted aged 15 for Argentinos Juniors. Calls for his inclusion in the 1978 World Cup squad were ignored by Argentina's coach, Cesar Luis Menotti, but he would appear at the next four tournaments. His finest hour came in 1986, when Maradona was the player of the tournament as he skippered an unremarkable side to World Cup victory (see pages 54–55). Maradona captained Argentina at the 1990 World Cup, where he reached the final, but the following year he failed a drugs test and was banned for 15 months. A further failed test during the 1994 World Cup saw him sent home after playing the first two games. His international career was over. After retiring, Maradona battled with drug addiction, but in 2000 he was the joint winner of FIFA's Footballer of the Century award with Pelé.

▶ Maradona holds the Argentinian record for most World Cup appearances – 21 games.

ZICO
BRAZIL • BORN 1953
CAPS: 72 • GOALS: 52

Artur Antunes Coimbra (known as Zico) was given a special diet and training regime to build him up when he first arrived at the Brazilian club Flamengo. Sharp, quick-witted and with the ability to hit an explosive shot or a deadly free kick, Zico won four league titles with Flamengo, as well as the Copa Libertadores and the World Club Cup in 1981. He scored a staggering 591 goals in his first 11 seasons with Flamengo. He went on to play in Asia for Kashima Antlers and in 2002 he became manager of Japan's national team.

FACTFILE

Diego Maradona's moves to Barcelona in 1982 (for £4.2 million) and to Napoli in 1984 (for £6.9 million) were both world-record transfers. After nine years at Napoli and a spell at Sevilla, he returned to Argentina with Newell's Old Boys and Boca Juniors.

RUUD GULLIT
N'LANDS • BORN 1962
CAPS: 66 • GOALS: 17

In 1978, the dreadlocked Gullit started out as a sweeper for Dutch side Haarlem. He possessed great attacking flair, stamina, a tough tackle and a sweet pass. He was the subject of feverish transfer activity, moving to Feyenoord, PSV Eindhoven and AC Milan, with whom he won European Cups in 1989 and 1990. After a season at Sampdoria he moved to Chelsea, and in 1996 he was appointed player-manager of the London club. By winning the 1997 FA Cup he became the first non-British manager to lift a major domestic trophy in England.

◀ Ruud Gullit initiates an attack at EURO 88.

ALFREDO DI STEFANO
SPAIN • 1926–2014 • CAPS: 31 • GOALS: 23

To many people, di Stefano was the complete player, years ahead of his time. His astonishing energy helped him play all over the pitch – defending, tackling, unselfishly distributing the ball and creating chances for others as well as for himself. Born in a poor suburb of Buenos Aires, he played for River Plate in a relentless forward line known as *La Máquina* (the Machine). A move to Europe in 1953 saw him become part of the legendary Real Madrid side that dominated Europe in the 1950s and early 1960s. Di Stefano formed a deadly partnership with Ferenc Puskas, scoring in five European Cup finals in a row. Real Madrid player and coach Miguel Muñoz explained: 'The greatness of di Stefano was that with him in your side, you had two players in every position.'

▶ As well as appearing for Real Madrid (pictured) and Spain, di Stefano also played seven unofficial games for Argentina and four for Colombia.

EUSEBIO
PORTUGAL • 1942–2014 • CAPS: 64 • GOALS: 41

Eusebio da Silva Ferreira was the first African footballing superstar. Lethal in the air and equipped with a power-packed right-foot shot, he scored an incredible 727 goals in 715 professional games. Eusebio played his early football for Sporting Lourenço Marques in his home country of Mozambique – a Portuguese colony at the time. The striker was at the centre of one of the fiercest transfer disputes when he arrived in Portugal. He was virtually kidnapped by Benfica to keep him away from rivals Sporting Lisbon. Benfica's £7,500 purchase proved to be one of the buys of the century. Over a 15-year career with Benfica, Eusebio scored at an awe-inspiring ratio of more than a goal a game. He was the Portuguese league's top goalscorer seven times, twice the leading goalscorer in the whole of Europe and the 1966 World Cup's top scorer, with nine goals for Portugal.

▲ Eusebio won the Portuguese league title with Benfica an incredible 11 times in 15 seasons between 1960 and 1975.

VIVIANNE MIEDEMA
NETHERLANDS • BORN 1996
CAPS: 106 • GOALS: 85

Losing her two front teeth aged six in a collision with a goalkeeper did not diminish Miedema's appetite for attacking football. She began her senior career with SC Heerenveen, where she scored at a rate of more than a goal per game. This attracted the attentions of more than 30 clubs, including Bayern Munich, whom she joined in 2014 and helped propel to their first league title since 1976. Her international goal record, not far short of a goal per game, is astonishing. It includes her setting a new Olympic record in 2021 when scoring ten goals in just four games.

◣ Miedema moved to Arsenal in 2017 and by the start of 2022 had struck 109 goals in just 116 games.

GEORGE WEAH
LIBERIA • BORN 1966 • CAPS: 61 GOALS: 22

In 1988, the Monaco manager Arsène Wenger shrewdly plucked the young, raw Weah from Cameroon side Tonnerre Yaoundé. Weah exploded onto the European scene, winning the French league with Monaco in 1991 and Paris Saint-Germain in 1994, before moving to AC Milan. A truly devastating finisher, Weah scored many spectacular goals to help AC Milan win two Serie A titles. He was voted African Footballer of the Year four times, and also won European and World Player of the Year awards in 1995 and FIFA's Fair Play Award the following year. He had short spells at Chelsea, Manchester City and in the United Arab Emirates late in his career, before retiring in 2002. A UNICEF ambassador since 1997, Weah entered politics and was elected president of Liberia in 2018.

JÜRGEN KLINSMANN
WEST GERMANY / GERMANY
BORN 1964 • CAPS: 108
GOALS: 47

Sharp and athletic around the penalty area and an outstanding goal poacher, Klinsmann was German Footballer of the Year in his first spell at VfB Stuttgart. He then moved to Internazionale, where he won the 1989 Serie A title. He was part of West Germany's 1990 World Cup-winning side, scored five goals in the 1994 competition and captained the team at the 1998 tournament. Klinsmann enjoyed spells with Monaco and, in 1994, the first of two stints with Tottenham Hotspur. After 29 goals in his first Premiership season, Klinsmann was voted England's Footballer of the Year in 1995. The striker moved to Bayern Munich, Sampdoria and Tottenham once more, before retiring in 1998. In 2004, he was appointed Germany's manager and coached an exciting side to third place at the 2006 World Cup.

◢ Jürgen Klinsmann is in sixth place on the World Cup scoring list, with 11 goals over three tournaments.

▶ An outstanding playmaker as well as goalscorer, Marta was voted best player of the 2007 Women's World Cup.

MARTA VIEIRA DA SILVA
BRAZIL • BORN 1986 • CAPS: 171 • GOALS: 115

Short for a striker, at under 1.6m tall, Marta is a goal-scoring dynamo who was voted the world's best female player six times (2006–10, 2018). She played her early football for several Brazilian clubs before two spells in Sweden, either side of three seasons in the USA, where she won the Women's Professional Soccer (WPS) championship twice with two different clubs – FC Gold Pride and Western New York Flash. A truly prolific finisher, Marta has scored more World Cup finals goals (17) than any player, male or female. She has also won seven Swedish league titles, two Olympic silver medals and three Copa América Femenina titles with Brazil, the latest in 2018. After her three goals at the Tokyo games in 2021, she became the first footballer to score in five consecutive Olympics.

RONALDO
BRAZIL • BORN 1976
CAPS: 98 • GOALS: 62

Ronaldo Luis Nazario de Lima became hot property as an 18-year-old by scoring 58 goals in just 60 games for Brazil's Cruzeiro. Ronaldo moved to PSV Eindhoven and then Barcelona, where his close control and devastating bursts of pace helped him become Europe's top scorer in 1996–97, with 34 goals. Sold to Internazionale, he was their top scorer in his first season. He then endured four injury-ravaged years. After a poor World Cup final in 1998, many doubted his ability, but he bounced back in 2002 as the tournament's top scorer. A month later, Real Madrid paid £28.49 million for the Brazilian, and in 2006 Ronaldo became the highest scorer in World Cup history, with 15 goals. In 2007, he moved to Italian giants AC Milan, and in 2009 to Brazilian team Corinthians.

MIA HAMM
USA • BORN 1972 • CAPS: 276 • GOALS: 158

Born with a partial club foot that had to be corrected by plaster casts, Mia Hamm went on to become the world's most famous female footballer. She was the youngest ever player for the US women's team when she debuted against China at the age of 15, and the youngest member of the US side that won the 1991 World Cup. Hamm played in three more World Cups, as well as winning two Olympic gold medals and one silver. A phenomenal all-round player with an icy-cool finish, she was the leading scorer in the history of women's international football for a decade. Hamm was also a founding member of WUSA, playing for Washington Freedom when the league began in 2001.

NEYMAR
BRAZIL • BORN 1992
CAPS: 117 • GOALS: 71

Heralded as the heir to Ronaldo and Pelé when he debuted for Santos aged 17, Neymar has spent his entire career under the pressure of expectation. He won the Copa Libertadores as well as the South American Footballer of the Year twice as a teenager before moving to Barcelona, where his trickery and vision saw him score 105 goals. Two of these came in an electric display in 2017 when he masterminded Barça's 6-1 victory over PSG, overturning a 4-0 first-leg loss – the biggest comeback in UEFA Champions League history. Within six months he was a PSG player after a world-record £198-million transfer. Injuries and disciplinary issues have affected his later career but he is still capable of magical dribbling or goalscoring moments that can turn the course of a game.

FACTFILE
Ronaldo's ex-wife, Milene Domingues, broke the world record for keeping a football off the ground in 1995. She kept the ball in the air for nine hours and six minutes, making 55,187 touches in the process.

▶ Neymar has won eight league titles – three at Santos, two at Barcelona and three in a row at PSG.

◤ Mia Hamm drives forwards during a 1999 Women's World Cup game versus China.

◀ Ronaldo in action for Brazil in 2002, the year he won his third FIFA World Player of the Year award.

PELÉ
BRAZIL • BORN 1940 • CAPS: 92 • GOALS: 77

Edson Arantes do Nascimento simply had it all. Considered the finest footballer of all time, Pelé was a masterful attacker with seemingly limitless skills, creativity and vision. He was magnificent in the air, lethal on the ground, could dribble, pass and take swerving free kicks, and saw passes and opportunities that other players could not. Aged 11, Pelé was spotted by a former Brazil player, Waldemar de Brito, who took him to Clube Atletico Bauru. Four years later, Pelé made his debut for Santos aged 15. He would play for the São Paulo side for the next 18 years. Pelé was only 17 when he appeared at the 1958 World Cup, scoring a hat-trick in the semi-final and two superb goals in the final as Brazil won their first World Cup. A pulled muscle cut short Pelé's involvement in the 1962 competition and he had to be content with winning the World Club Cup for Santos. Injured by brutal tackling in the 1966 World Cup, Pelé was outstanding at the 1970 tournament. He retired from international football in 1971 – in front of around 180,000 fans at the Maracanã Stadium – and from club football in 1974. In tribute, Santos removed the number ten shirt from their team line-up. Pelé later came out of retirement to play in a star-studded line-up at New York Cosmos. He went on to become Brazil's minister of sport and a UN and UNICEF ambassador. One of the most respected figures in world football, he was voted Athlete of the Century by the International Olympic Committee in 1999.

BIRGIT PRINZ
GERMANY • BORN 1977
CAPS: 214 • GOALS: 128

Apart from a spell in the United States in 2002, where her 12 goals in 15 games helped Carolina Courage to win the WUSA championship, Prinz played all her club football for FFC Frankfurt. Here, she won six German league titles, eight German Cups and scored over 250 goals (at a rate better than a goal a game). With Germany, she won two World Cups (2003, 2007), five European Championships and three Olympic bronze medals – a staggering haul. She was also awarded the FIFA World Women's Footballer of the Year on three occasions and finished second a further four times, the last in 2010, a year before she announced her retirement.

▶ Kane is closing in on Wayne Rooney's England goalscoring record of 53.

HARRY KANE
ENGLAND • BORN 1993
CAPS: 69 • GOALS: 49

Starting out at Ridgeway Rovers, the same Essex club as David Beckham, Kane used rejection by Arsenal and doubts about his potential as a spur to improve his game. Joining Tottenham Hotspur, he was loaned out to four English league clubs before making his first Premier League start in 2014. The following season, he scored 31 goals and established himself as Spurs' first-choice striker, capable of releasing thunderous shots and delicate chips or leaping to power or glance headers in on goal. He led the goals-scored charts in three Premier League seasons while developing his assisting and passing game to provide devastating through balls for team-mates. England's captain and talisman has led the national team to a World Cup semi-final in 2018 and the EURO 2020 final.

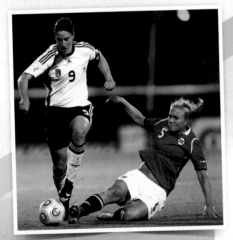

▲ Germany's Birgit Prinz is challenged by Norway's Anneli Giske during the UEFA Women's EURO 2009.

▲▲ Pelé at the 1970 World Cup, where he was Player of the Tournament.

KYLIAN MBAPPÉ
FRANCE • BORN 1998 • CAPS: 54 • GOALS: 26

Courted by Real Madrid and Chelsea while still a boy, Mbappé played for AS Bondy where his father was coach, often in age groups older than himself. He joined Monaco's B side in 2015 but was thrown into first-team action as a 16-year-old and quickly established himself as a phenomenal attacking talent. Mbappé's explosive acceleration, pace and power couple with tactical intelligence and a wicked shot. PSG came calling, making him the world's most expensive teenager in 2017. He repaid the investment rapidly with 100 goals for PSG before the end of 2020. His international debut came a year before the 2018 World Cup, where he became the first teenager since Pelé to score two World Cup goals in a match. At the same tournament he won FIFA's Best Young Player award.

◀ Kylian Mbappé kisses the World Cup trophy. The striker scored four goals in the tournament.

LEADING INTERNATIONAL GOALSCORERS

PLAYER	COUNTRY	CAPS	GOALS
Men			
Cristiano Ronaldo	Portugal	186	115
Ali Daei	Iran	149	109
Mokhtar Dahari	Malaysia	142	89
Ferenc Puskás	Hungary	84	83
Lionel Messi	Argentina	160	81
Godfrey Chitalu	Zambia	111	79
Women			
Christine Sinclair	Canada	306	188
Abby Wambach	USA	256	184
Mia Hamm	USA	276	158
Carli Lloyd	USA	316	134
Kristine Lilly	USA	352	130
Birgit Prinz	Germany	214	128

MARCO VAN BASTEN
N'LANDS • BORN 1964
CAPS: 58 • GOALS: 24

One of the coolest finishers in world football, van Basten was just 29 when an ankle injury in the 1993 European Cup final effectively ended his playing career – although he struggled on until 1995. Renowned for spectacular goals in crucial contests, van Basten was European Footballer of the Year three times (1988, 1989 and 1992) and in 1988 he hit the headlines as the Netherlands won the European Championships. He scored a hat-trick against England in the quarter-final, the semi-final winner versus Germany and a breathtaking volley from the tightest of angles in the final against the Soviet Union. With Ajax he won three league titles, scoring 128 goals. He then moved to AC Milan, hitting 90 goals in 147 games and winning three Serie A titles and two European Cups.

▶ Marco van Basten on the rampage in the Netherland's 3-1 win over England at EURO '88.

HUGO SANCHEZ
MEXICO
BORN 1958
CAPS: 57 • GOALS: 26

Mexico's most famous player, Sanchez spent the peak of his playing career in Spain, scoring over 230 goals for Atlético Madrid and Real Madrid. He formed a lethal partnership with Emilio Butragueno at Real as they won five league titles in a row. Sanchez was La Liga's top scorer in five different seasons and in 1990 he won the European Golden Boot for a record 38 goals in one season. Sadly, his commitments to European football and frequent bust-ups with Mexican football officials meant that he appeared in only a fraction of the international games played by his home country. He had a disappointing tournament at the 1986 World Cup on home soil, scoring just one goal.

SNAPSHOT
MARADONA'S WORLD CUP

Diego Maradona, the Argentinian striker with magical balance and touch, ended the 1986 World Cup with his hands on the trophy and a highly impressive five goals and five assists. Yet these statistics do not tell the story of his true impact, for Mexico '86 was Maradona's tournament. He roused a relatively ordinary Argentinian side into recapturing football's biggest prize (the South Americans had won the trophy on home soil in 1978) and wiped out the memory of a disappointing tournament in 1982. In a tense quarter-final against England, controversy raged over Maradona's infamous 'Hand of God' goal (see below), but his second and winning goal was pure genius. The Argentinian collected the ball in his own half, then dribbled, twisted and turned through the English defence to score what was later voted the goal of the century. He would score a goal of similar brilliance in the semi-final versus Belgium. At this point, at the age of just 25, Maradona was without doubt the greatest footballer on the planet.

◀ Diego Maradona, clutching the World Cup after his team's epic 3-2 victory over West Germany in the 1986 final, is carried around the Azteca Stadium on the shoulders of ecstatic Argentinian supporters.

▼ Maradona uses his hand to get the ball past England goalkeeper Peter Shilton to score Argentina's first goal in a 2-1 victory.

THE BRAIN GAME

Football is a sport that calls for pace, power, stamina and skill, but it also demands mental agility. Footballers with the ability to think one step ahead of the opposition are highly prized, and such skills can win a match for their team. The same applies to managers and coaches. In the run-up to a match, they have many key decisions to make. They must decide who to select, which formation to play, and choose the tactics they will use in their bid to outwit the opposition.

TEAM SELECTION

With large squads of players and endless analysis of opponents, managers fret over picking their starting XI in the days ahead of a big game. Teams need flair, skill, composure, aggression, sound defensive skills and goalscoring abilities – all in the right quantities. Some players, despite being footballing superstars, may not play well with each other or work with the rest of the team, while other, less heralded players may actually perform a more effective job in a particular game. The way the opposition plays can dictate which players are selected, as can the fitness and performances of individuals. Star players, who would normally be first on the team sheet, may not be picked if they are recovering from injury or suffering from a lack of confidence or form. Both young, talented players emerging from the reserve team and experienced veterans at the end of their careers will have strong cases for a place in the side. It all adds up to a complex puzzle that managers must solve.

◀ In November 2021, Canada beat CONCACAF giants Mexico for the first time since 2000. Manager John Herdman brought into his side 38-year-old veteran Atiba Hutchinson and striker Cyle Larin (left), who scored both goals in the famous victory.

▼ In the past, club squads were much smaller. In 1983–84, Liverpool's league- and European Cup-winning team (below) played 66 games with a squad of just 16. Bruce Grobbelaar, Alan Kennedy, Sammy Lee and Alan Hansen played in every game.

FACTFILE
In a 2021 World Cup qualifier versus Poland, Gareth Southgate became the first England manager since 1996 not to make a single substitution. His opposing coach, Paulo Sousa, made five.

REST AND ROTATION

With large squads and matches coming thick and fast in the middle of a season, coaches at the top sides often rest and rotate players to keep them fresh and fit. They may also adjust their team game-to-game to counter the opposition's strengths and prey on their weaknesses.

Some coaches, such as Pep Guardiola, are particularly keen to tinker and rarely field the same starting XI two or three times in a row. Other coaches prefer a more settled side, resting key players only against weaker opposition such as lower-league opponents in cup competitions – but even this can come with a risk. In 2021, Leeds United manager Marcelo Bielsa rested his first-choice goalkeeper and striker only to crash out of the FA Cup, losing 3-0 to Crawley Town, three divisions below.

SUBSTITUTIONS

Replacing a player with a substitute was not a part of the competitive game for almost a century. Richard Gottinger became the first official World Cup substitute, for example, in a 1953 qualifier when he came on for West Germany. The lack of subs made for some amusing and heroic moments, with strikers having to play in goal and teams occasionally reduced to eight or nine men through injury. Gradually, the number of substitutions a manager can make has risen. In the UEFA Champions League, for example, managers can make five substitutions. The timing and choice of substitutes can be crucial. Coaches use them to change tactics and the shape of the team or to seek a match-winning impact. At the 2018 World Cup, Belgium manager Roberto Martinez made two attacking substitutions with his side 2-0 down to Japan, bringing on Marouane Fellaini and Nacer Chadli. Both scored in a memorable 3-2 turnaround.

▶ Netherlands coach Sarina Wiegman prepares a sub. During her reign, the Dutch lost just 11 of 72 games, won EURO 2017 and reached the 2019 World Cup final.

▲ 150 of Ole Gunnar Solskjaer's 366 appearances for Manchester United were as a substitute. He scored 33 goals in the last 15 minutes of matches, including the memorable winner in the 1999 UEFA Champions League final.

◤ Christophe Galtier managed Lille to a surprise Ligue 1 title in 2021 with a team built around a core of promising young players.

FORMATIONS

The way in which a team lines up is known as its formation. In the first football international, in 1872, Scotland set up in a 2-2-6 formation, with two backs, two half-backs (similar to midfielders) and six attackers. England went even further, playing 1-1-8 (eight forwards), but crowded goalmouths saw the game end 0-0.

▶ Marcela Bielsa is famous for playing unusual formations such as 4-1-4-1 and 3-3-1-3 as coach of Leeds United, Marseille and Chile.

CHANGING SHAPES

Attack-heavy formations persisted until 1925, when Arsenal's Herbert Chapman capitalized on changes to the offside law with an innovative new W-M formation. Similar to a modern-day 3-2-2-3, W-M was adopted by many other teams and it was only the arrival of a flat back four that changed things. Sometimes thought of as negative, a flat back four was employed by a Brazil side that dazzled at the 1958 World Cup with a 4-2-4 formation. Up front, the team's two wingers fed into two central strikers, one of whom was a teenaged Pelé.

In the World Cups that followed, many sides kept the back four defenders but adjusted the rest of the formation to less-attacking 4-3-3 and 4-4-2 shapes. These are still employed today – the USA won the 2019 Women's World Cup playing 4-3-3 – but they are just two of a large selection of different formations at a manager's disposal. Teams may even change formation once or twice during a game.

FORMATION VARIATIONS

Some modern coaches, such as Jürgen Klopp, favour four at the back but expect their wide defenders to be a major attacking threat as well. To cover for them, defensive midfielders may be employed. Some sides adopt a 3-5-2 formation with three central defenders and two wing-backs who need exceptional stamina, as they are expected to both attack and defend throughout the game. Up front, different shapes and roles drift in and out of fashion, such as split strikers with one playing ahead of the other and the 'false 9'. This innovation was championed by Vicente del Bosque's EURO 2012-winning Spain side and by Pep Guardiola at Barcelona. He moved Lionel Messi from playing wide in attack to the centre, but expected him to head back into midfield to drag defenders out of position, receive the ball, turn and dribble. Other common false 9s include Roberto Firmino, Paulo Dybala and Nabil Fekir.

▲ Wing-backs, such as Bayern Munich's Alphonso Davies, play on the flanks. They act like full-backs in defence, but also make attacking runs upfield.

PROTECTING THE DEFENCE

Made popular by Italian teams from the early 1950s onwards, a sweeper plays behind the main bank of defenders to offer further protection. German legend Franz Beckenbauer turned the sweeper role from ultra-defensive to attacking, moving forwards with the ball and linking defence with attack. Today, few sides play with a sweeper. Instead, some teams rely on a goalkeeper who is skilled with their feet to do the job or they prefer one or more holding midfielders who are stationed in front of the defence. Their job is to close down attacks, tackle and intercept the ball. This role is so important that top holding midfielders – from Declan Rice and Rodri to Julie Ertz and N'Golo Kante – are highly prized.

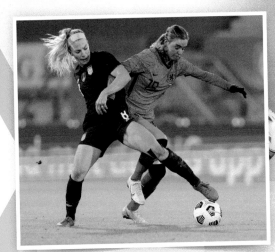

▲ US holding midfielder Julie Ertz stops the Netherlands' Jill Roord. Ertz is excellent at denying opponents time and space.

FLUID FOOTBALL

Inspired by Rinus Michels when he was in charge of Ajax and the Netherlands in the 1960s and '70s, 'total football' saw gifted players swap positions with dizzying regularity all over the pitch. A defender might pop up in attack, a wide midfielder could cover in defence, or a striker would drift into midfield. For most sides – who played rigidly in their formations, often with man-to-man marking – it could be a nightmare to defend against. It did, however, require players with great energy and intelligence to work. Today, many top teams play fluid football that is not strictly total football, but in which players do regularly exchange positions and roles.

◀ Nabil Fekir of Real Betis can be a devastating false 9, finding gaps between an opposing team's banks of defenders and midfielders.

FORMATIONS

Formations are given as numbers of outfield players from the defence forwards. In a 3-5-2, wing-backs operate in wide areas, while 4-4-2 is often more compact, with wide midfielders expected to deliver crosses. 4-3-3 can be all-out attack or more cautious, especially if the three midfielders don't get forward to support attacks. 4-2-3-1 is flexible and popular, with two defensive or pivoting midfielders in front of four defenders.

4-3-3

3-5-2

4-4-2

4-2-3-1

TACTICS

Teams may kick off a game in one of several common formations, but there can be great variation in how they play within that formation and in the tactics they use. For example, a team that lines up as a 4-4-2 side may choose to play defensively, with midfielders tucking in, or aggressively, with one or more midfielders joining the strikers in attack.

TAILORING TACTICS

Managers start a game with what they feel are the best tactics for the players available and the opposition they face. They watch how a match unfolds closely, knowing they can change tactics at any time to exploit an opponent's weakness or to fix problems in their own team's play. Most top footballers can play in several positions. A manager may switch formations using the same players or bring on a substitute with different attributes and skills. Some managers take this to extremes. In the 2021 UEFA Super Cup final against Villareal, Chelsea coach Thomas Tuchel substituted his world-class keeper, Edouard Mendy, with Kepa Arrizabalaga in the 119th minute with the scores tied. Tuchel felt that Kepa would have more success in the penalty shootout. The coach's hunch proved inspired as Kepa saved two penalties and Chelsea won.

◀ Liverpool's Mohamed Salah dribbles at speed. Salah can play on the wing, as a second striker, or as a central attacking midfielder, and can even switch positions throughout a match.

▼ Atlético Madrid's Stefan Savic lunges to block a shot from Real Sociedad's Alexander Isak, confident that he has support from team-mates behind him.

TACTICS IN DEFENCE

Teams have several choices about how they defend. Some managers prefer defenders to patrol areas of space that overlap, a system known as zonal marking. This tactic is often used by Argentinian clubs and many national sides. It requires good communication between defenders. Some coaches set their team up to perform a low block. This is stationing eight, nine or ten outfield players in two banks deep inside their own penalty area. The idea is to restrict the time and space available for their opponents in dangerous areas. Alternatively, a coach may opt for each of their defenders and, sometimes, their defensive midfielders as well, to mark individual opponents, tracking their attacking runs and positions when the defenders' team does not have the ball. Sometimes, a coach asks a player to mark a particularly dangerous opponent – such as a midfield playmaker who controls the opposing team's attacks – for an entire game. Denying them the ball or the space to move forwards can reduce their threat greatly.

▶ Some coaches, such as Julian Nagelsmann and Jürgen Klopp, like their attacking players to press opponents who have possession high up the pitch, looking to win the ball back as early as possible. This tactic is called gegenpressing. Here, RB Leipzig striker Alexander Sørloth chases down the ball, aiming to get there ahead of Bayern Munich goalkeeper Manuel Neuer.

FACTFILE

Barcelona lost the first leg of their 2017 UEFA Champions League quarter-final against PSG 4-0. In an astonishing comeback, they won the second leg 6-1 to go through.

LONG OR SHORT

All teams seek to pass and move the ball into the attacking third of the pitch, where goalscoring chances can be fashioned. For many decades, British managers believed that hitting long balls towards tall strikers created more goal chances, often through a defensive mistake. In continental Europe and South America, a shorter, pass-and-move game was preferred, with sides keeping possession for relatively long periods as they looked for an opening. Another tactic is to rely on pinpoint passing and skilful dribbling to get into the opposition penalty area. Some teams play a counter-attacking game, defending in large numbers and soaking up pressure. When they retrieve the ball, they move it rapidly out of defence with a long pass or by running with the ball. Fast counter-attacking can catch opponents off guard and outnumbered, but requires speedy, aware players. Many coaches mix up their passing and movement tactics – if their team is behind with only minutes to go, they may switch to a direct style, pushing extra players up into the opposition penalty area to look for headers and knock-downs.

▲ The offside trap is a defensive tactic in which the back three or four players move upfield in a straight line to catch an opponent offside. It can be very effective, but may be beaten by a player dribbling through the line or by a well-timed through pass combined with an attacking run.

THE COACH'S ROLE

A successful team needs more than great tactics. It needs to be prepared, instructed and inspired to produce great performances. This is the role of the manager or head coach.

INS AND OUTS

A manager may seek to change the shape and performance of their side by bringing in new players. If money is tight, they may have to bring in loan players, promote youth-team players or shop around lower leagues. At the other end, top football clubs are huge businesses and buy and sell footballers for many tens of millions of pounds. Bargains can still be had, though. Riyad Mahrez and Jamie Vardy cost Leicester City just £450,000 and £1 million respectively, whilst Borussia Dortmund bought striker Robert Lewandowski for a mere £4 million. Mahrez was eventually sold to Manchester City for well over 100 times the fee Leicester paid! Lewandowski, on the other hand, eventually left Dortmund for free.

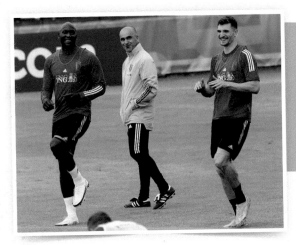

◀ Belgium coach Roberto Martinez oversees a training session at EURO 2020.

◢ Thomas Tuchel celebrates winning Ligue 1 with PSG in 2020, alongside his assistant coaches and a video analyst.

ON A FREE

Many clubs swoop for free transfers of players who are out of contract, offering high wages. In summer 2021, for example, Paris Saint-Germain secured Lionel Messi, Gianluigi Donnarumma, Achraf Hakimi, Sergio Ramos and Georginio Wijnaldum all on frees. On occasion, it's the manager not a player who is subject to a transfer fee! The record fee is £21.7 million paid by Bayern Munich in 2021 to RB Leipzig for their coach, Julian Nagelsmann. It's all a far cry from the women's game where, according to FIFA, just £880,000 was spent globally on transfer fees in 2020.

THE TEAM BEHIND THE TEAM

A manager or head coach is in charge of an increasingly large team of staff, all devoted to ensuring the side performs at its best. They include assistant coaches, some of whom may specialize in training goalkeepers or strikers; others might focus on set-piece moves. Fitness coaches, dieticians, masseurs, physiotherapists and other medical staff prepare players for training and games, and work with injured players on their recovery. Teams often work with sports psychologists, coordination and balance specialists, and sprint or strength trainers.

Performance, data and video analysts are increasingly influential at top clubs. They compile detailed breakdowns of players' strengths, weaknesses and where they can make better decisions during play. Analysts often prepare a detailed dossier on upcoming opponents. The manager digests the report and then communicates the key points to their players. Knowing that an opposing defender makes a particular pass when under pressure or that a striker always feints to the left before shooting can be the crucial detail that wins a game.

◀ Top managers, such as France's Didier Deschamps, talk to the press before and after every game.

▶ Lyon coach Sonia Bompastor passes on new instructions – which might include a change of tactics – to Amandine Henry.

◀ Leicester City paid £5.6 million for N'Golo Kanté in 2015, then sold him for £32 million a year later. Despite that price tag, he's proved to be a bargain for Chelsea, helping them to Premier League and Champions League titles.

MANAGERIAL MIGRATIONS

More and more clubs and national teams look beyond their borders when seeking a new manager. Top coaches may switch countries and continents frequently, especially as the time they are likely to spend in charge of a team gets shorter and shorter. Former England manager Roy Hodgson has managed 17 clubs in eight different nations but even he cannot compete with globetrotting Luiz Felipe Scolari, who has managed 21 clubs everywhere from China to Uzbekistan – including four spells in charge of Brazilian club Gremio in four different decades.

▶ Afshin Ghotbi has coached in the US, South Korea, Iran, China, Thailand and Japan.

UNDER PRESSURE

Few people in sport are under as much pressure as the manager of a major club or national side. Managers stand or fall by their results. In the past, some managers stayed at clubs for season after season. Miguel Munoz, for example, managed Real Madrid for 417 games during the 1960s. At the top level today, few coaches stay in charge of the best teams for more than a handful of seasons. In the short summer period between seasons in 2021, 37 clubs in the top five European leagues changed manager. Many more went on to switch managers during the season. Club owners, chairmen and some fans have short memories, and even recent success does not guarantee job stability. Maurizio Sarri was sacked days after winning the 2019–20 Serie A title with Juventus while Unai Emery was fired as PSG boss in 2018 straight after securing the Ligue 1 championship with a record points-per-game tally. In such an unforgiving climate, Alex Ferguson's remarkable record of 1,500 games in charge of Manchester United across 26½ years may never be beaten.

FACT FILE

In 2015, Chan Yuen Ting became the world's first female coach of any men's top division side when she took charge of Hong Kong team Eastern SC and coached them in the Asian Champions League.

GREAT MANAGERS

There have been dozens of truly great managers in football. Some have been masters at putting together successful teams on tight budgets; others are visionaries who have improved the skills of the world's biggest stars. Below are profiles of seven of the finest managers in the history of football.

JOSEP 'PEP' GUARDIOLA
BORN 1971

Guardiola played over 380 games for Barcelona after making his debut under manager Johan Cruyff in 1990 as a deep-lying midfielder. He retired in 2006 and went on to manage three European heavyweights: Barcelona (2008–12), Bayern Munich (2013–16) and Manchester City (since 2016) with great success. At each club, Guardiola's obsessive preparation and mostly possession-based tactics led to long winning runs and at least three league titles per club. He lost a mere 19 out of 161 games at Bayern and just 21 out of 247 at Barcelona. UEFA Champions League glory has only come twice so far, in 2009 and 2011, although he led Manchester City to the final in 2021.

▶ Pep Guardiola has set many Premier League records at Manchester City, including most points (100) and most goals scored (106) in a season.

FACTFILE
Alex Ferguson was sacked only once, in 1978, when St Mirren fired him for a range of offences that included 'unpardonable swearing at a lady'.

RINUS MICHELS
1928–2005

▲ Rinus Michels at Barcelona, where he won La Liga in 1974.

The man behind 'total football', which revolutionized both Ajax and the Dutch national team, Marinus 'Rinus' Michels had been a centre-forward as a player, winning five caps for the Netherlands in the 1950s. As coach of Ajax in the mid-1960s, he gave 17-year-old Johan Cruyff his debut. Michels later managed Cruyff at Spanish giants Barcelona and in the Dutch team that finished runners-up at the 1974 World Cup. Michels returned to Ajax in 1975 and became coach of German side Cologne five years later. He rejoined the Dutch national side in 1984 and, with a star-studded team, won the 1988 European Championships – the Netherlands' first major trophy. Michels' achievements were acknowledged in 1999, when he was named FIFA's Coach of the Century.

HELENIO HERRERA
1917–97

The well-travelled Argentinian Helenio Herrera was a tough manager who liked to control almost every aspect of a club. At Spain's Atlético Madrid, he won back-to-back league titles. After spells with Malaga, Valladolid and Sevilla, he joined Barcelona. Under his management, they won two Spanish titles and two Inter-Cities Fairs Cups. Internazionale headhunted him in 1960. Herrera's reign and his use of defensive *catenaccio* tactics coincided with Inter's most glorious era, in which they won three Serie A titles, two European Cups and two World Club Cups. Herrera was also in charge of Italy during qualification for the 1962 World Cup, but by the time the tournament began, he was manager of Spain.

▶ Helenio Herrera poses with two footballs in 1971, while coach of Italian side Roma.

◀ Alex Ferguson celebrates his final Premier League title in 2013, finishing 11 points clear of Manchester City.

JÜRGEN KLOPP
BORN 1967

The Best FIFA Football Coach winner in 2019 and 2020 began his career as a striker-turned-defender with German lower league club Mainz 05. Becoming Mainz's manager in 2001, Klopp guided them to the top tier of German football for the first time in their history. He moved to Borussia Dortmund in 2008, where his brand of pressing and rapid counterattacking re-established the club as a dominant force. He won three major cups and two Bundesliga titles (2011, 2012) before joining Liverpool. Passionate and popular, Klopp built an attractive side with a three-pronged attack of Mo Salah, Sadio Mané and Roberto Firmino. He endured three losses in major finals before winning the 2018–19 UEFA Champions League and the World Club Cup. Liverpool's first league title in 30 years followed the next season.

ALEX FERGUSON
BORN 1941

As European football's longest-serving top-flight manager, Alex Ferguson took Manchester United to a record 13 Premier League titles and the 1999 and 2008 Champions League crowns. A ruthless and highly driven manager, Ferguson won three Scottish league titles and the 1983 European Cup-Winners' Cup with Aberdeen. He managed Scotland at the 1986 World Cup before joining Manchester United. Ferguson developed young talents such as David Beckham and Ryan Giggs, and proved to be a masterful player of mind games with rival managers. Knighted in 1999 for his services to the game, Sir Alex announced his retirement at the end of the 2012–13 season, after 26 years with United.

▶ Under Jürgen Klopp, Liverpool won 18 league games in a row from October 2019 – a joint record in the English top flight.

ANTONIO CONTE
BORN 1969

A Juventus legend with over 400 games as a player, Conte managed the club in 2011 after spells at S.S. Arezzo, Bari, Atalanta and Sienna. He is a famously hard taskmaster whose intense coaching style does not suit every player, but his well-drilled teams have enjoyed great success, often in 3-5-2 formation with attacking wingbacks. He won three Serie A titles in a row at Juve, coached Italy at EURO 2016 and managed Chelsea to a Premier League title in 2017. Joining Inter Milan, he broke Juventus's Serie A dominance with a momentous title win in 2021. He left after disagreements over future player transfers, but later in 2021 he was appointed manager of Tottenham Hotspur.

EMMA HAYES
BORN 1976

With her own playing career cut short by injury at 17, Hayes turned to coaching, first with US college sides and then as assistant coach at Arsenal Women. After spells advising several US clubs on transfers, she was appointed Chelsea Women's manager in 2012. There, she has enjoyed a 69% win rate as Chelsea won four Women's Super League titles in six seasons as well as three FA Cups and two League Cups. The longest-serving manager in Women's Super League history, Hayes also led Chelsea to the UEFA Women's Champions League final in 2021, the first female coach in 12 years to do so.

▶ Antonio Conte issues instructions to Tottenham's players during a training session.

▶ Emma Hayes lifts the WSL trophy in 2021, the same year in which she won the Best FIFA Women's Coach award.

US attacker Megan Rapinoe celebrates scoring the opening goal against the Netherlands in the 2019 Women's World Cup final. Rapinoe was the star of the tournament, winning the Golden Ball as best player, the Golden Boot as top scorer with six goals, and becoming the first woman to start three World Cup finals in a row.

SNAPSHOT
AT THE DOUBLE

The US Women's National Team had entered the 2015 FIFA Women's World Cup hurting from not winning the competition for 16 years and losing out to Japan in the final of the 2011 edition. The two teams met in a riveting 2015 final, in which a stunning hat-trick from Carli Lloyd ensured the US gained revenge with a 5-2 victory, and secured their third Women's World Cup.

Only Germany had ever successfully defended the Women's World Cup, but the US arrived in France in 2019 in good shape and began the tournament in emphatic style, hammering Thailand by a record scoreline of 13-0, with five goals for Alex Morgan. Games tightened up during the knockout stages and the US recorded three successive 2-1 victories over Spain, France and England to reach the final. There, they met a talented Netherlands team but came out on top thanks to a penalty from the tournament's Golden Boot winner, Megan Rapinoe, and a 69th-minute strike from dynamic midfielder Rose Lavelle. It could have been more were it not for heroics from the goalkeeper of the tournament, Sari van Veenendaal. The victory made the US the only four-time winners of the competition and also made Jill Ellis the first coach to win two Women's World Cups. She retired after the tournament, leaving with an exceptional record of just seven defeats in 132 games.

GREAT SIDES

Great footballers, managed well and playing with spirit and intelligence can make a great team. Sometimes, less heralded individuals gel together to form an unstoppable side, such as the Leicester City team that won the English Premier League in 2016. Other sides made up of stellar players form a powerful dynasty with long runs of success. This section focuses on teams that at one point in their history were especially exciting, revolutionary or dominant in the competitions in which they played.

NATIONAL SIDES

HUNGARY
FOUNDED: 1901

The Hungary side of the 1950s changed the way many teams played football. The side brimmed with talented attacking players, and coach Gusztáv Sebes devised a simple but devastating alternative to the W-M formation to get the best out of them. Nándor Hidegkuti was the team's nominal centre-forward, but he played deep, allowing Ferenc Puskás, Sándor Koscis and others to raid ahead of the striker into space. Opposition teams couldn't cope, and the side recorded an incredible run of 50 matches with only one defeat, scoring 220 goals along the way. They won the 1952 Olympics, and in the following year thrashed England 6-3 and 7-1. However, their one defeat was heart-breaking, as it came in the 1954 World Cup final where they lost to West Germany 3-2.

SWEDEN WOMEN
FIRST INTERNATIONAL MATCH: 1973

Sweden won the first Women's European Championship in 1984 and have shown remarkable consistency since, finishing second or third on seven occasions. World Cup and Olympic glory has just evaded their grasp, with two back-to-back Olympic silver medals (2016, 2021), one World Cup runners-up spot (2003) and three World Cup third places (1991, 2011, 2019). They remain a very difficult team to beat, and after going undefeated for 18 matches in open play in 2020–21, find themselves placed second in the world at the start of 2022 according to the FIFA rankings.

◀ Hungarian goalkeeper Gyula Grosics gathers the ball under pressure from England's Stan Mortensen. Hungary's 6-3 win condemned England to their first home defeat to a team from the continent.

▶ Swedish defender Magdalena Eriksson (right) challenges US forward Carli Lloyd. Eriksson has played over 80 times for the Blue-and-Yellows.

WEST GERMANY
FOUNDED: 1900

West Germany staged a major shock when they courageously toppled the favourites, Hungary, to win the 1954 World Cup thanks to two goals from Helmut Rahn. Their side of the mid-1960s finished runners-up at the 1966 tournament and third in 1970. Manager Helmut Schön then rebuilt the team shrewdly, keeping the superb Sepp Maier in goal and moving Franz Beckenbauer from midfield into defence, where he played alongside Hans-Georg Schwarzenbeck and one of the best full-backs of the 1970s, Paul Breitner. Schön incorporated the talented Günter Netzer into midfield and often played a 4-3-3 formation, with Uli Hoeness in attack alongside goal machine Gerd Müller. West Germany's players had an incredibly strong team spirit because they came almost exclusively from just two clubs – Bayern Munich and Borussia Mönchengladbach. Their self-belief was evident as they powered to the 1972 European Championships title and then went a step further, winning the 1974 World Cup on home soil. By this time, the talented but outspoken Netzer had been replaced by Wolfgang Overath, while midfielder Rainer Bonhof had also played his way into the side. A defeat to Czechoslovakia in the 1976 European Championships final signalled the end of a remarkable period in which West Germany had become the first team to hold the European and World crowns at the same time.

◀ Right-back Benjamin Pavard in action for France against Hungary in a Group F match at EURO 2020.

▲ West German striker Uli Hoeness powers towards Spain's goal in a 2-0 quarter-final second-leg win over Spain at the 1976 European Championships.

FRANCE
FOUNDED: 1919

France has a long and illustrious football pedigree. It has produced several superb sides, particularly in the late 1950s – the era of Raymond Kopa and Just Fontaine – and in the early 1980s, with an attractive team led by Michel Platini. But it was the side of the late 1990s that finally translated great promise into World Cup success.

As World Champions, France entered EURO 2000 with the majority of their key players still at their peak, including flamboyant keeper Fabien Barthez and strong, skilled defenders in Marcel Desailly, Lilian Thuram and Bixente Lizarazu. In midfield, a blend of flair and dynamism was headed by the world's best attacking midfielder, Zinedine Zidane. Up front, young livewires such as Sylvain Wiltord and Thierry Henry were intent on making their mark. Five players scored two or more goals in their six-match EURO 2000 campaign, which ended with France beating Italy 2-1 to become the second team (after West Germany in 1974) to hold European and World titles at the same time.

USA WOMEN
FIRST INTERNATIONAL MATCH: 1985

Women's international football came of age during the 1990s and early 2000s, with the arrival of World Cup and Olympic competitions. The period's most successful nation was the USA, who won two Olympic titles (1996 and 2004) and two Women's World Cups (1991 and 1999). Their record in World Cup matches during the 1990s was remarkable, with 20 wins, two draws and just two defeats. Mia Hamm was considered to be the world's finest female striker, while Kristine Lilly became the first female player to pass 300 international caps in 2006. For a number of the US women's team, 2004 proved a successful swansong, with victory over Brazil to win Olympic gold – a feat that a new generation of US players such as Carli Lloyd, Christie Rampone and Abby Wambach repeated in 2008 and 2012. The team has dominated the Women's World Cup in recent years, finishing as runner-up in 2011, lifting the trophy for the third time in 2015, and going unbeaten in 2019 when they defeated the Netherlands 2-0 to become world champions for the fourth time.

◀ US midfielder Sam Mewis shoots during a 4-0 victory over Mexico in 2021. It was the 43rd game in a row that the US team had gone unbeaten.

FACTFILE

Ahn Jung-Hwan struck the goal that knocked Italy out of the 2002 World Cup. Ahn played for Italian side Perugia, whose president was so enraged that he terminated the South Korean midfielder's contract.

▼ South Korea celebrate a famous victory over Spain in the quarter-finals of the 2002 World Cup. The match ended at 0-0 after extra time, with the Koreans winning the penalty shootout 5-3.

SOUTH KOREA
FOUNDED: 1928

At the 2002 World Cup, co-hosts South Korea were given little chance of success by many people. In truth, the country boasted an improving side and had qualified for the previous three World Cups. Under the guidance of Guus Hiddink – a former Real Madrid and Netherlands coach – the South Koreans beat Poland 2-0 to record their country's first win at the World Cup finals. After a 1-1 draw with the USA, South Korea dumped a strong Portugal side out of the tournament courtesy of Park Ji-Sung's goal. An extraordinary second-round game versus Italy saw South Korea miss a penalty, then go behind, only to equalize two minutes before the final whistle. Urged on by an entire nation, the hardworking side defended resolutely and attacked with energy, skill and surprise. A golden goal three minutes before the end of extra time knocked Italy out of the tournament and sent the country into raptures. The drama was not over, however. A tense quarter-final against Spain ended in a thrilling penalty shootout, with keeper Lee Woon-Jae pulling off a magnificent save from Joaquin before captain Hong Myung-Bo slotted home the winning penalty. A narrow 1-0 defeat to Germany in the semi-final did not dampen the co-host nation's enthusiasm, and attendances at club level rocketed in the following seasons.

SPAIN
FOUNDED: 1904

Spain had been the perennial underachievers on the international stage, producing dozens of world-renowned players – from Ricardo Zamora and Andoni Zubizarreta in goal to Raul and Emilio Butragueño in attack – yet rarely producing the goods at major tournaments. The 2000s, however, saw a major change with the arrival of a clutch of supremely talented, technically gifted players, many from Barcelona, who thrived on a style of play – dubbed tiki-taka – where control of the ball, frequent short passing and quick, nimble movement are paramount. Players like Xavi Hernández and Andrés Iniesta in midfield kept possession of the ball in front of no-nonsense defenders such as Carles Puyol and Gerard Piqué. It yielded great results. Between November 2006 and June 2009, Spain went unbeaten in 35 international games until suffering a shock defeat to the USA at the Confederations Cup. Spain won EURO 2008 and became the first champions to successfully defend their European title in 2012. In between came Spain's first ever World Cup triumph, achieved after qualifying with a perfect record (ten wins out of ten) and victories over Portugal, Paraguay, Germany and the Netherlands at the tournament.

◥ Xavi Hernández unleashes a shot during Spain's comprehensive 4-0 victory over Italy in the final of the 2012 European Championships.

FACTFILE

In the semi-final of the 1938 World Cup, the string of Giuseppe Meazza's shorts broke and they fell to the ground just as he went to take a penalty. Holding his shorts up with one hand, Meazza calmly stroked the penalty home past the bemused Brazilian goalkeeper, Valter.

ITALY
FOUNDED: 1898

Italy and Uruguay emerged as the leading sides during the first decade of the World Cup. The Italians chose not to enter the first tournament, in 1930, but were hosts of the second, where they were managed by Vittorio Pozzo, who was nicknamed the Old Maestro. Pozzo deployed several *oriundi* – Argentinians of Italian descent – including Raimundo Orsi and the captain, Luisito Monti. His side also included one of the world's finest attackers of the inter-war years in Giuseppe Meazza. Italy won the 1934 World Cup under Pozzo's leadership and also triumphed at the 1936 Olympics. Recognizing the fact that his side was ageing, the wily Pozzo introduced more and more youngsters, so that by the time of the 1938 World Cup only two members of the 1934 team, Meazza and Giovanni Ferrari, remained. Pozzo's overhaul of the side proved a triumph, as Italy beat the highly fancied French, Brazilian and Hungarian teams to reclaim the trophy, and make Pozzo the only manager in men's football to have won two World Cups.

◀ Italy's national team pictured after their 1938 World Cup victory, with coach Vittorio Pozzo holding the trophy. The Italians comfortably beat Hungary 4-2 in the final.

ENGLAND
FOUNDED: 1863

As an England player, Alf Ramsey's last match had been the nation's 6-3 demolition by Hungary in 1953 – the game that punctured English belief in its footballing superiority. Ramsey was made England manager in 1962, and for the 1966 World Cup, he assembled a solid team with a strong spine – Gordon Banks in goal, Jackie Charlton and Bobby Moore in central defence, Bobby Charlton in midfield and, up front, Roger Hunt and the free-scoring Jimmy Greaves (who was injured during the tournament and replaced by Geoff Hurst). Propelled by goals mainly from Hunt and Bobby Charlton, and by a miserly defence that did not concede a goal until the semi-final, England beat Mexico, France, Argentina and Portugal. In the final at Wembley, a memorable hat-trick by Geoff Hurst and a goal from Martin Peters saw England beat West Germany 4-2 to win the trophy. After reaching the semi-finals of the 1968 European Championships, England were one of the favourites for the 1970 World Cup. In the quarter-final they were leading 2-0 with just 20 minutes left to play, before West Germany struck back to win 3-2. They would only reach two semi-finals in the next 12 World Cups (1990 and 2018).

▶ England captain Bobby Moore sits on the shoulders of Geoff Hurst (left) and Ray Wilson (right) as he holds the World Cup at Wembley.

▲ Nigerian forward Daniel Amokachi is tackled by Flavio of Brazil at the Centennial Olympic games in 1996.

NIGERIA
FOUNDED: 1945

In 1985, Nigeria's youngsters captured the World Under-17 Championship to become the first African nation to win a world tournament. Eleven years later, the 'Super Eagles' were the stars of the Atlanta Olympics thanks to their attacking verve, team spirit and will to win. Featuring players such as Celestine Babayaro, Emmanuel Amunike and Daniel Amokachi, Nigeria beat Hungary 1-0 and Japan 2-0, before losing to Brazil 1-0 in the group stages. They then beat Mexico 2-0 in the quarter-finals to set up a second meeting with Brazil. That match is considered to be the finest in Olympic history. With 13 minutes to go Nigeria were losing 3-1, but they pulled one goal back before their captain, Nwankwo Kanu, scored a last-gasp equalizer. In a frenetic period of extra time, Kanu struck again to seal a 4-3 victory. Another great comeback in the final saw Nigeria win gold by defeating Argentina 3-2.

NETHERLANDS
FOUNDED: 1889

Rinus Michels, a former Netherlands centre-forward, masterminded a revolution in Dutch football in the mid-1960s. First at club side Ajax, and then with the national team, he developed a system in which all his players were comfortable on the ball and would switch positions, often with devastating results. Called 'total football' (see page 59), the system revolved around such world-class talents as Johan Cruyff, Johan Neeskens and Ruud Krol. With Michels at the helm, the Dutch powered to the 1974 World Cup finals, scoring 14 goals and conceding just one in qualifying. They soared through the rounds, demolishing Argentina 4-0 and beating Brazil 2-0 on the way to the final against West Germany. Despite taking a one-goal lead within 80 seconds, the Netherlands suffered heartbreak, losing 2-1. Two years later, they reached the semi-final of the 1976 European Championships, going out to the eventual winners, Czechoslovakia, in extra time. The Dutch entered the 1978 World Cup without Cruyff, but could still call upon many of the 1974 squad, including Neeskens, Krol and strikers Johnny Rep and Robbie Rensenbrink. They reached the final again, this time losing 3-1 to Argentina. Considered the most talented team never to win the World Cup, the Dutch enthralled millions of fans with their exploits and flair.

▶ Alexandra Popp can play anywhere in attack or midfield. By 2022, this versatile player had scored 53 goals for Germany.

GERMANY WOMEN
FIRST INTERNATIONAL
MATCH: 1982

Germany struggled to be competitive in the 1980s, but received a massive boost in 1989 when they won the first of their eight European Championships. The 21st century proved remarkably fruitful for the side as they won the 2003 Women's World Cup and continued their European dominance with their sixth championship crown in a row in 2013. Before retiring in 2011, Germany's goal machine, Birgit Prinz, scored an incredible 128 goals for her country. In the 2007 World Cup, Germany's 11-0 demolition of Argentina and feat of not conceding a goal throughout the tournament were undoubted highlights. The Olympics eluded this talented side until Brazil 2016, when the team defeated China, Canada and Sweden to win the gold medal.

◀ The Netherlands line up before the 1978 World Cup final, which was held at River Plate's home stadium.

MEXICO
FOUNDED: 1927

Having reached the quarter-finals of the two World Cups it has hosted (1970 and 1986), the football-mad nation of Mexico had much to cheer in the 1990s, when its national team dominated the continental championships, the CONCACAF Gold Cup. In the inaugural competition of 1991, Mexico lost to the USA at the semi-final stage, but in the next three competitions they were unstoppable. They were rampant in 1993, beating Canada 8-0 and Jamaica 6-1, before humbling the USA 4-0 in the final. At the 1996 Gold Cup, they defeated invited guests Brazil to win the title and, four years later, beat the USA again to secure a hat-trick of wins. At the heart of Mexico's authoritative displays was the defender Claudio Suarez, nicknamed the Emperor for his commanding performances. Suarez made his national debut in 1992 and played his 177th game in 2006 against the Netherlands. A new generation of Mexican talent has added to this success, winning the Gold Cup in 2009 and 2011, and beating Brazil to grab more gold at the 2012 London Olympics.

FACTFILE
Mexico striker Javier Hernandez was timed as the fastest player at the 2010 World Cup – reaching a speed of 32.15km/h.

◀ Mexican defender Darvin Chávez at the 2012 Olympics. Chávez played 31 times for the Mexican under-23 team which won Olympic gold.

BRAZIL
FOUNDED: 1914

The 1958 World Cup signalled the arrival of Pelé and the start of a magnificent era for Brazil in which they won three out of four World Cups. The side that claimed the 1970 World Cup is considered by many to be international football's greatest team. In attack, few nations before or since have been able to field a side so blessed with flair and skill on the ball, as well as superb vision and movement off it. Opposition teams sometimes tried to mark Pelé out of the game, but this would only give opportunities to marvellous players such as centre-forward Tostao, the bustling Roberto Rivelino, midfield general Gerson or powerful winger Jairzinho. At the back, high-class players such as Carlos Alberto maintained a solid defence, but this side was all about attack. After going a goal down to Czechoslovakia in their first match at the 1970 World Cup, Brazil responded by scoring four times. They scored three to beat Uruguay in the semi-final and four in the final, in which they outclassed a strong Italy with one of the greatest displays of attacking football. Brazil dazzled with their wit and invention, and the 4-1 scoreline was completed by a marvellous team move ending in a thunderous shot by Carlos Alberto. In his last match for Brazil, Pelé was chaired off the field by his team-mates. The departure of other members of the side meant that by the 1974 World Cup, only Rivelino and Jairzinho remained from the team that had captured the imagination of millions.

◀ Brazil's team that beat England at the 1970 World Cup. Back row, left to right: Carlos Alberto, Brito, Wilson Piazza, Félix, Clodoaldo, Everaldo, Mario Zagalo (coach); front row: Jairzinho, Roberto Rivelino, Tostao, Pelé, Paulo Cesar.

FACTFILE
Brazil's first international match was in July 1914, when they played English league side Exeter City. In 2004, the 1994 Brazilian World Cup-winning side played a rematch against Exeter, winning the game 1-0.

▲ Pelé kisses the Jules Rimet trophy after Brazil's 1970 triumph. He was the first World Cup winner to score in four successive tournaments.

▼ Mo Salah celebrates with Essam El Hadary as Egypt progress to the 2017 African Cup of Nations final.

EGYPT
FOUNDED: 1920

In 1934, Egypt became the first African nation to appear at a World Cup, but have made only two further appearances since. In between, there was the brilliance of twin brothers Hossam and Ibrahim Hassan, and a spell of dominance in Africa underpinned by the excellence of Essam El Hadary in goal and Ahmed Hassan as captain. The Pharaohs won three Africa Cup of Nations in a row (2006, 2008, 2010), without losing a single game in all three tournaments. El Hadary was voted the competition's best keeper in all three editions and Ahmed Hassan the best player overall in two. In 2012, Hassan became Egypt's most capped player, while El Hadary's story took a remarkable twist when he helped Egypt to another Cup of Nations final in 2017 and played at the 2018 World Cup at the age of 45, making him that competition's oldest ever player. Most of the national team today play in Egypt, but fans of the Pharaohs also enjoy the exploits of foreign-based stars including Mohamed Salah, their current captain.

JAPAN WOMEN
FIRST INTERNATIONAL
MATCH: 1985

Japan enjoyed a rich spell of form in the 2010s that saw them challenge the dominance of Germany and the USA as women's football's pre-eminent sides. With a world-class midfield pairing of Homare Sawa and Aya Miyama at the heart of the team, Japan won a silver medal at the 2012 Olympics but the year before had shocked the footballing world with victories over Mexico, England, Germany and Sweden to reach the final of the Women's World Cup. There, they defeated the US to become the first Asian nation to win women's football's ultimate prize. They came close to repeating the feat in 2015, reaching the final again, only to suffer a heavy defeat to the US. The retirement of much of the golden generation, including Sawa in 2015 and Miyama a year later, saw Japan undergo a lengthy rebuild. Within their continent, however, they remain peerless. Japan went unbeaten through two Asian Cups to be crowned double champions (2014, 2018) and never finished outside of the top four in the previous 12 tournaments – a remarkable record.

◀ Japan's inspirational captain Homare Sawa shoots during a group game against Mexico at the 2011 Women's World Cup. Sawa scored a hat-trick as Japan won 4-0.

LONGEST UNBEATEN INTERNATIONAL RUNS (IN GAMES)

36	Brazil 1993-96
35	Spain 2007-09
31	Argentina 1991-93
	Spain 1994-98
30	France 1994-96
	Hungary 1950-54
29	Brazil 1970-73
28	South Korea 1977-79
27	Colombia 1992-94
	Spain 2016-18
26	Spain 2011-13
25	Italy 2004-06
	Netherlands 2008-10

FACTFILE

Idriss Carlos Kameni was just 16 when he played in goal for Cameroon in the 2000 Olympic final. He was a hero as early as the fifth minute, when he saved a Spanish penalty. Cameroon went on to win gold in a penalty shootout, making their coach, Jean-Paul Akono, the first African manager to win a major world football competition.

CAMEROON
FOUNDED: 1960

Cameroon threatened a major shock at the 1982 World Cup, drawing against Italy (the eventual winners) and Poland, yet failing to reach the second round by a hair's breadth. In 1990, a team led by Roger Milla lit up the tournament, winning a tough group containing the Soviet Union, Argentina and Romania, beating Colombia in round two and taking England to extra time before losing 3-2. Many of Cameroon's footballers have played for Europe's top clubs – Geremi at Real Madrid, Samuel Eto'o at Barcelona and Salomon Olembe at Marseille, for example. After a disappointing 1998 World Cup, Cameroon roared back in 2000. They won the African Nations Cup, beating Nigeria. They then triumphed at the Olympics, stunning Brazil in the quarter-finals, Chile in the semis and Spain in the final to win gold.

◀ Roger Milla races past Romania's Gheorghe Popescu to score his first goal at the 1990 World Cup. Milla struck again to give Cameroon a 2-1 victory.

CLUB SIDES

BARCELONA
SPAIN • FOUNDED: 1899
STADIUM: NOU CAMP

With their own bank, radio station and one of the most impressive stadiums in the world, Barcelona can easily claim to be one of the world's largest football clubs. Barcelona's domestic achievements are impressive – their sixth-place finish in the Spanish league, La Liga, in 2003 was their worst since 1942. The club have won 26 league titles, finished runners-up 26 times and top the list of Copa del Rey winners, with 31 victories. They have also won the European Cup-Winners' Cup four times – more than any other team. Barcelona smashed the world transfer record in 1973 when they paid £922,000 for Dutch maestro Johan Cruyff. Fifteen years later, he returned as the club's manager. In his first season, Cruyff steered the club to second place in La Liga and to victory over Sampdoria to collect the European Cup-Winners' Cup. Dutchman Ronald Koeman and Denmark's Michael Laudrup were signed to play alongside Spanish stars such as keeper Andoni Zubizarreta and midfielder José Bakero. In 1991, Barcelona won the first of four league titles in a row, and a year later won their first European Cup, beating Sampdoria. Their second triumph in the competition came in 2006, along with the Spanish league title. Barcelona have won the prized double of La Liga and Champions League three times (2009, 2011 and 2015).

▶ Barcelona midfielder Frenkie de Jong in action against Napoli in the Champions League round of 16 in 2020. Barcelona won 4-2 on aggregate to progress to the quarter-finals.

▲ Al-Ahly's Waled Suleiman (left) and Hossam Ashour (centre) in action against Zamalek in a 2018 Cairo derby.

AL-AHLY
EGYPT • FOUNDED: 1907
STADIUM: AL-AHLY WE STADIUM

Cairo-based Al-Ahly can lay claim to being the most successful club in Africa. They have notched up 42 Egyptian Premier League titles, 37 Egypt Cup wins and ten African Champions League triumphs – five more than the next best club, their fierce domestic rivals, Zamalek. After winning the first Egyptian league competition in 1949, Al-Ahly enjoyed a long spell of league success until the 1960s, and another period of supremacy in the 1980s. Intent on continuing their dominance after being named CAF's African Club of the 20th Century, Al-Ahly won 13 out of 15 league titles up to 2021. The year 2020 also saw Al-Ahly record their seventh CAF Super Cup victory and their second third-placed finish at the Club World Cup.

FACTFILE

Two of Al-Ahly's youngest stars during the 1990s were the twins Hossam and Ibrahim Hassan, the most-capped players in Egyptian football. The brothers were idolized as they helped Al-Ahly to four league titles, but turned from heroes to villains when they sensationally quit the club to join rivals Zamalek in 2000.

FLAMENGO

BRAZIL • FOUNDED: 1895
STADIUMS: GÁVEA, MARACANÃ

Brazil is full of famous football sides, including Vasco da Gama, São Paulo, Botafogo and Corinthians. Flamengo are the most heavily supported of them all, having recorded 42 attendances of 100,000 or more at their games. Many gifted players have worn the side's distinctive black-and-red striped shirts. One of the greatest was Léonidas da Silva, known as the Black Diamond and the star of the 1938 World Cup. After a successful period in the 1950s, when the team won three Rio state league titles and earned the nickname the Steamroller, Flamengo had to wait more than 25 years for their next great era. Inspired by Zico and his strike partner, Nunes, the side won the Rio Championship (the Carioca) in 1978, 1979 and 1981, and the Brazilian National Championship in 1980, 1982 and 1983. In 1981, they captured the Copa Libertadores and a month later went on to claim the World Club Cup, beating Liverpool 3-0.

▶ Gabriel Barbosa kisses the trophy in 2020 after Flamengo secured their second Campeonato Brasileiro Série A in a row.

▼ Cristiano Ronaldo and Bruno Fernandes celebrate a 4-1 victory over Newcastle. The 2021 game marked Ronaldo's return to Manchester United, 18 years after his debut.

MANCHESTER UNITED

ENGLAND • FOUNDED: 1878
STADIUM: OLD TRAFFORD

Sir Alex Ferguson, the Premiership's longest-serving and most successful manager, led Manchester United to a unique treble in English football when they won the Premier League, the FA Cup and the UEFA Champions League in 1999. Forty years earlier, a Manchester United side managed by Sir Matt Busby – another Scot who became a knight – had captured the hearts and minds of supporters everywhere. The story began in the mid-1950s. Great things were expected of the young 'Busby Babes' side that had won two league titles (in 1956 and 1957) and included, among other talents, the young England stars Roger Byrne and Duncan Edwards. But in 1958, a tragic plane crash in Munich killed 23 people on board, including eight members of the Manchester United first team. Busby had to build a new side, which contained tough defenders like Nobby Stiles, young midfielders such as Brian Kidd, and two survivors from the Munich crash, Bobby Charlton and central defender Bill Foulkes. Although often playing in midfield, Charlton formed a glittering attacking trio with Denis Law and George Best. Busby's side won the league title in 1965 and 1967, but the pinnacle of their achievements came in the 1968 European Cup. After beating Real Madrid in the semi-final, Manchester United faced Benfica in the final. Two goals from Charlton, one from Best and one from the 19-year-old Kidd secured a memorable 4-1 victory. The Red Devils, as the team is nicknamed, had become the first English side to win the European Cup.

◀ Bobby Charlton (right) carries the trophy with team-mate Shay Brennan after Manchester United's defeat of Benfica to win the European Cup in 1968.

► Inter forward Lautaro Martinez in action in a 5-1 Serie A win over Sampdoria in 2021.

INTERNAZIONALE (INTER MILAN)
ITALY • FOUNDED: 1908
STADIUM: GIUSEPPE MEAZZA (SAN SIRO)

Also known as Inter Milan, Internazionale was formed by a group of former AC Milan players. During the rule of dictator Benito Mussolini, the club was forced to change its name to Ambrosiana-Inter, but switched it back in 1942. Argentinian coach Helenio Herrera joined Inter in 1960 and pioneered a new tactical system, playing a sweeper behind a back four and using fast-moving defenders to build attacks. Known as the *catenaccio* (doorbolt) system, it was seen as negative and defensive by some. But Inter won Serie A in 1963, 1965 and 1966 and also triumphed over Real Madrid in 1964 and the mighty Benfica in 1965 to win the European Cup twice. They added the World Club Cup to their list of honours in 1964 and 1965, but did not add to their European tally until the 1990s, when they won the UEFA Cup three times. In 2006, Inter were controversially awarded the Italian league title when Juventus were stripped of the trophy. They followed up with four further Serie A titles in 2007, 2008, 2009 and 2010, and a fifth in 2021, when 24 goals and 11 assists by Romelu Lukaku helped break Juventus' league dominance.

SLAVIA PRAGUE
CZECH REPUBLIC
FOUNDED: 1892
STADIUM: SINOBO STADIUM

Enjoying golden spells in the 1930s, 1940s and 1990s, Slavia Prague have often been overshadowed by their city rivals, Sparta. That has changed in recent years, however. Bolstered by new owners, the Red-and-Whites – whose colours have not changed since their formation – won the Czech First League in 2017, followed by league success again in 2019 and 2020. Despite the loss of midfield lynchpin Tomáš Souček and enterprising full-back Vladimír Coufal – both to West Ham in 2020 – Slavia achieved a league and cup double in 2021. They also fared relatively well in the 2020–21 Europa League, with wins over Bayer Leverkusen, Nice, Leicester City and Rangers, before defeat at the quarter-final stage to Arsenal.

◄ Slavia's Jakub Hromada holds off Leicester City's Youri Tielemans during a 2021 Europa League clash.

SANTOS
BRAZIL • FOUNDED: 1912 • STADIUM: VILA BELMIRO

Santos are most famous as being Pelé's club. They had won few honours before he began playing for them in 1956, aged only 15. During his 19 years at the club, Santos won the São Paulo Championship ten times and the Copa Libertadores twice, in 1962 and 1963. They also won the World Club Cup in those years, the first with an extraordinary 5-2 win away at Benfica, which included a sensational hat-trick from Pelé. Santos have fared less well in the years since, but a number of bright young stars emerged at the turn of the century. The club took a gamble on many of these players in the 2002 Brazilian National Championship, fielding a side with an average age of just 22. With 17-year-old midfielder Diego and 18-year-old striker Robinho especially prominent, Santos rolled back the years and delighted many neutral fans by winning the competition.

◀ Santos defender Lucas Verissimo (right) clashes with Luiz Adriano of Palmeiras in the 2020 final of the Copa Libertadores. Due to the COVID-19 pandemic, the match was played in 2021.

▼ The Dick, Kerr Ladies team pictured during their historic and successful 1922 tour of North America.

BOCA JUNIORS
ARGENTINA • FOUNDED: 1905
STADIUM: LA BOMBONERA

Best known in Europe as the club for which Diego Maradona played, Boca Juniors were founded by a group of Italian immigrants and an Irishman, Patrick MacCarthy. With their Buenos Aires neighbours River Plate, they form one of the fiercest rivalries in world football. Boca have the edge in the derby matches and have won two more Copa Libertadores than River. Boca had a strong resurgence at the end of the 20th century. Beginning in May 1998, they went 40 league games unbeaten to set an Argentinian record. The run helped them to win the Clausura and Apertura league titles in 1999, a feat followed by an incredible four Copa Libertadores triumphs in 2000, 2001, 2003 and 2007, as well as two Intercontinental Cups in 2000 and 2003.

◀ Boca Juniors forward Norberto Briasco (left) battles for the ball with Patronato defender Facundo Cobos in an Argentinian Primera División match in 2021.

DICK, KERR LADIES
ENGLAND • FOUNDED: 1917
NO STADIUM

W. B. Dick and John Kerr owned a rail and tram equipment-making factory in Preston, northwest England. During World War I, women began to work in factories, taking the jobs of the men serving in the war. In 1917, the women at Dick, Kerr challenged their male colleagues to a game of football and went on to organize matches against male and female opposition to raise money for war charities. By 1920, Dick, Kerr Ladies were playing matches to sell-out crowds. One fixture against St Helen's Ladies attracted 53,000 spectators to Everton's Goodison Park. In 1921, at the peak of their popularity, Dick, Kerr Ladies played 67 games, and a tour of the USA the following year saw the team win three and draw three out of nine matches against male sides. The Football Association felt threatened by a team that, in some cases, was drawing bigger crowds than the men's game. In 1921, the FA banned all women from playing football on the pitches of its member clubs. Incredibly, the ban remained in force for 50 years. As a result, support for women's football dwindled, and by 1926 Dick, Kerr Ladies had disbanded. Yet the team left an important legacy by showing that women could play highly entertaining, competitive football.

AC MILAN

ITALY • FOUNDED: 1899
STADIUM: GIUSEPPE MEAZZA
(SAN SIRO)

AC Milan's first period of notable success came in the 1950s, when a trio of Swedish stars – Gunnar Gren, Nils Liedholm and Gunnar Nordahl – followed by Uruguayan striker Juan Alberto Schiaffino, helped them to four Serie A titles. Nordahl remains the club's highest scorer, with an amazing 210 goals in 257 games. The 1960s saw AC Milan emerge as one of the leading clubs in Europe, winning two European Cups and a Cup-Winners' Cup trophy. A period of decline followed, which included an enforced relegation in 1980 after a betting scandal. Milan's fortunes were revived by the arrival of a new chairman, Silvio Berlusconi, in 1986. The wealthy media tycoon appointed Arrigo Sacchi as coach the following year. An exciting team was assembled, which included the superb Dutch trio of Ruud Gullit, Marco van Basten and Frank Rijkaard, alongside Franco Baresi, Roberto Donadoni and Paolo Maldini. Milan won Serie A in 1988 and went on to win it five times during the 1990s. Starting in 1991, Milan went unbeaten in Serie A for an incredible 58 games. In Europe, Milan beat Real Madrid 5-0 and then Steaua Bucharest 4-0 in the final to collect the European Cup in 1989 – a competition they also won in 1990, 1994 and 2003, and in which they were runners-up in 1993, 1995 and 2005. They won their seventh Champions League title in 2007. In Italy, Milan claimed the Serie A title for the 18th time in 2011.

▲ Kaka sprints away from Liverpool's defence during the 2007 Champions League final. Milan beat Celtic, Bayern Munich and Manchester United on the way to the final.

RIVER PLATE

ARGENTINA • FOUNDED: 1901
STADIUM: MONUMENTAL

River Plate are one of Argentina's leading sides. In the late 1930s, they moved to a wealthy suburb of Buenos Aires which, along with a team of expensive players, led to their nickname, the Millionaires. River are renowned for their attacking style. In the late 1940s, their powerful forward line became known as *La Maquina* (the Machine), and the club has produced a succession of world-class attackers, including Omar Sivori, Mario Kempes, Hernan Crespo, Javier Saviola and the legendary Alfredo di Stefano. River Plate have won 36 Argentinian league titles, yet it was not until 1986 that they triumphed in the Copa Libertadores. The team had made the final twice previously (in 1966 and 1976) before a side featuring Norberto Alonso, Juan Gilberto Funes and the great Uruguayan striker Enzo Francescoli beat America Cali of Colombia. River have enjoyed three further Copa Libertadores triumphs, the latest in 2018, in which they beat fierce rivals Boca Juniors 5-3 in the final.

▶ Striker Rafael Santos Borre celebrates scoring for River Plate against LDU Quito in the 2020 Copa Libertadores. The club reached the semi-final in that year, and the final in the year before.

MAMELODI SUNDOWNS
SOUTH AFRICA • FOUNDED: 1970
STADIA: LUCAS MORIPE / LOFTUS VERSFELD

Formed by a group of friends in Pretoria and formerly owned by a pair of doctors, Sundowns have enjoyed great success under the ownership of millionaire businessman Patrice Motsepe. He experimented with foreign coaches including Johan Neeskens, Hristo Stoichkov and former France manager Henri Michel, but it was the arrival of former player and South Africa national team coach Pitso Mosimane in 2012 that triggered the most sustained period of success in the club's history. Eleven league titles have come since 1998, including four-in-a-row up to 2021. The club also finished runners-up three times during that period, and in 2012 defeated Powerlines in a Nedbank Cup fixture by a record 24-0 margin. The year 2016 was a landmark one for 'The Brazilians', so named for their yellow and blue kit. Having reached the final of the CAF Champions League in 2001, they went one step further, defeating Egyptian giants Zamalek 3-1 on aggregate in the two-legged final. The win meant Sundowns became only the second South African team (following Orlando Pirates) to win the continent's biggest club prize.

◤ Midfielder Thapelo Morena strikes the ball on the volley as the Sundowns play title rivals Kaiser Chiefs in 2019.

MOST CONSECUTIVE LEAGUE CHAMPIONSHIPS

15	Tafea FC (Vanuatu)	1994-2008
14	Lincoln (Gibraltar)	2003-16
14	Skonto Riga (Latvia)	1991-2004
13	Al-Faisaly (Jordan)	1959-66, 1970-74
13	BATE Borisov (Belarus)	2006-18
13	Rosenborg (Norway)	1992-2004
11	Al-Ansar (Lebanon)	1988, 1990-99
11	Dinamo Zagreb (Croatia)	2006-16
11	Loto Ha'apai FC (Tonga)	1998-2008
11	Nauti (Tuvalu)	1980-90

PARIS SAINT-GERMAIN
FRANCE • FOUNDED: 1970 • STADIUM: PARC DES PRINCES

Formed to provide an elite club in Paris to challenge for trophies, PSG was initially owned by businesspeople and around 20,000 fans. The Coupe de France in 1982 was the club's first major piece of silverware; they have won the trophy 13 more times since. Their first Ligue 1 title came in 1986, but only one further success and six runners-up spots followed in the 1990s and early 2000s. In 2012, the Emir of Qatar became PSG's owner. This triggered a glut of big-money signings, starting with the French transfer record being broken for Javier Pastore (€42 million). Fourteen signings of £30 million or more followed, including the world-record fee of £198 million to sign Neymar, and around £158 million for Kylian Mbappé. Edinson Cavani (£55 million) remains the club's all-time top scorer, with 200 goals. Between 2013 and 2021, PSG won seven out of nine Ligue 1 championships. In 2016, a record 9-0 thrashing of Troyes confirmed their status as Ligue 1 champions again with eight games still to play. While a 2020 runners-up spot is their highest Champions League placing, a staggering 20 domestic cups won since 2012, in addition to the league titles, confirms their status as France's leading club, augmented by the summer 2021 signings of Lionel Messi, Sergio Ramos, Nuno Mendes and Gianluigi Donnarumma.

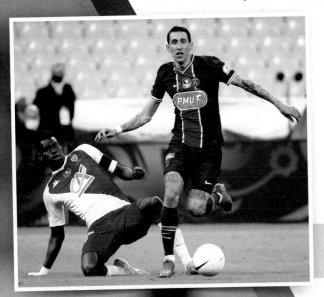

◀ PSG's Ángel di María chases down the ball. The winger has made over 300 appearances since joining the club in 2015.

▲ Fluminense celebrate a 3-1 victory over their local rivals Flamengo in 2021. The derby between the Rio de Janeiro clubs takes place at their shared ground, the Maracanã.

FLUMINENSE
BRAZIL • FOUNDED: 1902
STADIUMS: LARANJEIRAS, MARACANÃ

Founded in 1902, Fluminense have traditionally been supported by the middle classes, while their fierce Rio de Janiero rivals Flamengo drew support from the working class. Derby games between the two always guarantee big crowds. One 'Flu v Fla' derby in 1963 attracted a world-record attendance for a club match, with 177,656 supporters crammed inside the enormous Maracanã Stadium. Fluminense also contest Rio's oldest derby, the Classico Vovô (Grandpa Derby), with Botafogo, co-founders of the Rio league. Despite being the home club of a series of Brazilian footballing legends, including Didi during the 1950s and Carlos Alberto and Roberto Rivelino in the 1960s and 1970s, Fluminense have always disappointed on the international stage. They have never won a major South American competition. However, they have achieved much in Brazil, winning the Rio Championship 31 times. One of their most impressive runs came when the Tricolores – so nicknamed for their green, red and white colours – won three Rio Championships in a row from 1983 to 1985. Fluminense have also won the Brazilian National Championship four times, and won the inaugural Primeira Liga in 2016.

ARSENAL
ENGLAND • FOUNDED: 1886
STADIUM: EMIRATES

First known as Dial Square FC, Arsenal were formed by workers from the Royal Arsenal munitions factory in Woolwich, south London – hence their nickname, the Gunners. After a move to the north of the city in 1913, the club's rise to the top of the English game coincided with the appointment of Herbert Chapman as manager in 1925. Chapman was innovative both on and off the pitch, and he built a counter-attacking team featuring inside-forwards Alex James and David Jack, and winger Cliff Bastin, whose 178 goals for the club remained a record for over half a century. Arsenal were league runners-up in Chapman's first season and won the title in 1931 with a points total that would not be beaten for 30 years. Runners-up in 1932, they then claimed three league titles in a row (1933–35) and two FA Cups (1930 and 1936). Despite a league and FA Cup double in 1971, the closest Arsenal have come to their earlier dominance has been under French manager Arsène Wenger. With a team boasting Thierry Henry, Dennis Bergkamp and Patrick Vieira, they won three Premier League titles and four FA Cups from 1998 to 2005. Arsenal were unbeaten through the 2003–04 season, recording a total of 49 league games without defeat, a record in English football. They have won the FA Cup a record 14 times.

FACTFILE
Under Herbert Chapman, 'The Arsenal' became just 'Arsenal', allegedly to make them appear at the top of an alphabetical list of Division One clubs. Chapman also successfully campaigned for Gillespie Road underground station, close to the ground, to be renamed Arsenal.

▶ Arsenal striker Pierre-Emerick Aubameyang celebrates with the trophy at Wembley after his team's record-breaking victory over Chelsea in the 2020 FA Cup final.

CORINTHIANS WOMEN
BRAZIL • FOUNDED: 1997, REFOUNDED 2016
STADIUM: PARQUE SÃO JORGE

Sport Club Corinthians Paulista Futebol Feminino was disbanded in 2009 and then reformed as a short-lived partnership with Audax before Corinthians went it alone. Inspired by stellar performances from players such as Tamires Dias de Britto, club captain Grazi and young goalscorer Gabi Nunes – who struck 77 times in her first 115 matches for the club – the team have truly prospered. They have won the Campeonato Paulista twice (2019, 2020), the Campeonato Brasileiro twice (2018, 2020) and the Copa do Brasil once (2016). They scooped the continental prize, the Copa Libertadores Femenina, in 2017 and 2019, announcing them as a major force in women's football.

◀ Victória (left) and Tamires of Corinthians celebrate a goal in the 2020 Women's Copa Libertadores semi-final.

▲ Striker Hakan Sükür (centre) scored more than 290 goals for Galatasaray in over 500 games.

◢ Juve forward Paulo Dybala celebrates a Champions League goal against Lokomotiv Moscow in 2019.

GALATASARAY
TURKEY • FOUNDED: 1905
STADIUM: ALI SAMI YEN

Turkey's three biggest clubs – Galatasaray, Fenerbahçe and Besiktas – are all based in Istanbul and their passionate supporters are fierce and occasionally violent rivals. Galatasaray have won the league title 22 times (three more than Fenerbahçe), the latest being in 2019, as well as the Turkish Cup 18 times, including victory over Akhisarspor in 2019. They are the best-known Turkish club abroad, partly through their competitive performances in Europe during the 1990s. Visiting foreign teams often encounter an intimidating atmosphere – from 'Welcome to Hell' banners displayed at the airport by fans, to a stadium that turns into a cauldron of colour and noise on match nights. Galatasaray went unbeaten at home in Europe from 1984 to 1994, the year in which they drew 3-3 at Old Trafford to knock Manchester United out of the Champions League. In 2000, they won their first major European trophy by beating Arsenal to win the UEFA Cup.

JUVENTUS
ITALY • FOUNDED: 1897
STADIUM: DELLE ALPI

Formed by high-school students in Turin, Juventus used to play in pink shirts until they switched to black-and-white stripes in 1903. The club won five consecutive league titles from 1931 to 1935, and its successful 1980s team won Serie A four times and the 1985 European Cup. Financed by the wealthy Agnelli family, owners of the Fiat car company, Juventus spent lavishly on top-class players in the 1990s, including Roberto Baggio, Gianluca Vialli, Attilio Lombardo, Angelo di Livio, Fabrizio Ravanelli and Christian Vieri. After capturing the UEFA Cup twice in the early 1990s, Juve won an Italian league and cup double in 1995, and beat Ajax to win the Champions League in 1996. They lost the final of that competition in 1997 and 1998, but their fans could console themselves with Serie A titles in both years. Following a match-fixing scandal, Juventus were stripped of the 2005 and 2006 Serie A titles and relegated to Serie B for the first time. They bounced back into Serie A in 2009 and built a new era of dominance, winning their ninth Serie A title in a row in 2020, their 14th Supercoppa Italiana in 2021 and reaching Champions League finals in 2015 and 2017.

BAYERN MUNICH
GERMANY • FOUNDED: 1900
STADIUM: ALLIANZ ARENA

Germany's most famous club was formed in 1900 from rebels who had split from their former club, MTV 1879. The new team beat their old side 7-1 in the first match between the clubs. Although Bayern won a league title in 1932, by the early 1960s they were one of West Germany's less fashionable clubs and did not merit a place in the Bundesliga when it was formed in 1963. They achieved promotion soon after, and by the late 1960s were a dominant force in the domestic game. At the helm were future footballing legends such as Sepp Maier, Franz Beckenbauer and Gerd Müller, who was the Bundesliga's top scorer in seven seasons (1967, 1969–70, 1972–74 and 1978). With that squad, Bayern won German Cups in 1966 and 1967, and a European Cup-Winners' Cup in 1967. In the early 1970s, Bayern's stars were joined by more world-class players such as Paul Breitner and Uli Hoeness. The team won three Bundesliga titles in a row and three consecutive European Cups from 1974 to 1976. Success has continued with 2012–13 proving a stellar season, with a notable Bundesliga, German Cup and Champions League treble under outgoing coach Jupp Heynckes. In 2021, Bayern celebrated winning their 31st Bundesliga title, their ninth in a row. The year before they had secured their sixth European Cup/Champions League crown.

▼ Bayern's Kingsley Coman celebrates after scoring the only goal of the Champions League final against PSG in 2020.

▶ Benfica pose during the 1968-69 season. Having reached the final of the European Cup in 1968, they started their next campaign with an 8-1 win over Iceland's Valur, but were eventually knocked out by Ajax in the quarter-finals.

ZENIT SAINT PETERSBURG
RUSSIA • FOUNDED: 1925
STADIUM: PETROVSKY STADIUM

Founded by a group of local metal workers, Zenit originally played in the Soviet league and in the 1950s could count on the support of famous classical composer Dmitri Shostakovich in the stands. The break-up of the Soviet Union saw Zenit, known as the Blue-and-Whites, enter the Russian league, which it won for the first time in 2007 – with Andrei Arshavin the team's standout performer. Six further league titles followed, including three-in-a-row (2019, 2020 and 2021). The club frequently competes in the Champions League, but in 2008 Zenit won the UEFA Cup for the first time and beat Manchester United later the same year to lift the UEFA Super Cup.

BENFICA
PORTUGAL • FOUNDED: 1904
STADIUM: ESTADIO DA LUZ

Benfica remain Portugal's most famous and successful club, despite the long periods of glory enjoyed by rivals Porto and Sporting Lisbon. Their greatest era was undoubtedly the 1960s, which began under the management of Hungarian Bela Guttmann. The side played with a mix of pace, power and skill, typified by the midfielder Mario Coluna and the brilliant Eusebio. Benfica began the decade by defeating Barcelona 3-2 to win the 1961 European Cup. The following year, facing the mighty Real Madrid in the final, they found themselves 3-1 down to a Ferenc Puskas hat-trick, but fought back to beat the Spanish giants 5-3. They featured in five European Cup finals during the 1960s and won eight out of ten league championships. Defending another league title in the 1972–73 season, Benfica went unbeaten through 30 league matches, scoring 101 goals in the process.

LOS ANGELES GALAXY
USA • FOUNDED: 1995
STADIUM: DIGNITY HEALTH SPORTS PARK

A founder member of Major League Soccer (MLS), the Los Angeles Galaxy are one of its most successful sides, with five MLS Cups (2002, 2005, 2011, 2012, 2014) and four MLS Supporters' Shields trophies (1998, 2002, 2010, 2011). In addition, they have won the Lamar Hunt US Open Cup twice (2001, 2005) and, in 2000, the CONCACAF Champions League. Attracting homegrown talents such as Cobi Jones and Landon Donovan, the Galaxy have also bought in foreign stars including David Beckham and, in 2018, Zlatan Ibrahimović. After previously playing at the Rose Bowl and Titan Stadium, since 2005 the Galaxy's games have been held at the Dignity Health Sports Park.

◢ Mexican midfielder Jonathan dos Santos joined LA Galaxy in 2017. He scored the winning goal against the United States in the 2019 Gold Cup.

ANDERLECHT
BELGIUM • FOUNDED: 1908
STADIUM: LOTTO PARK

Anderlecht took 39 years to win their first league title in 1947 but have won 33 more since, along with 21 runners-up spots to make them Belgium's most successful side. Such consistency saw the club qualify for European competition every year from 1964 to 2007. A golden period during the 1970s under the management of Raymond Goethals saw Franky van der Elst and Arie Haan play behind a talented strike force of Benny Nielsen and Robbie Rensenbrink. Four Belgian Cups, two European Cup-Winners' Cups and two European Supercups were won during this period in great, attacking style.

▶ Anderlecht and Belgium forward Francis Amuzu controls the ball during a Belgian Pro League tie with Royal Antwerp in 2021.

VFL WOLFSBURG WOMEN
GERMANY • FOUNDED: 2003
STADIUM: AOK STADION

After relegation, promotion and rebuilding in the mid-2000s, *Die Wölfinnen* (The She-wolves) won a remarkable treble in 2012–13. They won their first DFB-Pokal Frauen cup competition, their first Frauen-Bundesliga title and the Women's Champions League. Wolfsburg repeated their league and Champions League feats the following year, which included twin 14-0 and 13-0 thrashings of Pärnu JK. Emphatic results were often achieved by the tactical excellence of Alexandra Popp and the free-scoring play of Conny Pohlers and Martina Müller. Wolfsburg added to their success throughout the 2010s, with a further seven cup wins and five league titles. The 2017 signing of Pernille Harder helped maintain their momentum as they battled fierce rivals Bayern Munich for domestic bragging rights.

◀ Members of the Wolfsburg team pose for photos after winning the DFB-Pokal Frauen in 2021. Striker Ewa Pajor holds the trophy.

OLYMPIQUE LYONNAIS FÉMININ
FRANCE • FOUNDED: 1970
STADIUM: PARC OLYMPIQUE LYONNAIS

Aligned to Olympique Lyonnais since 2004, this team has become known for pacy, powerful and skilful women's football. OL Feminin have been dominant in France, winning a record 14 league titles in a row up to 2020. They have also won nine Coupe de France Féminine. In 2011, they secured their first Women's Champions League title. Propelled by a free-scoring attack led by prolific Norwegian striker Ada Hegerberg and anchored by a tough defence, OL Féminin have won six further Champions League titles and finished runners-up twice, to make them the most successful women's club in Europe.

▲ OL Féminin celebrate their 2020 Champions League win. The team features French stars such as Wendie Renard and Amandine Henry and talented imports such as Chilean goalkeeper Christiane Endler (centre).

ESPERANCE SPORTIVE TUNIS
TUNISIA • FOUNDED: 1919
STADIUM: EL-MENZAH

With a distinctive strip that gave them their nickname – the Blood and Golds – Esperance have long been one of the leading clubs in Tunisia and North Africa. Back-to-back Tunisian league wins in 1993 and 1994 paved the way for their 1994 African Champions League triumph where, in front of a delirious home crowd, they beat the Egyptian holders Zamalek 3-1. In 1997, Esperance began a record-breaking league run. Seeing off the challenge of leading rivals such as Etoile Sportive du Sahel and Club Africain, the team captured an incredible seven straight league championships. No Tunisian club had won more than three in a row before, and many of the side's best players were part of the Tunisia side that won the 2004 African Cup of Nations on home soil. The club went on two more back-to-back league-winning runs: four from 2009 to 2012 and five from 2017 to 2021, along with their fourth African Champions League in 2019.

◀ ES Tunis's Anice Badri (right) battles for the ball during the 2019 CAF Super Cup against Raja Casablanca.

▼ Peñarol's Facundo Torres (left) battles for the ball with Fagner of Corinthians in the 2021 Sudamericana.

PEÑAROL
URUGUAY
FOUNDED: 1891
STADIUM: CAMPEÓN DEL SIGLO

Along with Nacional, Peñarol dominate Uruguayan football. Peñarol are marginally the more successful with 50 titles, the latest in 2018, leaving them four ahead of their rivals. In addition, they have finished league runners-up 41 times. The club's first golden era came in the 1960s. Led by Ecuadorian striker Pedro Spencer, the side won three Copa Libertadores (1960, 1961 and 1966) and two World Club Cups (against Benfica in 1961 and Real Madrid in 1966). Peñarol's side of the 1980s added to this tally, winning two more Copa Libertadores and, in 1982, beating Aston Villa to win a third World Club Cup. Peñarol hold a number of Copa Libertadores records: the largest win (11-2 against Valencia of Venezuela in 1970), the highest aggregate win (14-1 versus Everest of Ecuador in 1963) and the most consecutive participations in the competition (15 between 1965 and 1979).

LIVERPOOL
ENGLAND • FOUNDED: 1892
STADIUM: ANFIELD

In 1959, Liverpool were struggling in the English second division and had been knocked out of the third round of the FA Cup by amateur side Worcester City. Then Bill Shankly arrived as manager. He was a passionate, no-nonsense Scot who went on to build a successful Liverpool side that won the league championship three times and lifted the UEFA Cup in 1973. A year later he resigned, and Bob Paisley – Shankly's assistant for 15 years – was promoted to manager. Paisley's Liverpool won 19 major trophies in nine years, making him the most successful British manager of the 20th century. The club won six league titles and three League Cups thanks to a watertight defence, a quick, accurate passing game and intelligent attacking by players such as Kevin Keegan, Steve Heighway, John Toshack and Kenny Dalglish. A UEFA Cup win in 1976 was followed by European Cup triumphs in 1977 and 1978, making Liverpool the first British side to successfully defend the trophy. In 1981, the club beat Real Madrid to win the European Cup for a third time, and a fourth win came (after penalties) in 1984 against Italian side Roma. Two further Champions League titles followed (in 2005 and 2019), the latter under the leadership of their popular German coach, Jürgen Klopp. Klopp's Liverpool side, led by his three-pronged attacking spearhead of Roberto Firmino, Mo Salah and Sadio Mané, were in imperious form in 2019–20, when the Reds finished 18 points ahead of Manchester City to win their first league title since 1990.

FACTFILE

Between January 1978 and January 1981, Liverpool set an all-time record of 85 home games unbeaten in all competitions. Included in this run were an incredible 63 home league matches in a row.

◀ Ajax star Ryan Gravenberch holds off Oussama Tannane of Vitesse in the 2021 Dutch Cup final. Ajax won 2-1, with Gravenberch scoring the opening goal.

▲ Joël Matip and Virgil van Dijk hold the Champions League trophy after Liverpool's 2-0 defeat of Tottenham Hotspur in 2019.

AJAX
NETHERLANDS • FOUNDED: 1900 • STADIUM: AMSTERDAM ARENA

Rinus Michels arrived as Ajax's coach in 1965, saved the team from relegation and transformed the club with his brand of 'total football', where the emphasis was on fluid play and players interchanging positions freely. In 1969, they became the first Dutch club to reach the final of the European Cup and triumphed in the competition in 1971, 1972 and 1973. Their stylish side was led by Ruud Krol, Johan Neeskens and Johan Cruyff, with the club providing the bulk of the Netherlands' 1974 World Cup final-reaching side. In total, Ajax have won 35 Eredivisie and 20 KNVB Cups, one Cup Winners' Cup and the UEFA Cup in 1992. A further night of European glory came in 1995, when a young Ajax side won the Champions League. The club continues to be a production line of promising young talent, and won two Dutch league and cup doubles in three years (2019 and 2021).

COLO COLO
CHILE • FOUNDED: 1925 • STADIUM: DAVID ARELLANO

With around 60 per cent of the country's football fans following them, Colo Colo are easily the most heavily supported and successful of all the Chilean club sides. The team has won a record 32 league championships (14 more than fierce rivals Universidad de Chile) as well as the Copa Chile 13 times. Under their coach Arturo Salah, Colo Colo captured league titles in 1986 and 1989, before former Yugoslavia under-20 coach Mirko Jozic took up the manager's post during the 1990 season. The team completed a sequence of three league titles in a row in 1991, the same year that they enjoyed fantastic success abroad. In 1973, Colo Colo had been the first Chilean side to contest a final of the premier South American club cup competition, the Copa Libertadores. In 1991, the club went one stage further, beating the mighty Argentinian side River Plate in the semi-finals and the cup holders Olimpia 3-0 on aggregate to win the trophy. Whilst further international success has been restricted to a runners-up spot in the Copa Sudamericana in 2006, the club won nine league titles between 2006 and 2017.

◀ Pablo Solari (right) celebrates his winning goal for Colo Colo in a 2021 relegation play-off match versus Universidad de Concepcion.

MANCHESTER CITY
ENGLAND • FOUNDED: 1887 (1894 RENAMED MANCHESTER CITY) STADIUM: CITY OF MANCHESTER STADIUM

City won the first of their six FA Cups back in 1904 and their first English league title in 1937. They then spent many years as also-rans until Joe Mercer became manager in 1965 and they won the league, FA Cup and European Cup-Winners' Cup in a three-year spell. The club bounced between divisions for much of the 1980s and 1990s, but have remained in the Premier League since 2002. City were bought by the Abu Dhabi United Group in 2008 and investment poured in. Some of the expensive signings weren't successful, but others – including David Silva, Vincent Kompany and Sergio Agüero – had a major, long term impact. City clinched their first English league title since 1968 in 2012 and have since been crowned EPL champions four more times (2014, 2018, 2019, 2021) and reached the Champions League final in 2021.

◀ Manchester City's record signing Jack Grealish shields the ball from Arsenal's Martin Ødegaard. Grealish cost City over £100 million in 2021.

CELTIC
SCOTLAND • FOUNDED: 1888 STADIUM: CELTIC PARK

With 51 league titles, Celtic have dominated Scottish football for decades alongside their Glasgow-based rivals Rangers. But before Jock Stein's arrival as manager in 1965, Celtic hadn't won the league for 11 years. Stein built a home-grown team, all of whom hailed from Glasgow and the surrounding area. The team was full of youth, pace and adventure with tricky winger Jimmy Johnstone, prolific strikers Steve Chalmers, Bobby Lennox and Willy Wallace and a defensive rock behind in Billy McNeill. Celtic won nine Scottish league championships in a row (1967-74), yet contested the 1967 European Cup Final as underdogs. Against the odds, Celtic recovered from a goal down to beat the Italian giants Internazionale 2-1 and become the first British side to win the trophy. The 'Lions of Lisbon' narrowly failed to repeat their achievement after reaching the final again in 1970. It would be 33 years before Celtic played in another European final, losing 3-2 to Porto in the 2003 UEFA Cup.

▶ Celtic and Rangers clash in a 2021 Old Firm derby – the fiercest rivalry in Scottish football. The clubs have met over 425 times in the competition.

DYNAMO KYIV
UKRAINE • FOUNDED: 1927
STADIUM: NATIONAL SPORT KOMPLEX OLIMPIYSKIY

Originally the football team of the Soviet secret police, Dynamo Kyiv were the first club outside Moscow to win the Soviet league championship. A player in that 1961 side, Valery Lobanovsky, became Kyiv's coach 13 years later. He led the club through its greatest era, which began spectacularly with back-to-back Soviet league titles. In 1975, Kyiv won the Cup-Winners' Cup, becoming the first Soviet side to win a European competition. They also beat Bayern Munich 3-1 to win the European Supercup. In total, Lobanovsky (in three separate spells) managed Kyiv to eight league titles, six Soviet Cups and two European Cup-Winners' Cups. In 1991, after the break-up of the Soviet Union, Kyiv played in the newly formed Ukrainian league. They have dominated there, winning 16 league titles including the 2020–21 competition.

▼ Dynamo Kyiv midfielder Vitaliy Buyalskyi holds off Villarreal's Etienne Capoue during a 2021 Europa League match. Buyalskyi was made club vice-captain for the 2021-22 season.

REAL MADRID
SPAIN • FOUNDED: 1902
STADIUM: BERNABEU

Real Madrid are one of the world's most famous and successful sides. They have won 34 league titles, eight more than rivals Barcelona and 23 more than their neighbours, Atlético Madrid. In the 1940s and 1950s, Real's president, Santiago Bernabeu, began to transform the club with foreign signings and a huge desire to win the newly formed European Cup competition. Real did not disappoint, capturing the first European Cup, in 1956, and the next four as well. The team included two of the world's outstanding attacking talents in Ferenc Puskas and Alfredo di Stefano, as well as pacy winger Paco Gento, central defenders Marcos Marquitos and Juan Zarraga, and attacking midfielder Hector Rial. From 1957 to 1965, Real remained unbeaten at home in 121 Spanish league matches and won five La Liga titles in a row (1961–65). A new-look side captured the European Cup for a sixth time in 1966. Today, Real are one of the world's richest clubs, with a habit of buying football's most famous and expensive players, from Zinedine Zidane to James Rodriguez, Cristiano Ronaldo and Gareth Bale. Real have won seven La Liga titles in the 21st century, including the 2019-20 competition and have taken their European Cup and Champions League triumphs to a total of 13, plus four Club World Cups.

▶ Real Madrid players celebrate their 2020 Spanish Super Cup victory, the 11th time that they won the trophy.

SNAPSHOT
LES BLEUS TRIUMPH AGAIN

France was where the idea of a World Cup was formed yet the country had never won the competition until 1998. That triumphant team, featuring global superstars such as Zinedine Zidane, had been captained by the hardworking defensive midfielder Didier Deschamps. Twenty years later, in 2018, Deschamps was head coach of the French team, packed full of outstanding attacking flair but with questions about their ability to perform on the biggest stage of all. Doubts also surrounded Deschamps' selection as he left talented attackers Karim Benzema, Anthony Martial and Alexandre Lacazette out of his squad. After topping their group, France beat Argentina 4-3, with two goals for striker Kylian Mbappé, who finished as the tournament's second-highest scorer alongside his strike partner, Antoine Griezmann. Victories over Uruguay and Belgium took France to the final, in which they prevailed over Croatia 4-2 in the highest-scoring final since 1966.

The French team, captained by their goalkeeper, Hugo Lloris, celebrate with the 2018 World Cup trophy after their victory over Croatia in front of over 78,000 fans at Moscow's Luzhniki Stadium.

FOOTBALL DREAMS

From Beijing to Buenos Aires, Manchester to Mexico City, millions of children, teenagers and adults play football for fun, sport and exercise. Many are content to take part at an amateur level, but for some, the dream of emulating the stars they read about, watch and worship is a passion.

FACTFILE

In 2015, Vanuatu's U23 team beat Micronesia by a record scoreline of 46-0. It was the second heavy defeat for Micronesia, who earlier that year lost 38-0 to Fiji.

▲ USC Trojans take on UCLA Bruins in the NCAA Division I, the pinnacle of the US women's college game.

YOUTH TEAMS AND COMPETITIONS

As young players approach the pinnacle of the game, there are international matches for schoolboys and schoolgirls as well as under-17 and youth competitions. These reach a peak with the FIFA U-20 World Cup. At the 1991 tournament, Portugal swept to the title with a midfield containing teenagers João Pinto, Rui Costa and Luis Figo. Argentina won five of the ten competitions held between 1993 and 2011, whilst Erling Haaland scored nine goals in a single game at the 2019 competition, which was won by Ukraine with South Korea second and Ecuador third. FIFA's Under-17 World Cup has also unearthed its own stars from Landon Donovan to Phil Foden, the most valuable player of the 2017 tournament.

Some players are thrown into their club or national team at a very early age. Steven Appiah was 14 when he debuted for Ghana, Ellie Carpenter 15 when she first appeared for the Australian women's team and Pelé 16 when he turned out for Brazil.

YOUNG DREAMS

In most countries, young footballers can play at a regional, county or state level in organized youth team competitions. Major football clubs run youth sides and football academies, and also send scouts to watch games in the hope of spotting new talent. Young players may be invited to an open day or trial, where scouts and coaches can observe them in action at close hand. A club may then offer a contract or a place at its youth academy to a promising player. Famous academies exist at Barcelona, Bayern Munich and Porto. One of the most famous is Ajax's De Toekomst youth academy, which has been responsible for a host of great players – from Johan Cruyff and Dennis Bergkamp in the past to Christian Eriksen, Frenkie de Jong and Sven Botman in recent years.

▶ Martin Ødegaard was just 15 when he played in the top Norwegian league for Strømsgodset and made his debut for Norway (pictured). By the age of 17 he had played for Real Madrid before moving to Arsenal for 35 million euros in 2021.

▼ Jadon Sancho was just 14 when he was transferred for £66,000 from Watford to Manchester City. He was 17 when sold to Borussia Dortmund for around £8 million, and aged 21 when sold to Manchester United for 85 million euros in 2021.

HANDLING REJECTION

For millions of wannabes, the hope of playing professional football remains just a dream. As players rise through the footballing ranks, the vast majority find that their talents are surpassed by others and they are unable to progress further. Some talented young footballers are rejected because coaches believe their slight build or lack of height would put them at a disadvantage. As youngsters, Antoine Griezmann was rejected by Lyon, Roy Keane by Brighton and Marcus Rashford by Manchester City, all for being too small.

Rejection is hard to take for many junior players, but it spurs some on to train harder and smarter and overcome barriers to prove their doubters wrong. Argentinian wide player Javier Zanetti was turned down by Independiente's youth academy for not being robust enough to play professional football. He eventually signed for Italian giants Inter Milan, for whom he played a record 858 matches. In 2002, a very young Harry Kane was released from Arsenal's youth academy. He joined Tottenham's academy two years later and went on to become one of the world's most feared centre-forwards.

▼ Blind football matches last for 50 minutes. Here, Tomonari Kuroda of Team Japan holds off Spain during a Paralympic match in 2021.

FOOTBALL FOR ALL

Football can be enjoyed in all climates and conditions and by people of all ages and abilities. It is also played competitively by footballers with disabilities that range from being wheelchair-bound to having impaired hearing. At the 2017 Deaflympics, Turkey won the men's gold and Russia the women's gold. Amputee football is played by outfield players using crutches, but no artificial leg, and by goalkeepers who are single-arm amputees. Football for blind and visually impaired athletes uses a special ball. It contains a noise-making device that makes a distinctive sound as the ball moves. Teams consist of four blind outfield players, a keeper (who can be partially sighted) and five substitutes. In 2004, the sport made its debut at the Paralympics. Brazil have won all five Paralympic tournaments so far, including in 2021, when they beat Argentina in the final.

FACTFILE
In 2014, Gloriana Villalobos made her debut for Costa Rica at the age of 14. The following year she appeared at the 2015 Women's World Cup.

A PRO'S LIFE

Viewed from the outside, a professional footballer's life appears glamorous, exciting and rewarding. But behind the appearances in top matches, on television shows and at celebrity events, lies much hard work and sometimes frustration and disappointment.

MAKING THE GRADE

Only a tiny handful of talented players get to play professional football. In 2019, a study showed that just 180 out of the 1.5 million boys playing youth football in England will ever play a single minute in the Premier League. Even getting signed by a big club as a youth player is no guarantee of success. Most players do not make the grade and either drop out of pro football or have to move down a division or two to play first-team football. Jamie Vardy was released by Sheffield Wednesday at age 16 and played in non-league football until he was 25 before being signed by Leicester City, with whom he won the Premier League and FA Cup.

LOANED OUT

In many top leagues, clubs loan out to other clubs many of their young players as well as some senior players who currently don't feature in the manager's plans. Some are loaned to lower-division or overseas clubs, although in some leagues, players are loaned out to rivals. In 2021-22, for example, Atalanta took central defender Merih Demiral on loan from rivals Juventus but loaned out a staggering 62 of their own players. In the same season, Chelsea sent out on loan more than 20 players, including Conor Gallagher to Crystal Palace and Tiémoué Bakayoko – on his fourth loan spell since joining for £40 million in 2017 – who was loaned out to AC Milan until 2023. If they play well, a loaned player may be signed permanently or their parent club may bring them back into the first-team squad.

◀ Nathaniel Chalobah reached the Chelsea substitutes bench at the age of 15, but played just ten Chelsea league games over the next seven years as he went on six season-long loans.

▶ Alexia Putellas left Barcelona's youth academy aged 12. After spells at Levante and Espanyol, she re-joined Barça six years later and has now scored more than 150 goals for the club.

REWARDS AND RESPONSIBILITIES

Top players are globally famous and multi-millionaires. Some put their celebrity to good use, helping charities and schools and publicizing worthy causes. They often have to deal with the media, give interviews and make appearances for their club or sponsors. What can be harder for young footballers to handle is the way in which the press can invade their private lives. Photographers and reporters may besiege a player's home and follow their family and friends. Footballers are seen as important role models for young people and any wrongdoing, such as being fined for speeding, snubbing autograph hunters, or partying, attracts much negative media attention.

◀ Lionel Messi has won FIFA's Ballon d'Or a record seven times (2009–12, 2015, 2019 and 2021).

▶ Marcus Rashford with Alex Ferguson after receiving an honorary degree for his campaign against child poverty.

FACTFILE

Not all injuries are caused on the pitch. Heerenveen left-back Rami Kaib broke his jaw eating a raw carrot in 2021. Twenty years earlier, Spanish goalie Santiago Canizares missed the World Cup after dropping a bottle of aftershave on his foot!

TRAINING, INJURIES AND RECOVERY

A typical week for a footballer involves training, resting, going to club functions and travelling to one or more games. Training usually involves a mixture of fitness, strength and flexibility exercises to boost a player's stamina, pace and sharpness. Players also practise skills and tactics – improving their heading or working on free kicks and other set plays, for example. Football is a high-speed contact sport in which impacts, bad tackles and falls cause significant numbers of injuries, especially leg muscle tears and ankle and knee joint problems. At any one time, it is not unusual for a top team to have between three and nine of their leading players injured or on the way back to full fitness. An injured footballer's recovery may involve surgery and recovery before full rehabilitation can start. This is usually headed by the club's physiotherapists and other members of the medical and fitness teams. It can be a long, frustrating period out of the side, with the player hungry for action as they gradually build up strength and mobility in the injured body part. During this time, the player is aware that a veteran, young starlet or newly transferred player may seize their chance and establish themselves in the side. They also have the worry of suffering a reoccurrence of the injury – as happened to England women's captain Steph Houghton in 2022, just a few weeks after making her comeback from a tendon injury that had kept her out for four-and-a-half months.

◀ Recovery from an injury can be a difficult and lonely time as players miss key games. England captain Steph Houghton looks on as she battles an Achilles tendon injury whilst Raul Jimenez of Wolves trains after eight months out with a fractured skull.

THE PLAYERS' STAGE

Without stadiums, football would still be played, but games would be far quieter and a lot less exciting. Stadiums spring to life on match days when they are transformed from empty silent steel and concrete structures into a seething sea of colour and noise.

GREAT STADIUMS

The mighty Maracanã Stadium in Rio de Janiero, Brazil, holds the official world record for a football crowd – in 1950, around 199,850 people watched a World Cup game there between Brazil and Uruguay. In 2014, the Maracanã became only the second venue, after Mexico City's Azteca Stadium, to have hosted the World Cup final twice. Many of the world's biggest football arenas were built to host the World Cup or European Championships – from the Centenario in Uruguay, the venue for the first World Cup in 1930, to Poland's National Stadium that hosted EURO 2012 matches. Eight venues were used for the 2022 World Cup in Qatar, seven of which were newly built. These included the 80,000-capacity Lusail Stadium that hosted the final of the tournament.

BEHIND THE SCENES

The forgotten people of football are often the staff who run a stadium and ensure that the day of a match goes smoothly. We tend to think of them only when there is a problem such as crowd trouble or a pitch that is unfit for play. The club or stadium owner liaises with police and local authorities and employs stewards to prevent pitch invasions, violence and other problems. Box office staff do their best to ensure that tickets are sold and distributed correctly, while turnstile operators and sellers of programmes and food and drink all work at a ground on a match day.

The groundstaff are in charge of the goals, the pitch and its markings. They work especially hard when the pitch is in poor condition because of bad weather – clearing snow, thawing out the pitch or soaking up excess moisture. Before the match, the referee examines the pitch and talks to the groundstaff before deciding whether the game can go ahead.

◀▼ Groundstaff prepare the goal nets and clear snow before a match.

FACTFILE

A railway runs between the pitch and seats of Slovakian club Tartan Čierny Balog. The fans' view is sometimes obscured by puffs of smoke from the steam trains that run along it!

◥ The Timsah Arena is green and shaped like a crocodile's head. Completed in 2015, it's the home of Turkish club Bursaspor and seats around 45,000.

STADIUM INNOVATION

Stadium tragedies (see page 103) have prompted governments and football authorities to bring in stricter rules and safety measures. Most spectators stood in the past, but now large stadiums are usually all-seater. New stadium designs include features like electronic ticketing, solar panels and other energy-conscious innovations. Inside, hybrid pitches may have grass reinforced with plastic fibres and undersoil heating – consisting of hundreds of metres of pipes through which warm water runs – to stop them freezing. Many of these stadiums form part of a hotel, leisure or shopping complex.

The USA staged the first indoor World Cup qualifier (at the Seattle Kingdome) and the first indoor World Cup finals match (at the Pontiac Silverdome). Stadiums with a sliding roof have become more and more popular, allowing the venue to host music concerts and other indoor events. The Johan Cruyff Arena was opened in 1996 as Ajax's new ground. The first European stadium with a retractable roof, it seats 55,000 spectators. The Millennium Stadium in Cardiff, Wales, and London's Wembley Stadium also have sliding roofs. Inside a new stadium, fans may find a removable pitch, corporate boxes for business entertaining, and giant screens. The 72,000-seat Zenit Arena in Russia has two giant LED TV screens, 30.7m long and 10.2m high, which replay action from the game, interviews and stadium messages.

▲ Benfica's dramatic Estádio da Luz has hosted two UEFA Champions League finals as well as matches at EURO 2004.

▼ The state-of-the-art Zenit Arena was opened in 2017.

FACTFILE
At the 1986 World Cup, eagle-eyed officials spotted that the pitch markings at the edge of the penalty area for the France-Hungary game were in the wrong place. They had to be hastily repainted.

SUPPORTERS AND TEAMS

Dreams are not only held by players and coaches. Everyone connected to a club or national side hopes that their team will achieve glory and success, especially the fans.

FOLLOWING A TEAM

For millions of supporters, following their club or national side is a lifelong passion. Fans may chant for a manager to leave or be unhappy with certain players or the team's form, but their love of the club tends to remain. Dedicated fans go to great lengths to follow their side, putting up with poor weather, great expense and long hours of travelling to away games. Many fans spend much of their income every season on getting to as many games as possible and buying replica shirts and other merchandise – from T-shirts and scarfs to club-branded toothpaste and credit cards.

Every loyal fan loves to feel the rush of excitement as they approach their home ground, chant with the crowd and witness the start of a match. What comes next is a 90-minute rollercoaster ride of highs and lows, ending at the final whistle and followed by a post-match examination of what went right and wrong, before hope and expectancy build for the next game.

TOP TEN AVERAGE LEAGUE ATTENDANCES (2017–18)

1	Borussia Dortmund	79,496
2	Bayern Munich	75,000
3	Manchester United	74,976
4	Tottenham Hotspur	67,953
5	Barcelona	66,603
6	Real Madrid	66,161
7	FC Schalke 04	61,197
8	Arsenal	59,323
9	Inter Milan	57,529
10	Celtic	57,523

▲ Draped in scarves, a Bayern Munich supporter celebrates his team's Bundesliga title in 2016.

▼ Senegal fans drum up the atmosphere during their team's 2-1 victory over Poland at the 2018 World Cup.

FACTFILE

Charlotte FC set an MLS regular-season attendance record in 2022 as 74,479 fans flocked to the Bank of America Stadium to watch their match against the LA Galaxy.

FANS AND THE MEDIA

Television coverage and Internet streaming have opened up the game to millions of new fans. Some supporters, however, criticize TV for concentrating on the top teams and moving matches to different days and new starting times. TV companies spend a fortune on buying the rights to show live games and highlights from the top leagues. Back in the studio, famous ex-players and managers comment on the action, while reporters and statisticians provide interviews and highly detailed analyses of matches.

Coverage of football in other media has boomed, too. Fans manage their own sides in computer simulations or fantasy football leagues, while results, news and video clips are sent to their smartphones and tablets. They can read about their club in books, magazines, fanzines and blogs. The rise of radio phone-ins and social media has allowed fans to voice their opinions on games, players, managers and referees.

▲ South African defender Janine van Wyk poses for a selfie with fans at the 2019 Women's World Cup.

MORE THAN A GAME

Fans look forward to certain matches in particular – a clash between two teams at the top of the league table, for example. A game between a small club and a top side allows fans to dream of a famous giant-killing victory. In March 2022, North Macedonian fans went wild when their team, a lowly 67th in the FIFA rankings, knocked reigning European champions Italy out of the World Cup qualifying play-offs with a last-gasp winner in the 92nd minute.

The most passionate of all games tend to be derby matches between two neighbouring sides. Most clubs have some form of derby match, but certain rivalries have passed into football folklore. Among them are the Milan derby between Internazionale and AC Milan and, in Greece, the battle between Olympiakos and Panathinaikos. One of the most intense derbies in South America is between the two great Argentinian sides Boca Juniors and River Plate. For some fans, beating their rivals in a derby can be even more important than league or cup success.

Some of the biggest derbies are not between neighbouring sides, but between the top clubs in the country. Spain's *Superclassico*, for example, is contested by two teams 500km apart – Real Madrid and Barcelona.

▲ A face-painted fan cheers on the Netherlands at EURO 2020.

▶ Ettie the chicken gees up the crowd at the 2019 Women's World Cup. The first World Cup mascot was Willie the lion in 1966.

WHEN FANS TURN BAD

Fighting between fans has sadly occurred since football's early days. Attempts to stop violence and hooliganism – through policing, video surveillance, all-seater stadiums, and lifetime bans for identified culprits – has reduced trouble in many stadiums, but not all. A 2021 Slovak Super Liga match between fierce rivals Spartak Trnava and Slovan Bratislava was abandoned after fans of both teams started fighting on the pitch.

Sometimes, players and officials are the target of violence. In 2013, AC Milan's Kevin-Prince Boateng walked off the pitch followed by the rest of both teams after he and other black players were racially abused by some supporters. In 2012, a Dutch referee's assistant was attacked by teenagers from Nieuw Sloten B1, one of the teams taking part. He died the next day. These deeply disturbing events should not mask the fact that the vast majority of games are peaceful and attended by fans who are there for the football, not fighting or abuse.

BIG BUSINESS

When it comes to the world's biggest leagues, football is big, big business. In 2020, the top five leagues in Europe generated over 15.1 billion euros of annual revenue. The pressure to achieve success, though, has seen some clubs overspend and fall deeply into debt.

VALUE FOR MONEY?

Spending huge sums can seem essential to top clubs, but does not guarantee success. Tottenham Hotspur spent over £419 million on players in the five seasons up to 2021-22, yet they last won a league championship in 1961. Both Paris Saint-Germain and Manchester City have spent lavishly. PSG hold the record for the largest transfer fee – £198 million for Neymar – and City have spent over £1.6 billion on transfers since 2008. While both have won domestic honours, neither club has ever won the UEFA Champions League.

Less wealthy clubs can still succeed. The entire Leicester City squad that won the 2015-16 English Premier League cost under £60 million – less than Chelsea paid for one goalkeeper, Kepa Arrizabalaga, in 2018. Porto are outside of the top 50 richest football clubs yet they won the UEFA Champions League in 2004, the UEFA Europa League in 2011, and Portuguese league titles in 2018 and 2020.

MONEY MATTERS

In the past, football clubs received most of their money from selling programmes, tickets and food and drink. Today, these items contribute just 13% of the income of clubs in La Liga and the English Premier League and only 11% of club income in Ligue 1, Serie A and the Bundesliga. Sales of shirts and other merchandise as well as sponsorship and advertising deals with companies accounts for 30–40%. The lion's share of revenue for big clubs comes from selling broadcasting rights to television in particular, but also to radio and Internet services. In the 2020-21 season, for example, Atlético Madrid received 158 million euros in La Liga TV rights alone.

Some clubs succeed through the backing of a wealthy state, company or individual such as Chelsea's former chairman Roman Abramovich, Inter Milan owner Zhang Jindong, and the Agnelli family, who own Inter's rivals Juventus. Theoretically, the richest club in the world by benefactor is now Newcastle United following the club's £302-million purchase by Saudi Arabia's state-owned Public Investment Fund in 2021.

Some top clubs have run up huge debts through the collapse of business deals, high stadium construction costs, or the Covid pandemic causing competitions to be cancelled or games played without paying fans. Most debts, though, are run up through excessive transfer fees and wages that don't result in success. Some teams go into administration and have to drop down many divisions or reform as a new team. Others struggle on. In 2021, Barcelona were more than £1.1 billion in debt. The year before, another Spanish club, Malaga CF, released their entire first-team squad to play elsewhere in order to survive.

▶ Lille defenders Sven Botman (left) and José Fonte cost a total of £7.5 million but helped guide Lille to the Ligue 1 title in 2021, conceding just 23 goals.

▶ Tottenham's new stadium cost around £1 billion and has left the club with one of the largest debts in European football.

FACTFILE

French striker Karim Benzema has a release clause in his Real Madrid contract. He can leave if another club bids more than £850 million for him.

◀ Lionel Messi is thought to earn more than £25 million a year by endorsing products and through sponsorship deals.

FACTFILE

In 1999, Romanian club Nitramonia Fagaras were so cash-stricken that they could not pay a £14,000 gas bill. They had to transfer two players, Gabor Balazs and Ioan Fatu, to Gazmetan Medias (the gas company's football club) as payment.

PLAYER POWER

Spiralling transfer fees can be a lifeline to smaller, struggling clubs, because selling just one young talent for many millions can keep the club afloat for seasons. But for other clubs, the cost of keeping pace with richer rivals is huge. In summer 2021, Ligue 1 clubs spent £325 million on transfers. Bundesliga teams spent £360 million, Serie A clubs £475 million and English Premier League teams an eye-watering £1,140 million.

With big fees often come big wages. PSG spent £354 million on wages in 2021, with star players such as Kylian Mbappé and Neymar reported to be on at least £300,000 per week. That's what an average MLS footballer earns as a salary in a year, and four times the salary of a typical footballer in Australia's A-League. The women's game is even more underfinanced. While marquee signings may be paid £200,000 a year, typical NWSL and Women's Super League players earn around £35,000–£45,000 a year. Away from the bigger leagues, footballers are often semi-professional. They are paid expenses or a small fee to play, but need to work a second job to make ends meet.

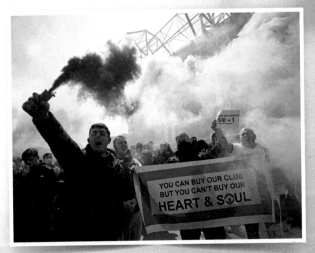

◀ Despite their wealth, big clubs don't always get their own way. Fan protests forced Europe's elite teams to scrap their Super League project in 2021.

◀ In 2021, Chelsea paid a club-record fee of £97.5 million for Romelu Lukaku, a player they owned in 2011-14 but loaned out to other clubs before selling. Following further transfers to Manchester United and Inter Milan, a record £285 million has been spent in fees on this Belgian striker.

FOOTBALL NIGHTMARES

Football sadly has a dark side. With passions running high on and off the pitch and with so much at stake in big matches, the game has sometimes lurched into a nightmare world of cheating, abuse, violence and even death.

CUT OFF IN THEIR PRIME

A number of players have died suddenly through on-pitch collisions or because of a medical problem. In 2003, during a Confederations Cup match against Colombia, Cameroon's 28-year-old midfielder Marc-Vivien Foé collapsed and died shortly afterwards. According to FIFA's Sudden Death Report, 614 amateur or professional footballers died, mostly of heart attacks, between 2014 and 2018.

In 2019, Cardiff City's Argentinian striker, Emiliano Sala, died in a plane crash before he had played a game for the Welsh club. Other plane crashes have wiped out entire teams, including Bolivia's most popular team, The Strongest, in 1969, 18 members of the Zambian national squad in 1993, and Brazilian club Chapecoense in November 2016. One of the most famous air crashes was the 1958 Munich disaster that killed eight Manchester United players and 11 officials and journalists.

FACTFILE

In 2013, the players and officials of four Nigerian second-division teams were banned for life for match-fixing after two highly suspect scorelines. Police Machine FC won 67-0 and Plateau United Feeders recorded a 79-0 victory on the same day.

MATCH-FIXING AND CHEATING

In 1909, George Parsonage was banned for life after asking for a £50 signing-on fee when he joined Chesterfield (the maximum allowed was £10). This looks quaint compared to today's examples of corruption, bribery and match-fixing. In 1999, the former head coach of Romania's Dynamo Bucharest, Vasile Ianul, was sentenced to 12 years in prison for stealing £1.6 million from the club. German football was rocked in 2004 when referee Robert Hoyzer owned up to fixing matches. He was sentenced to more than two years in prison. In 2006, after a match-rigging scandal, Juventus were relegated to Serie B while AC Milan, Lazio, Fiorentina and Reggina Calcio were fined, removed from European competitions and had league points deducted. Further match-fixing or corruption scandals have rocked South Korean football in 2013 and Greek and Italian football in 2015. Four Swedish players received long bans for match-fixing in 2021.

▼ After scoring an own goal in a 2-1 loss to the USA at the 1994 World Cup, Colombian defender Andrés Escobar was murdered, shot 12 times by an unknown gunman.

▲ Denmark players form a barrier around Christian Eriksen after he suffered a heart attack at EURO 2020. Remarkably, he returned to action just 259 days later for Premier League team Brentford.

STADIUM DISASTERS

Crumbling stadiums, overcrowding, poor safety rules and bad crowd control have caused many stadium disasters. The worst ever football tragedy occurred in Lima, Peru, in 1964 when over 300 fans were killed and more than 500 injured in panic stampedes and riots. Two major disasters occurred in 1985 – a wooden stand at Bradford City's ground caught fire, killing 56 people, while the European Cup final also ended in tragedy. A wall collapsed at the Heysel Stadium in Belgium and a riot flared when some Liverpool fans charged at Juventus supporters. One Belgian and 38 Italian spectators died as a result. In January 2022, a crush outside Olembe Stadium before the African Cup of Nations match between Cameroon and Comoros resulted in eight deaths.

▶ Brazilian midfielder Oscar was banned for eight games for provoking this mass brawl between Shanghai and Guangzhou in 2017.

POOR ROLE MODELS?

Most professional footballers are dedicated to the game and are considered excellent role models to young people. Some, however, abuse their position by their actions on or off pitch or have been convicted of crimes related to drugs, assault or theft. A handful of footballers have even fought with fans, most famously Eric Cantona, who kung fu-kicked a Crystal Palace supporter in 1995.

▼ Lionel Messi of PSG and Manchester City's Raheem Sterling protest against racism by taking the knee before a 2021 Champions League game.

RACISM

After concerted efforts by anti-racism groups, from Kick Racism Out to FARE (Football Against Racism in Europe), racism was thought to be declining in football. The truth, sadly, is different. There has been a rise in the amount of non-white players, officials and supporters suffering racist abuse both at games and on social media. On occasion, teams have been punished for their fans' racism with fines and being forced to play games in empty stadiums. In 2021, UEFA handed Hungary a two-game crowd ban and a £158,000 fine after a section of fans abused England's Raheem Sterling and Jude Bellingham in a World Cup qualifier. However, many people feel that governments and football authorities are doing nowhere near enough, and punishments are often criticised as slow or too lenient. Some famous players have taken to social media to publicize incidents and to urge people to speak out and report racism when it occurs. In a handful of instances, players and team-mates have walked off the pitch in protest.

Lionel Messi holds the Copa América and savours finally winning a senior trophy with the Argentinian national team. He was joint top goalscorer at the tournament and named its most valuable player.

FINALLY, FINALLY, MESSI

It had been a long wait but, 16 years after his senior-team debut, Lionel Messi had finally won a major international trophy with Argentina – the 2021 Copa América. He sunk to his knees at the final whistle as his team defeated their fiercest rivals, Brazil, 1-0 in the iconic Maracanã Stadium. Messi had endured a quiet final but his role in the march to the Maracanã had been immense, as he scored or provided the assist for nine of Argentina's 11 goals.

Messi had burst onto the international scene at the 2005 FIFA World Youth Championship alongside Sergio Agüero and Fernando Gago. There, he celebrated his 18th birthday and scored six goals, winning the Golden Boot and netting a further award as its best player. Two of his goals came in the final as Argentina narrowly defeated Nigeria. At the start of what would be a glittering club career in which he won 35 cups or titles with Barcelona, it was inconceivable that it might be his only trophy in Argentinian colours. There was an Olympic gold medal in an under-23s tournament in 2008, but that failed to make up for the heartbreak of reaching four major international finals – three Copa Américas and the 2014 World Cup – only to finish as runner-up on each occasion. For Messi and Argentina, who had not won the Copa since 1993, it would be a case of fifth time lucky.

THE WORLD CUP

Friendlies or charity matches are entertaining, but for a football match to have meaning it has to be part of a wider competition. Football has spawned hundreds of different competitions, but none can compete in global interest and prestige with the World Cup. From small beginnings with 13 competing countries, it has grown to the point where 207 nations attempted to qualify for the 2022 competition.

▲ Austria are in on goal in a first round tie against France in 1934. Austria won 3-2 in what was the first World Cup match to go to extra time.

URUGUAY 1930
FINAL
URUGUAY 4 · ARGENTINA 2
SEMI-FINALS
URUGUAY 6 · YUGOSLAVIA 1
ARGENTINA 6 · USA 1
Games **18** · Goals **70** · Goals per game **3.89**

It took 19 minutes for France's Lucien Laurent to write his name in the record books as the scorer of the first World Cup goal. France beat Mexico 4-1, but it was their only victory and, like Belgium and Romania, they went out at the group stage. Four European sides made the long trip to South America by boat, but only Yugoslavia reached the semi-finals. They and the USA were thrashed in the semis, by Uruguay and Argentina respectively. Argentina boasted the best forward of the competition, Guillermo Stabile, but Uruguay – on home soil and as reigning Olympic champions – were firm favourites. In the final, they came back strongly after Argentina had taken a 2-1 lead, to become the first World Cup winners.

▶ Uruguay captain Jose Nasazzi (left) and Argentina's Manuel Ferreira exchange team pennants before the 1930 World Cup final.

ITALY 1934
FINAL
ITALY 2 · CZECHOSLOVAKIA 1
SEMI-FINALS
ITALY 1 · AUSTRIA 0
CZECHOSLOVAKIA 3 · GERMANY 1
Games **17** · Goals **70** · Goals per game **4.12**

In 1934, the South American teams had not forgotten the lack of European entrants for the first World Cup. As a result, world champions Uruguay chose not to defend their title, while Brazil and Argentina sent understrength sides to Italy. Yet 32 nations, mostly European, were keen to enter the competition. With 16 places available, qualification matches began in June 1933. Italy's 4-0 win over Greece marked the first and only time that a World Cup host has had to play a qualifier to get into the finals. Egypt were the first nation outside of the Americas or Europe to qualify, but following one round of knockout games, the eight remaining teams were all European. After a 7-1 thrashing of the USA, Italy's goals dried up and they only just sneaked past Spain and Austria on their way to the final. In that match, Italy's Luisito Monti (formerly of Argentina) became the only player to have appeared in a World Cup final for different countries. Against a battling Czech side, a goal five minutes into extra time from Italy's Angelo Schiavio secured the Jules Rimet trophy for the hosts.

◄◄ Italy and Hungary in action in the 1938 final.
◄ The poster for the tournament in France – the last World Cup to be held before the Second World War.

FRANCE 1938
FINAL
ITALY 4 · HUNGARY 2
SEMI-FINALS
ITALY 2 · BRAZIL 1
HUNGARY 5 · SWEDEN 1
Games 18 · Goals 84 · Goals per game **4.67**

With the threat of war looming over Europe, Spain and Austria were forced to pull out of the tournament. But the 1938 World Cup did feature the first team from Asia, the Dutch East Indies (now Indonesia), as well as a Cuban side that sprang a major shock by beating Romania in a replay. Sweden thrashed Cuba 8-0, but were then on the receiving end of a 5-1 semi-final mauling by the first great Hungarian side. The other semi-final saw one of the great managerial blunders when the Brazil coach, Adhemar Pimenta, either because of arrogance or through injury fears, rested his star player, Léonidas da Silva. Léonidas had lit up the tournament, most notably in an epic 6-5 thriller against Poland in which he became the first player to score four goals in a World Cup finals match, only for Poland's Ernest Wilimowski to do the same five minutes later. Without the tournament's top scorer, Brazil crashed to defeat against Italy, who went on to become champions for the second time.

FACTFILE
At the 1930 World Cup, not one of the 18 games was drawn. Neither was there a play-off game to decide third place.

BRAZIL 1950
FINAL POOL
URUGUAY 5 PTS · BRAZIL 4 PTS
SWEDEN 2 PTS · SPAIN 1 PT
Games 22 · Goals 88 · Goals per game **4.00**

The only World Cup to feature a final pool of four instead of a final, the 1950 tournament started poorly. Scotland and Turkey withdrew, only 13 nations attended and the mighty Maracanã Stadium was not ready to host the first match. But the competition built in excitement and drama as the goals flowed, often from the boots of the hosts who, after topping their group, ran rampant in the final pool stages, scoring seven against Sweden and six against Spain. Before that point, there had been several notable shocks, including the USA's 1-0 defeat of a highly rated England team. The final pool format could have been an anticlimax, but the outcome went down to the very last game, with Uruguay and Brazil separated by one point and playing in front of around 199,850 fans. Despite falling a goal behind to the favourites, Uruguay won the match 2-1 to lift the World Cup once more.

WORLD CUP GOLDEN BOOT WINNERS (GOALS)

1930	Guillermo Stabile, Argentina (8)
1934	Oldrich Nejedly, Czech. (5)
1938	Léonidas da Silva, Brazil (8)
1950	Ademir Menezes, Brazil (9)
1954	Sandor Kocsis, Hungary (11)
1958	Just Fontaine, France (13)
1962	Garrincha, Brazil; Vava, Brazil; Valentin Ivanov, USSR; Leonel Sanchez, Chile; Florian Albert, Hungary; Drazan Jerkovic, Yugoslavia (4)
1966	Eusebio, Portugal (9)
1970	Gerd Müller, West Germany (10)
1974	Gregorz Lato, Poland (7)
1978	Mario Kempes, Argentina (6)
1982	Paolo Rossi, Italy (6)
1986	Gary Lineker, England (6)
1990	Salvatore Schillaci, Italy (6)
1994	Hristo Stoichkov, Bulgaria; Oleg Salenko, Russia (6)
1998	Davor Suker, Croatia (6)
2002	Ronaldo, Brazil (8)
2006	Miroslav Klose, Germany (5)
2010	Thomas Müller, Germany; Wesley Sneijder, Netherlands; Diego Forlán, Uruguay; David Villa, Spain (5)
2014	James Rodriguez, Colombia (6)
2018	Harry Kane, England (6)

▲ Brazilian keeper Moacir Barbosa gathers the ball during a 1950 group game against Yugoslavia. The match, watched by more than 142,000 spectators in the Maracanã, ended in a 2-0 victory to Brazil.

SWITZERLAND 1954

FINAL
WEST GERMANY 3 · HUNGARY 2

SEMI-FINALS
WEST GERMANY 6 · AUSTRIA 1
HUNGARY 4 · URUGUAY 2
Games **26** · Goals **140** · Goals per game **5.38**

As home to the headquarters of FIFA, which was celebrating its 50th birthday, Switzerland was an obvious host for the 1954 tournament. It featured newcomers such as Turkey, South Korea and the western half of a divided Germany (which had been barred from the 1950 competition). The fans saw plenty of drama and goals, none more than in Austria's 7-5 defeat of Switzerland (the highest-scoring game in the history of the World Cup finals). Hungary, boasting the incredible talents of Ferenc Puskas, Sandor Kocsis and Nandor Hidegkuti, were the most rampant side, scoring an incredible 27 goals in just five matches. At their third World Cup, Uruguay thrashed Scotland 7-0 and beat England 4-2 to reach the semi-finals. They were the only team never to have been beaten in the World Cup until they came up against Hungary, who won 4-2 and went into the final as favourites. West Germany, however, overturned the odds to record a highly emotional victory.

▼ Members of West Germany's triumphant 1954 team are carried off the pitch after two goals from Helmut Rahn and one from Max Morlock secured the country's first World Cup.

FACTFILE
Two pairs of brothers have played on winning sides in a World Cup final – Fritz and Ottmar Walter of West Germany (1954) and England's Jack and Bobby Charlton (1966).

▲ Brazil, pictured after their 1958 final win, during which a 17-year-old Pelé (front row, centre) scored two of Brazil's five goals.

SWEDEN 1958

FINAL
BRAZIL 5 · SWEDEN 2

SEMI-FINALS
BRAZIL 5 · FRANCE 2
SWEDEN 3 · WEST GERMANY 1
Games **35** · Goals **126** · Goals per game **3.60**

Fifty-five countries entered the 1958 qualifying tournament and some big names, including Italy, the Netherlands, Spain and Uruguay, failed to qualify. All four UK home nations (Scotland, England, Northern Ireland and Wales) reached the finals – the only time this has happened. England had lost key players in the Munich aircrash (see page 77), but were the only team to hold a rampant Brazilian side to a draw and to stop them scoring. It was the World Cup's first ever 0-0 draw. Yet it was the two smaller British nations, Wales and Northern Ireland, who qualified for the quarter-finals, with the Irish sensationally beating a strong Czech team. Free-scoring France and Brazil quickly emerged as the favourites, and their semi-final clash was an epic in which the 17-year-old Pelé blasted a hat-trick in Brazil's victory. France had to be content with a 6-3 mauling of West Germany to secure third place. Just Fontaine's four goals in that game propelled him to the Golden Boot with 13 goals in total, a record to this day. Hosts Sweden had quietly seen off Hungary, the Soviet Union and West Germany to reach the final, but they were no match for Brazil, who triumphed 5-2 to win the tournament for the first time.

▶ Jairzinho scores Brazil's third goal in the 1970 final to become the first player to score in every game at a World Cup tournament.

CHILE 1962

FINAL
BRAZIL 3 · CZECHOSLOVAKIA 1
SEMI-FINALS
BRAZIL 4 · CHILE 2
CZECHOSLOVAKIA 3 · YUGOSLAVIA 1
Games **32** · Goals **89**
Goals per game **2.78**

Chile was a controversial choice to host the World Cup, with its small population and its infrastructure damaged by an earthquake in 1960. As it turned out, most of the problems happened on the pitch. A series of bad-tempered matches occurred in the first round, including the infamous 'Battle of Santiago', during which armed police had to split up warring Chilean and Italian players. Chile made it through to a semi-final against Brazil by beating the Soviet Union, while two strong Eastern European sides, Yugoslavia and Czechoslovakia, battled it out in the other semi-final. The Brazilians lost Pelé to injury after only two games, but in Garrincha and Vava they had two of the best players of the competition. Brazil duly won the final with a team featuring eight World Cup winners from the 1958 tournament.

MEXICO 1970

FINAL
BRAZIL 4 · ITALY 1
SEMI-FINALS
BRAZIL 3 · URUGUAY 1
ITALY 4 · WEST GERMANY 3
Games **32** · Goals **95** · Goals per game **2.97**

For many seasoned football observers, the 1970 World Cup remains the best. Much of the brutal, physical play seen in the 1962 and 1966 tournaments was absent. In its place were fascinating tactical and skilful contests between the world's greatest sides. Although the tournament was the first to feature red and yellow cards, no player was sent off, and some of the games have passed into football legend. These include a chess-like battle between Brazil and England that the South Americans narrowly won 1-0; Italy's 4-1 defeat of Mexico; and the Italians' amazing 4-3 victory against West Germany in the semi-final. Brazil powered through the rounds, with stars such as Jairzinho, Pelé and Rivelino attacking with flair. In the final against Italy they were unstoppable, recording their third World Cup win and claiming the Jules Rimet trophy for good.

FACTFILE

Vava's goal in the 1962 final (to add to his pair of goals in the 1958 final) make him the only player to have scored in the finals of successive World Cups.

▼ Soviet keeper Lev Yashin saves at the feet of German striker Uwe Seeler in the 1966 semi-final. West Germany ran out 2-1 winners.

ENGLAND 1966

FINAL
ENGLAND 4 · WEST GERMANY 2
SEMI-FINALS
ENGLAND 2 · PORTUGAL 1
WEST GERMANY 2 · SOVIET UNION 1
Games **32** · Goals **89** · Goals per game **2.78**

The 1966 World Cup was a well-organized tournament and the first to feature a mascot (World Cup Willie). West Germany and Portugal were the most free-scoring sides in a competition characterized by defensive play. Two enormous shocks occurred early on – Brazil were eliminated by Portugal and newcomers North Korea knocked out Italy with a stunning 1-0 victory. The North Koreans won the support of many neutral fans, and their quarter-final meeting with Portugal was a classic. North Korea were 3-0 up within 20 minutes before Portugal, inspired by the tournament's eventual top scorer, Eusebio, hit back to win 5-3. In the semi-final, Eusebio's 82nd-minute strike could not stop England going through to meet West Germany in what proved to be an epic final. The Germans went ahead, then England scored twice to lead until a surprise last-minute German goal took the game into extra time. Geoff Hurst scored two more goals to secure a dramatic victory for the host nation (see page 72).

WEST GERMANY 1974
FINAL
WEST GERMANY 2 · NETHERLANDS 1
THIRD-PLACE PLAY-OFF
POLAND 1 · BRAZIL 0
Games **38** · Goals **97** · Goals per game **2.55**

Ninety-nine nations attempted to qualify for the 1974 tournament, which would see the winners lift a new trophy – the FIFA World Cup. Spain, France and England all failed to reach the tournament, while Zaire, Haiti, East Germany and Australia made their debuts. Changes to the competition format meant that there would be no semi-final games. Instead, the winners of the two second-round groups would contest the final and the group runners-up would play off for third place. The Netherlands, exhibiting their brand of 'total football', swept aside Bulgaria (4-1), Uruguay (2-0), Brazil (2-0) and Argentina (4-0) to top Group A and reach the final. Poland were the surprise package. Propelled by the goals of striker Gregorz Lato, they came second in Group B after narrowly losing 1-0 to West Germany. The West Germans started slowly, but with Franz Beckenbauer in charge and Gerd Müller in fine form, they made the final. There, they overcame the setback of a first-minute Dutch goal from a penalty to win the World Cup for a second time.

FACTFILE
On 14 June 1974, Carlos Caszely of Chile became the first player to receive a red card in a World Cup tournament.

▶ Italy forward Luigi Riva heads the ball above Arsene Auguste of Haiti. The Haitians were at the World Cup finals for the first time in their history.

ARGENTINA 1978
FINAL
ARGENTINA 3 · NETHERLANDS 1
THIRD-PLACE PLAY-OFF
BRAZIL 2 · ITALY 1
Games **38** · Goals **102** · Goals per game **2.68**

▶ Hugo Sánchez, Mexico's most famous player, during his team's shock defeat to Tunisia in 1978.

A colourful and at times controversial tournament, the 1978 World Cup may have lacked some standout stars, but it was rarely short of footballing drama. The hosts found themselves in the toughest of groups with France, Hungary and a young Italian side that beat them, but Argentina made it through to the second group stage. Tunisia caused a shock by drawing with holders West Germany and beating Mexico 3-1 to become the first African side to win a World Cup finals game. Austria, with their star striker Hans Krankl, played strongly in the early stages, beating Spain, Sweden and West Germany. But they were crushed 5-1 by a Dutch squad lacking Johan Cruyff, who had pulled out of the tournament for family reasons. Scotland's campaign promised much, but went badly wrong when they failed to beat Iran and lost to Peru. They then roused themselves, however, to beat the Netherlands 3-2. In the second group stage, Italy, Argentina, Brazil and the Netherlands emerged as frontrunners. Much controversy centred on the Argentina-Peru game. As the last Group B match, it would determine whether Argentina or Brazil reached the final. Peru had played well earlier in the tournament, winning their group ahead of the Netherlands, so their 6-0 loss to Argentina was suspicious. It meant that Brazil were knocked out without being defeated, while Argentina progressed to the final in which they beat the Netherlands.

SPAIN 1982
FINAL
ITALY 3 · WEST GERMANY 1
SEMI-FINALS
ITALY 2 · POLAND 0
WEST GERMANY 3 · FRANCE 3 (5-4 PENALTIES)
Games **52** · Goals **146** · Goals per game **2.81**

In 1982, the format of the tournament changed again so that 24 countries would appear at the finals. Teams played in six groups of four, with the top 12 sides playing in four groups of three to determine the semi-finalists. Belgium beat the holders Argentina to win their group, while England topped theirs ahead of France. Surprise packages Northern Ireland and Algeria beat Spain and West Germany respectively. Poland made the semi-finals, but the hosts, Spain, went out after just one win. The toughest second-round group, containing Brazil, Argentina and Italy, saw the Italians go through, beating Brazil in a 3-2 thriller. West Germany beat France in an equally exciting semi-final, but could not stop the Italians from winning their third World Cup.

MEXICO 1986
FINAL
ARGENTINA 3 · WEST GERMANY 2
SEMI-FINALS
ARGENTINA 2 · BELGIUM 0
WEST GERMANY 2 · FRANCE 0
Games **52** · Goals **132** · Goals per game **2.54**

Colombia had been due to host the 1986 World Cup, but troubles in that country meant they had to withdraw. When Mexico stepped in, they became the first nation to host the tournament twice. More than 120 nations battled for the 24 places in the finals, in which Canada and Iraq both made their debuts. Morocco became the first African nation to reach the second round when they won a group that contained Portugal, Poland and England. Denmark looked promising until they were thrashed 5-1 by Spain, while Belgium squeezed past the Soviet Union 4-3 in one of the best games of the tournament. The quarter-finals were extremely tight affairs. Three went to penalty shootouts, while the fourth game saw England face Argentina. Maradona arrived at the World Cup as the world's most expensive player and a heavily marked man. His incredible dribbling and scoring skills made him the best player of the tournament. In the quarter-final, his two goals (one a deliberate handball, the other a magnificent solo effort – see pages 54–55) sank England and he repeated the feat against Belgium in the semi-final. In the final, West Germany went 2-0 down, rallied to 2-2, but were beaten by a late Argentinian goal.

FACTFILE
The fastest sending-off in World Cup history occurred in 1986, when Uruguay's José Batista was dismissed against Scotland after just 55 seconds.

▶ Diego Maradona is sent flying over West German keeper Harald Schumacher during the final of the 1986 World Cup. The Argentinian legend was sensational as he helped his country win the trophy for a second time.

ITALY 1990
FINAL
WEST GERMANY 1 · ARGENTINA 0
SEMI-FINALS
WEST GERMANY 1 · ENGLAND 1
(4-3 PENALTIES)
ARGENTINA 1 · ITALY 1 (4-3 PENALTIES)
Games **52** · Goals **115** · Goals per game **2.21**

This fondly remembered World Cup had moments of
great theatre, from veteran Cameroon striker Roger Milla's
dance at the corner flag to Costa Rica's joy at defeating both
Scotland and Sweden to qualify for the second round. Sadly, the
tournament also saw much negative football and a record number of
bookings (164), as well as 16 sendings-off. Cameroon were the talk of
the tournament, beating Romania and Colombia to set up a quarter-final
against England. Cameroon went 2-0 up, but two Gary Lineker penalties
and a third England goal in extra time saw the neutral's favourites go out.

The Netherlands arrived as
European Champions, but
failed to win a match, while
Brazil and the Soviet Union also
disappointed. The semi-finals were
both full of drama, but the final was
deeply forgettable. West Germany beat
Argentina courtesy of an 85th-minute
penalty, while Pedro Monzon was the first
of two sendings-off for Argentina and the first
player to be red-carded in a World Cup final.

USA 1994
FINAL
BRAZIL 0 · ITALY 0 (3-2 PENALTIES)
SEMI-FINALS
BRAZIL 1 · SWEDEN 0
ITALY 2 · BULGARIA 1
Games **52** · Goals **141** · Goals per game **2.71**

Some feared that the crowds at the 1994 World Cup would be small
in a country where male football is not a dominant sport. But it
proved to be a lively and well-attended tournament. Attacking
play had been encouraged by the adoption of the backpass
rule (see page 24) and three instead of two points for a win
in the group games. Despite losing many players since
the break-up of the Soviet Union, Russia recorded
the biggest win, 6-1 against Cameroon, with Oleg
Salenko scoring five goals – the most by one player
in a World Cup match. Maradona went home
after he failed a drugs test, and the Republic
of Ireland shocked Italy with a 1-0 win in the
group stages. The Bulgarians were terrific,
beating Argentina, knocking out Germany
and finishing fourth overall. European
sides dominated the quarter-finals,
yet it was Brazil who beat the
Netherlands, Sweden and Italy
to lift the World Cup trophy for
a record fourth time.

▼ Midfielder Emmanuel Petit
celebrates as France beat
Croatia 2-1 to book a place
in the 1998 World Cup final
against Brazil.

FRANCE 1998
FINAL
FRANCE 3 · BRAZIL 0
SEMI-FINALS
FRANCE 2 · CROATIA 1
BRAZIL 1 · NETHERLANDS 1 (4-2 PENALTIES)
Games **64** · Goals **171** · Goals per game **2.67**

With places at this tournament increased to 32, newcomers included Jamaica, Japan
and South Africa. Iran caused a shock in their first World Cup for 20 years by beating the
USA. Nigeria upset the odds with a 3-2 defeat of Spain that effectively knocked out the
European side. Despite 22 red cards, the football was enthralling, with Croatia, Denmark,
Brazil, France and the Netherlands playing attacking football. England narrowly went out,
losing on penalties to Argentina in one of the games of the tournament. Croatia were the
dark horses, progressing quietly and then beating Germany 3-0 in the quarter-final. For
the second World Cup in a row, Italy were knocked out on penalties, this time to France at
the quarter-final stage. A France-Brazil final was an exciting prospect, but Ronaldo was ill
before the game and was extremely subdued, as were his team-mates. France won with
relative ease, aided by two goals from Zinedine Zidane.

SOUTH KOREA AND JAPAN 2002

FINAL
BRAZIL 2 · GERMANY 0
SEMI-FINALS
BRAZIL 1 · TURKEY 0
GERMANY 1 · SOUTH KOREA 0
Games **64** · Goals **161** · Goals per game **2.52**

An amazing 193 nations attempted to qualify for the first World Cup held in Asia. Surprise failures included the Netherlands, Uruguay and Colombia. A shock came in the opening game in which Senegal beat the World Cup holders, France, 1-0. France then lost to Denmark and exited the tournament, as did Russia, Poland and Portugal. Cheered on by passionate crowds, the South Koreans were headline news, knocking out Italy, Spain and Portugal to reach the semi-finals, along with Turkey who eventually finished third. The final saw Brazilian striker Ronaldo turn back the years to score two goals that defeated Germany.

▶ Senegal's Papa Bouba Diop in action against Turkey in their 2002 quarter-final tie. It was his country's first ever appearance at the tournament.

GERMANY 2006

FINAL
ITALY 1 · FRANCE 1 (5-3 PENALTIES)
SEMI-FINALS
ITALY 2 · GERMANY 0 (AFTER EXTRA TIME)
FRANCE 1 · PORTUGAL 0
Games **64** · Goals **147** · Goals per game **2.3**

▼ Japan's Yuichi Komano (left) battles for the ball with Lucas Neill of Australia in a Group F game in 2006. Australia won 3-1.

Despite a thrilling opening match (Germany 4-2 Costa Rica), this tournament saw defences on top and a record card count (345 yellow and 28 red). Italy's miserly defence, led by Fabio Cannavaro, let in just one goal on the way to the first all-European final since 1982. Elsewhere, only one (Ghana) of the five African nations present progressed from their group whilst Australia, Oceania's first team at a World Cup since 1982, surprisingly qualified from a group featuring Brazil, Japan and Croatia. In the final, Zinedine Zidane – playing his last competitive match – scored a penalty only for Italian defender Marco Materazzi to equalize. During extra time, Zidane was sent off for head-butting Materazzi in the chest. With the game ending in a stalemate, Italy won a tense penalty shootout to secure the World Cup for a fourth time.

SOUTH AFRICA 2010
FINAL
SPAIN 1 · NETHERLANDS 0
(AFTER EXTRA TIME)
SEMI-FINALS
NETHERLANDS 3 · URUGUAY 2
SPAIN 1 · GERMANY 0
Games **64** · Goals **145**
Goals per game **2.27**

The first tournament to be held in Africa will be remembered as a noisy, colourful affair with some 3.18 million spectators attending matches in ten stadiums. Serbia and Slovakia made their tournament debuts but failed to progress from their group, a fate which also befell Cameroon, Denmark, Italy and France.

The Germans would score the most goals (16) in the tournament but would finish in third place after being knocked out in the semi-finals. The Netherlands were also on a roll, taking their World Cup and World Cup qualifying winning run to 13 games when they knocked out Brazil in the quarter-finals. Spain lost their very first game, 1-0 against Switzerland, but they won each of their four knockout games 1-0, including a tense final against the Netherlands, to claim their first ever World Cup.

▲ Spanish keeper Iker Casillas intercepts the ball before Dutch striker Robin van Persie can pounce during the 2010 final.

▶ Russian striker Artem Dzyuba celebrates scoring against Spain in the Round of 16 at the 2018 World Cup. His side would go on to win the tie in a thrilling penalty shootout.

▼ Bastian Schweinsteiger (left) and Lukas Podolski celebrate with the trophy after Germany's fourth World Cup win. The champions scored 18 times in seven games, conceding only four goals.

BRAZIL 2014
FINAL
GERMANY 1 · ARGENTINA 0 (A.E.T.)
SEMI-FINALS
GERMANY 7 · BRAZIL 1
ARGENTINA 0 · NETHERLANDS 0 (4-2 PENALTIES)
Games **64** · Goals **171** · Goals per game **2.67**

The first World Cup in Brazil for 64 years saw the debut of Bosnia & Herzegovina, goal line technology and vanishing foam to mark out distances for free kicks. Defending champions Spain crashed out at the group stage after being thrashed 5-1 by the Netherlands and losing 2-0 to Chile. In Group D, Uruguay and Costa Rica progressed, knocking out England and Italy, while Algeria got through the group stage for the first time ever. The host's hopes were crushed in an extraordinary semi-final in which Germany scored five times in just 20 minutes to win 7-1. They met Argentina in the final where a Mario Götze goal made Germany the first European team to win a World Cup in the Americas. Colombia's James Rodriguez won the Golden Boot with six goals, while Lionel Messi was awarded the Golden Ball as the tournament's best player.

RUSSIA 2018

FINAL
FRANCE 4 · CROATIA 2
SEMI-FINALS
FRANCE 1 · BELGIUM 0
CROATIA 2 · ENGLAND 0
Games **64** · Goals **169** · Goals per game **2.64**

A celebration of football and fandom, Russia proved welcoming hosts. The football often dazzled and entertained with only one of the 64 games, France against Denmark, ending in a goalless draw. With a population of less than 340,000, Iceland became the smallest country to play in a World Cup. They failed to qualify out of their group, as did all the African nations and the defending champions, Germany. Losing to both Mexico and South Korea, it was the first time Germany had failed to qualify from their group since 1938. The hosts, however, fared better, progressing from their group then beating Spain in a penalty shootout that gripped spectators around the world. Exciting young stars like Kevin de Bruyne and Kylian Mbappé helped propel Belgium and France to the semi-finals, whilst England recorded their biggest ever World Cup win, overpowering Panama 6-1. England's Harry Kane would win the Golden Boot as top scorer whilst Luka Modric won the Golden Ball as the tournament's best player, but the glory and a second World Cup win went to France.

◢ Qatar built eight new stadiums at a cost of more than $6.5 billion for the 2022 World Cup.

▼ Mali's Ibrahim Kone celebrates scoring against Kenya in a 2022 World Cup qualifier. His country was aiming to make it to the tournament for the first time in its history.

HOPING TO HOST

Six nations expressed an interest in hosting the first World Cup, held in 1930, and ever since, countries have prepared their bid many years in advance to try and secure the World Cup within their borders. The tournament was first held in Africa in 2010 and was hosted in the Middle East – in Qatar — for the first time in 2022. Only one tournament has been co-hosted (Japan/South Korea in 2002), but the 2026 World Cup will feature three hosts – Canada, the United States and Mexico – with an expanded format containing 48 teams.

THE WOMEN'S WORLD CUP

Given how popular women's football is today, it is hard to believe that many countries only lifted their ban on women's competition in the 1970s. Asia was the first continent to hold a competition: in 1975, New Zealand defeated Thailand in the final of the AFC Women's Championship (now the AFC Women's Asian Cup). In the 1980s, increased lobbying and the success of Italy's invitational women's tournament, the Mundialito, led to FIFA running a test event in China in 1988. Three years later, the world's elite female footballers returned to take part in the very first Women's World Cup.

▲ Carla Overbeck (centre) celebrates with the 1999 US team she captained. Overbeck was also part of the winning team in 1991.

CHINA 1991
FINAL
USA 2 · NORWAY 1

The first Women's World Cup was a great success and proof that women's football had a major global audience. Twelve teams from all six FIFA confederations took part, and 65,000 spectators watched the final between the USA and Norway. The USA ran out 2-1 winners, with both their goals coming from Michelle Akers. Akers was awarded the Golden Shoe after scoring ten goals in the tournament.

▶ US forward Wendy Gebauer skips to avoid a challenge from Japan's Kyoko Kuroda at the 1991 World Cup.

SWEDEN 1995
FINAL
NORWAY 2 · GERMANY 0

The tournament's 26 games saw plenty of goals. Brazil were thrashed 6-1 by Germany, who then lost a 3-2 thriller to Sweden. The USA and China shared the spoils in an epic 3-3 encounter and Norway powered through their group, putting 17 goals past Canada, England and Nigeria, before knocking out the USA at the semi-final stage. Sweden's Ingrid Jonsson became the first woman to referee a FIFA final, in which Norway scored two first-half goals to secure the world crown.

USA 1999
FINAL
USA 0 · CHINA 0 (5-4 PENALTIES)

Expanded to 16 teams, the tournament was a huge success and saw Nigeria become the first African side to reach the quarter-finals. The USA, with Mia Hamm, Brandi Chastain and Tiffeny Milbrett all playing superbly, had to work hard to overcome both Germany and Brazil. China, in contrast, cruised to the final. Played in front of more than 90,000 fans at the Rose Bowl, the final was a very tense affair. The game went to penalties, with Briana Scurry saving Ying Liu's spot kick to see the USA win the shootout 5-4.

USA 2003
FINAL
GERMANY 2 · SWEDEN 1

Relocated to the USA from China at the last minute due to the SARS virus epidemic, the 2003 tournament was predicted to be a successful swansong for many of the USA's veteran players. However, a vibrant, attacking German side, led by the tournament's leading scorer, Birgit Prinz, knocked them out in the semi-finals. In a memorable final, a golden goal by substitute Nia Kuenzer secured Germany their first Women's World Cup.

CHINA 2007
FINAL
GERMANY 2 · BRAZIL 0

The tournament got off to a record start with Germany thrashing Argentina 11-0 in Group A whilst Brazil, led by top scorer Marta, mauled New Zealand 5-0 and China 4-0 in Group D. These two teams, along with Norway and the USA, made it out of their groups and into the semi-finals, where Brazil handed a surprise 4-0 defeat to the USA to join Germany in the final. Two second-half goals from Birgit Prinz and Simone Ladehr propelled Germany to their second World Cup final victory in a row.

CANADA 2015
FINAL
USA 5 · JAPAN 2

Canada hosted a competition expanded from 16 to 24 teams. All games were played on artificial turf, which caused player complaints but otherwise the tournament was a great success. Compelling matches and stunning displays showcased women's elite football. There were mismatches: Switzerland defeated Ecuador 10-1, while Germany thrashed the Ivory Coast 10-0, but many other games were tight affairs. Australia defeated a highly rated Brazilian team in the quarter-finals, lost narrowly to Japan but beat Germany in the play-off to finish third overall.

The USA met holders Japan in a repeat of the 2011 final, and the game was memorable for US midfielder Carli Lloyd's spectacular hat-trick, which included an incredible shot from the halfway line.

▲ Germany's Celia Sasic (left) shared the 2015 Golden Boot (six goals) with Carli Lloyd of the USA.

GERMANY 2011
FINAL
JAPAN 2 · USA 2 (3-1 PENALTIES)

An exciting, well-staged tournament saw almost a million spectators watch matches between the 16 teams, which included Colombia and Equatorial Guinea for the first time. Two quarter-finals went to penalty shootouts, with France defeating England and Brazil losing to the USA after an epic match. The Americans went down to ten players after a red card in the 65th minute, but managed to take the game into extra time and equalized in the 122nd minute. The US went through to the final where they came up against the newest force of women's football. Japan, led by the tournament's best player, Homare Sawa, became the first team from Asia to win a World Cup.

▼ US striker Abby Wambach (right) battles with Japan's Saki Kumagai during the 2011 final.

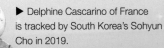

▶ Delphine Cascarino of France is tracked by South Korea's Sohyun Cho in 2019.

FRANCE 2019
FINAL
USA 2 · NETHERLANDS 0

France 2019 was the biggest Women's World Cup ever, with global television audiences passing one billion. There were goals galore as hosts France kicked off with an emphatic 4-0 win over South Korea, the first of 52 matches and 146 goals in total. The USA entered the competition as defending champions and firm favourites. They did not disappoint, hammering Thailand with a record-breaking scoreline of 13-0 in their opening match and a record-breaking five goals in one game for striker Alex Morgan. The USA knocked out Spain, France and England on their way to the final where they beat the Netherlands 2-0 in their fourth World Cup win. US co-captain Megan Rapinoe stole the headlines, bagging the Golden Ball for best player and the Golden Boot for six goals. More history was made when Brazilian legend Marta scored against Italy, bringing her World Cup record to 17 goals, more than any other player.

THE EUROPEAN CHAMPIONSHIPS

The European Championships began in 1958 as the UEFA European Nations Cup, but struggled to attract teams to compete. However, today it is the largest international football competition behind the World Cup. It is also held every four years.

HOSTS AND WINNERS

Year	Host	Final
1964	Spain	Spain 2-1 USSR
1968	Italy	Italy 2-0 Yugoslavia (after replay)
1972	Belgium	West Germany 3-0 USSR
1976	Yugoslavia	Czechoslovakia 2-2 W. Germany (5-3 pens)
1980	Italy	West Germany 2-1 Belgium
1984	France	France 2-0 Spain
1988	West Germany	Netherlands 2-0 USSR
1992	Sweden	Denmark 2-0 Germany
1996	England	Germany 2-1 Czech Republic
2000	Belgium / Neth.	France 2-1 Italy
2004	Portugal	Greece 1-0 Portugal
2008	Austria / Switz.	Spain 1-0 Germany
2012	Poland / Ukraine	Spain 4-0 Italy
2016	France	Portugal 1-0 France
2020	Europe-wide	Italy 1-1 England (3-2 pens)

GROWING COMPETITION

Early tournaments consisted of qualifying rounds with just four teams progressing to a mini tournament of semi-finals and a final. By 1980, this was extended to eight sides and it doubled again for the 1996 tournament, the first held in England. Before expansion, many talented sides missed out on the tournament, such as the Soviet Union in 1984 and Spain and Italy in 1992. EURO 2016 saw further growth with 24 teams taking part. Five nations made their EURO debuts at this tournament, with Iceland and Wales (the latter reaching the semi-finals) making the biggest impact.

SURPRISE WINNERS

EURO 1992 saw Denmark record a memorable triumph. They had failed to qualify and most of their players were on holiday when UEFA invited them to the tournament following Yugoslavia's disqualification. With little time to prepare, the Danes defeated the Netherlands and Germany to win the most unlikely of European Championship crowns. In 1976, Czechoslovakia surprised everyone by beating the World Cup holders, West Germany, in the final. EURO 2004 began with shocks aplenty when Spain and Italy were knocked out early, followed by Germany who had been held to a draw by minnows Latvia. Greece had defeated the tournament hosts Portugal in the opening match, only to face them again in the final. Greek forward Angelos Charisteas scored his third goal of EURO 2004 in the 57th minute, as Greece won 1-0 to secure their first major international trophy.

◀ Denmark celebrate in 1992. ▶ Spain's Jordi Alba tussles with Mario Balotelli of Italy in 2012. ▶▶ Ronaldo lifts the trophy as Portugal toast their 2016 victory.

FACTFILE

Spanish leader General Franco, a critic of communism, refused the Soviet team entry into Spain to play their qualifying game for the 1960 competition. The Soviets were awarded a win.

EURO 2020

Postponed for a year due to the Covid Pandemic, this was the first tournament with no single or shared hosts, but with games spread out across the continent. Spain's helter-skelter 5-3 defeat of Croatia, Switzerland knocking out France and Germany's 4-2 defeat of Portugal were amongst the highlights. England had suffered knockout infamy at the hands of Iceland in 2016, but five years later, Gareth Southgate's well-drilled team cruised past Germany, Ukraine and Denmark to reach the final. There, England faced an Italian team whose tight defence, well marshalled by veteran Giorgio Chiellini, saw them prevail in a tense tussle which went to penalties. Italian goalkeeper Gianluigi Donnarumma, the player of the tournament, twice proved a penalty shootout hero to give the Italians their first EURO title for 53 years.

◀ England's Raheem Sterling scores against Germany at EURO 2020. The 2-0 win was his side's first knockout victory over the Germans in 55 years.

WOMEN'S EUROS

Starting in 1984 with just four invited teams, the women's EUROs has expanded, with 16 sides taking part for the first time in 2017. That tournament was won by the Netherlands, the fourth time a host nation had triumphed. They joined Norway (1987, 1993) and Sweden (1984) as the only teams to stop Germany, who have dominated the competition with an astonishing eight tournament wins. The 2022 tournament, held in England, featured four groups of four teams including Northern Ireland, who qualified for the first time.

▶ Norway's Maria Thorisdóttir (left) and Daniëlle van de Donk of the Netherlands in action at EURO 2017.

THE OLYMPICS

Until the emergence of the World Cup, the Olympics provided football's leading world competition. Football appeared in the 1896 games as an exhibition event and became a full Olympic sport 12 years later. With the exception of the 1932 Los Angeles games, it has featured at every Olympics since. The competition was boosted in the 1990s by the admittance of professional stars and the emergence of African football, which produced two Olympic gold medallists in Nigeria and Cameroon.

AMATEURS ONLY

For most of its history, Olympic football was played by amateurs only. The rise of professional football in the 1920s meant that many of the world's best professionals were unable to appear at the Games. State-run teams from Eastern Europe dominated the Olympics after World War II – from 1952 to 1988, every Olympic winner came from Eastern Europe with the exception of the 1984 French side, while Hungary remain the only team to have won football gold three times. But as the Olympics began to accept professional athletes in other sports, so it changed the rules for football. Professionals who were part of their national under-23 team appeared at the 1992 games. In 1996, the rule was relaxed to allow each side to field three professional players over the age of 23. At Sydney 2000, Chile, led by 33-year-old striker Ivan Zamorano, won bronze. Zamorano's six goals made him top scorer at the Games.

▼ Mexico's Oribe Peralta is mobbed after scoring the winner in the 2012 Olympic final against Brazil.

EMERGING PLAYERS

Great professional players have emerged from the Olympics. For example, French midfielder Michel Platini and Mexican legend Hugo Sanchez burst onto the international scene at the 1976 Montreal games. The 1996 Brazil team included Rivaldo and Ronaldo. The 1952 Olympics in Helsinki, Finland, saw the arrival of a stunningly good Hungarian side. Featuring players such as Ferenc Puskas, Nandor Hidegkuti and Sandor Kocsis, the Hungarians conceded two goals but scored 20 on their way to the gold medal. These players went on to form the core of the Hungarian side that lit up international football through the 1950s (see page 68).

FACTFILE

The first official Olympic tournament, in 1908, saw a record average of eight goals per game. This tally was helped by Denmark's 17-1 thrashing of France. Sophus Nielsen scored ten times including three goals within the first six minutes!

▶ Cameroon's Samuel Eto'o in the gold-medal match at Sydney 2000. His team's win secured his country's first Olympic gold medal.

OLYMPIC WOMEN

Women's football finally became part of the Olympics at the 1996 Atlanta Games, after many years of lobbying for inclusion. With no time for a qualifying competition, the top eight nations at the 1995 Women's World Cup were invited to take part, with the exception of England, who were ineligible to compete. The final saw China beaten 2-1 by the USA in front of 76,481 spectators, a world record for a women's sporting event at that time. Five nations – the USA, China, Germany, Norway and Brazil – shared all the medals until 2012, when powerful Canadian and Japanese teams emerged. But the qualification system now in place will ensure that Asia, Africa and Oceania are all represented at future Olympics.

▶ Canada midfielder Julia Grosso (left) scored the decisive penalty in a shootout to win gold for Canada at Tokyo 2020.

2016 AND 2020 GAMES

The 2016 tournament saw new winners in both competitions. In the men's, Neymar was the hero for Brazil, scoring the winning penalty in a shootout to defeat Germany in the final. The Germans gained consolation from their female colleagues who defeated Sweden 2-1 in front of 52,000 spectators to win gold for the first time. The 2020 competition, delayed for a year due to the Covid pandemic, offered plenty of drama, from the Netherlands women's team thrashing China 8-2 to Canada's Jessie Fleming scoring the penalty that knocked the favourites USA out at the semi-final stage. In the men's tournament, Mexico had enjoyed a 4-1 win over France and a 6-3 victory against South Korea, but could not find the net against eventual champions Brazil, losing to them in a penalty shootout.

▼ Dani Alves, the oldest player in the tournament at 38, shows off his gold medal after Brazil's triumph at Tokyo 2020.

COPA AMÉRICA

▼ Peruvian striker Gianluca Lapadula (right) and Ecuador's Robert Arboleda in a 2021 Copa América Group B match. Lapadula scored the first of Peru's two goals in the game, which ended 2-2.

The oldest continental cup competition, the Copa América has been played under a bewildering array of names and formats ever since the first competition, a three-way affair between Argentina, Uruguay and Chile in 1910. One thing has remained constant – its status as a major footballing prize for the nations of South America.

CUP DOMINATION

The Copa América has had to contend with clubs reluctant to release players and the increasing popularity of international club competitions. Yet it still maintains a strong appeal. There have been 47 Copa América competitions, eight of which have been unofficial but are counted for the records. The tournament has been dominated by the big three South American nations of Argentina, Brazil and Uruguay. Fifteen Copas passed until another country, Peru, won it. Since then, Argentina and Uruguay (both with 15 titles) have maintained a strong grip. Brazil have won nine times; Paraguay and Peru twice and Bolivia, Chile and Colombia have each won once.

INVITED GUESTS

In 1993, the Copa was expanded to 12 sides. Teams are invited from outside South America, including Mexico (runners up twice), USA, Costa Rica and Honduras – who caused a sensation in 2001 by beating Brazil 2-0 in the quarter-finals. Mexico appeared for the sixth time at the 2015 Copa, drawing 3-3 with hosts Chile, who progressed to the final after beating Uruguay and Peru in the quarters and semis. Chile defeated Argentina 4-1 on penalties to win their first-ever Copa and won the tournament again the next year.

▶ Chile's Gonzalo Jara (left) and Arturo Vidal hold the trophy after winning the centenary edition of the Copa América in 2016.

COPA AMÉRICA WINNERS

Year	Winner	Year	Winner	Year	Winner
1910 *	Argentina	1942	Uruguay	1989	Brazil
1916 *	Uruguay	1945 *	Argentina	1991	Argentina
1917	Uruguay	1946 *	Argentina	1993	Argentina
1919	Brazil	1947	Argentina	1995	Uruguay
1920	Uruguay	1949	Brazil	1997	Brazil
1921	Argentina	1953	Paraguay	1999	Brazil
1922	Brazil	1955	Argentina	2001	Colombia
1923	Uruguay	1956 *	Uruguay	2004	Brazil
1924	Uruguay	1957	Argentina	2007	Brazil
1925	Argentina	1959 *	Argentina	2011	Uruguay
1926	Uruguay	1959	Uruguay	2015	Chile
1927	Argentina	1963	Bolivia	2016	Chile
1929	Argentina	1967	Uruguay	2019	Brazil
1935 *	Uruguay	1975	Peru	2021	Argentina
1937	Argentina	1979	Paraguay		
1939	Peru	1983	Uruguay	* unofficial	
1941 *	Argentina	1987	Uruguay	tournament	

AFRICA CUP OF NATIONS

When first held in 1957, the tournament was contested by just three of Africa's nine independent nations: Sudan, Ethiopia and eventual winners, Egypt. Since then, the number of nations has risen sharply and now teams strive to qualify for one of the 24 places at the finals.

UPS AND DOWNS

The Africa Cup of Nations has had to endure its ups and downs, with poor playing facilities in some countries, hostilities between nations and major controversies. These continue into the modern era. Nigeria, one of Africa's top sides, were expelled from the 1998 tournament after they had refused to travel to the 1996 competition. Since the early 1990s, the best teams in the competition have relied on calling back as many of their foreign-based stars as possible. In 2006, for example, not one player in the Ivory Coast and Cameroon squads was based in his home country. Four years later, Cameroon striker Samuel Eto'o notched his 18th goal, making him the tournament's all-time leading goalscorer.

◄ Sadio Mané of Senegal (right) battles Egypt's Emam Ashour in the 2021 final. Mané scored the winning penalty in the shootout that gave Senegal victory.

AFRICA CUP OF NATIONS WINNERS

Year	Winner	Year	Winner
1957	Egypt	1990	Algeria
1959	Egypt	1992	Ivory Coast
1962	Ethiopia	1994	Nigeria
1963	Ghana	1996	South Africa
1965	Ghana	1998	Egypt
1968	Congo-Kinshasa	2000	Cameroon
		2002	Cameroon
1970	Sudan	2004	Tunisia
1972	Congo-Brazzaville	2006	Egypt
		2008	Egypt
1974	Zaire	2010	Egypt
1976	Morocco	2012	Zambia
1978	Ghana	2013	Nigeria
1980	Nigeria	2015	Ivory Coast
1982	Ghana	2017	Cameroon
1984	Cameroon	2019	Algeria
1986	Egypt	2021	Senegal
1988	Cameroon		

WINNERS AND LOSERS

Champions have come from around the continent – from Africa's northernmost country, Morocco (winners in 1976), to its southernmost nation, South Africa, who returned from the international wilderness to win an emotional competition in 1996. Nine tournament finals have ended in penalty shootouts, including the 2015 tournament when the Ivory Coast defeated Ghana 9-8 despite missing their first two penalties. One of the most unlucky nations has to be Zambia, who lost an entire team in a tragic 1993 plane crash (see page 102), yet miraculously reached the final the following year. Zambia finally triumphed in 2012, after a period of dominance by Egypt – three wins in a row –which took them to the top of the winners' table with seven cups. The 2017 final was contested by the cup's most successful sides, Egypt (7 titles) and Cameroon (5 titles), while Algeria won their second title in 2019. The delayed 2021 edition saw Egypt in the final once again, this time against Senegal. After a tense penalty shootout, Senegal won the trophy for the very first time.

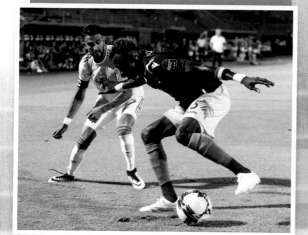

◄ Guinea's Issiaga Sylla holds off Algeria captain Riyad Mahrez in 2019. Mahrez scored a vital 95th-minute winner in the semi-final and led his team to the title with victory over Senegal.

ASIAN GAMES AND ASIAN CUP

Asia is the one continent that has two major football competitions for its nations – the Asian Games and the Asian Cup. Both tournaments are held every four years, but in cycles that keep them two years apart.

◀ Japan's Maya Yoshida out-jumps Almoez Ali of Qatar in the 2019 Asian Cup final.

THE ASIAN GAMES

The Asian Games is a multi-sport competition in which football is just one of a number of events. South Korea have shared the title twice, after the final was drawn. After a self-imposed exile from the Asian Games in the mid-1990s, Iran powered to victories in 1998 and 2002. By the 2002 games, the tournament had become an under-23 competition, with sides allowed to field up to three over-age players. The 2018 competition saw South Korea win again.

THE ASIAN CUP

First held in 1956 with just four teams, the Asian Cup has grown in importance, with 46 nations entering qualifying for the 2023 tournament. Japan are the competition's most successful team, winning the cup four times, followed by Iran and Saudi Arabia with three titles. Israel were a major force in the early years. They were in the final of the first four Asian Cups, winning in 1964. In 1975, however, Israel were expelled from the Asian Football Confederation, and joined UEFA in 1992.

China became hosts for the first time in 2004, when the tournament was expanded to include 16 teams. The Japan versus China final attracted enormous interest. The match was broadcast live to 60 nations; in China alone, the television audience was more than 250 million.

Australia entered the fray from 2007 onwards, finishing runners-up in 2011 but triumphing in 2015, defeating South Korea 2-1 in the final. They joined other recent first-time champions including Iraq in 2007 and, sensationally, Qatar in 2019. The Qataris went through the entire tournament unbeaten and, propelled by nine goals from Almoez Ali, reached the final where they defeated Japan 3-1.

◀ Iran run a lap of honour after their shock defeat of Japan to win the 2002 Asian Games.

ASIAN GAMES AND ASIAN CUP WINNERS

Games winners (since 1962)		Cup winners	
1962	India	1956	South Korea
1966	Burma	1960	South Korea
1970	Burma and	1964	Israel
	South Korea	1968	Iran
1974	Iran	1972	Iran
1978	North Korea and	1976	Iran
	South Korea	1980	Kuwait
1982	Iraq	1984	Saudi Arabia
1986	South Korea	1988	Saudi Arabia
1990	Iran	1992	Japan
1994	Uzbekistan	1996	Saudi Arabia
1998	Iran	2000	Japan
2002	Iran	2004	Japan
2006	Qatar	2007	Iraq
2010	Japan	2011	Japan
2014	South Korea	2015	Australia
2018	South Korea	2019	Qatar

CONCACAF CHAMPIONSHIP

GOLD CUP WINNERS	
Canada	2000
Mexico	1993, 1996, 1998, 2003, 2009, 2011, 2015, 2019
USA	1991, 2002, 2005, 2007, 2013, 2017, 2021

Of all the footballing regions of the world, North America, Central America and the Caribbean Islands have had the most complex history of competitions. Five different tournaments have been open to them, starting with the CCCF Championship in 1941.

THE GOLD CUP

For a number of years, competition in the CONCACAF zone was used as a direct way of qualifying for the World Cup. In 1991, the tournament was renamed the Gold Cup, which from 2019 features 16 teams in the finals. Every Gold Cup has been hosted by the USA, either alone or jointly with Mexico. Teams from outside CONCACAF have often been invited to play. In 1996, the Brazilian under-23 side lost to Mexico in the final. South Korea were guests in 2000, but they lost out on a quarter-final place to Canada on the toss of a coin. Canada went on to beat another guest, Colombia, in the final. Qatar were the invited guests for the 2021 tournament and reached the semi-final, only to fall to the eventual winners, USA. It was the seventh victory for the hosts, one behind their great rivals Mexico. In recent years, the two sides' dominance has been threatened by an enterprising Jamaican team that knocked the US side out of the 2015 tournament, Mexico out of the 2017 competition, and reached the semi-finals in 2019.

▲ USA defender Shaq Moore (right) gets past Haiti's Duckens Nazon in a 2021 Gold Cup match.

▶ New Caledonia (in red) defend against New Zealand's Chris Wood in the 2016 OFC Nations Cup.

THE OFC NATIONS CUP

Oceania's competition is the smallest and youngest of the continental championships. It has been held nine times since 1973, now every four years. The 2004 tournament saw a major surprise as the Solomon Islands beat New Zealand to make the final, losing to Australia. The 2012 Cup saw further surprises, with New Caledonia knocking out New Zealand and Tahiti emerging as champions. New Zealand triumphed in 2016, defeating Papua New Guinea on penalties in the final.

FOOTBALL LEAGUES

Clubs compete in leagues that are made up of several divisions. Rules, numbers of teams and the length of a league season vary around the world. Many top leagues – in Spain, Italy, France and Germany, for example – have 18 or 20 teams.

NUMBERS AND BREAKS

The top divisions of Sweden and Russia contain 16 teams whilst Australia has 12 and Latvia just ten. In most leagues the sides play each other twice, home and away, during a season. In Denmark, the 12 teams play each other three times. Scotland's top division has an unusual format – there are 12 teams, but the season lasts for 38 games. Sides play each other three times, before the league turns into two groups of six for a further round of matches. Some leagues – in Argentina and Mexico, for example – are split into two short seasons every year. League teams in Spain, France, Germany, Hungary and some other countries take a midwinter break, while in northern European nations, such as Norway and Finland, the league season begins in the spring. England's Women's Super League (WSL) has risen from eight clubs in 2015 to 12 by 2019.

▲ Lyon's Ada Hegerberg battles with Vanessa Gilles of Bordeaux in the 12-team Division1 Féminine.

PROMOTION AND RELEGATION

While leagues in Australia and the USA guarantee each team a place for the following season, most leagues have a system of promotion and relegation, with top and bottom sides switching places for the new season.

In Uruguay, relegation and promotion are determined by the performance of teams over two seasons. In Austria, one side is promoted and one relegated each season. In Hungary, the Czech Republic and South Korea, two teams go up and down, while in France, Spain, Egypt and Ghana it is three.

In Germany, the third-place team in the second division contests a two-game play-off with the team finishing 16th in the Bundesliga, to determine who will play in the top division the following season. Other nations, such as Italy and England, hold a play-off series featuring semi-finals and a final to determine which of four teams will be promoted along with others that won automatic promotion above them. In Italy, play-offs are also used to determine which side joins three other relegated teams from Serie A. Play-off systems are criticized for turning a whole season into a lottery over one, two or three games, but many people think they maintain interest and add drama.

◀ VfL Osnabruck captain Marc Heider is dejected after his team's relegation to the German 3. Liga in 2021.

HARD FALLERS

Just as clubs can rise, so can they fall. In the 2021-22 season, 15 former champions of the French league (with 31 titles between them) played outside the top division. A slide down the divisions can be sudden or gradual. Deportivo La Coruña won the Spanish League in 2000 and the Intertoto Cup in 2008 yet were relegated twice in three years, so that come 2021, they were playing in the third tier of Spanish football. Napoli was home to Diego Maradona and one of Italian football's aristocrats, winning the league title in 1987 and 1990 and finishing runners-up in the two intervening years. Yet, by the early 2000s they were bankrupt and playing in Serie C, two divisions down from the top flight.

Rarely, however, has a downturn been more dramatic than that experienced by Manchester City or Tasmania 1900 Berlin. In 1937, Manchester City were the English league champions. In the following season, they scored 80 league goals, more than any other side, but were relegated. Tasmania 1900 Berlin were joint first in the early stages of the 1965–66 Bundesliga season. By the end, they were bottom and holders of a series of unenviable records for a season, including: fewest wins (two), most losses (28), most goals against (108) and lowest points total (eight).

◀ Al-Ahly (in white) are Africa's most successful club side, with 42 Egyptian league titles.

◀ KV Mechelen have been promoted to or relegated from the Belgian First Division A 25 times.

FAST RISERS

Some leagues have been dominated by a small number of teams throughout their history. For 43 seasons from 1932, the Uruguayan league title was won by either Peñarol or Nacional (Defensor were champions in 1976). Scotland's Glasgow Rangers hold the world record for the most league championships, with a staggering 55 titles, four more than their arch rivals, Celtic. In some leagues, small teams have risen dramatically from humble beginnings to become champions or contenders. In Europe, the now mighty Bayern Munich were not considered successful enough to join the Bundesliga in the early 1960s, but since then they have become one of the pillars of German football.

FACTFILE

In 2017, newly promoted side Génération Foot won the Senegal Premier League by 13 points. The previous year's champions, US Gorée, finished bottom and were relegated.

▶ Jesús Medina in action for New York City FC on their way to winning the 2021 MLS Cup. It was the fast-rising club's first trophy, having joined the MLS just six years earlier.

▶ Inter Milan striker Lautaro Martinez is challenged in a 2021 clash with Serie A debutants Spezia Calcio.

SERIE A

For decades, Serie A was considered the ultimate test for the world's top players. Some clubs have since struggled with the results of their former lavish spending on players. Winning Serie A is sometimes referred to as the *scudetto* (small shield), as the champions' strip the following season bears a small coat of arms in Italian colours. Internazionale, for example, won the UEFA Cup in 1994, but could only manage 13th place in the league. Juventus are the most successful Serie A club, with 35 titles, followed by Internazionale (19), AC Milan (18) and Genoa (nine). In the 2021-22 season, only three former champions – Casale, Novese and Pro Vercelli – were playing in lower divisions.

THE BUNDESLIGA

Starting in 1965, the Bundesliga is considered one of the powerhouses of club football and a breeding ground for innovative coaches. It is the best-supported league in world football, with an average attendance during the 2018-19 season of 43,358 spectators per game – astonishing considering the league included SC Freiburg, whose stadium can only hold 24,000. Bayern Munich are the Bundesliga's most successful team by far, with 30 titles, followed by Borussia Dortmund and Borussia Mönchengladbach (five each) and Werder Bremen (four). Polish striker Robert Lewandowski's 308 goals puts him well ahead of current rivals, but still far behind the legendary Gerd Müller's record of 365 Bundesliga goals.

◣ Pedri of Barcelona (right) challenges Real Madrid's Nacho Fernandez as the La Liga giants meet in 2020.

▲ Borussia Dortmund's superstar striker Erling Haaland breaks through the Bayern Munich defence in a 2021 Bundesliga encounter.

LA LIGA

The Spanish league banned foreign players between 1963 and 1973, but since then it has been the home of some of the world's greatest footballers, from Johan Cruyff and Lionel Messi to current stars Luis Suárez, Jan Oblak and João Félix. The league can be highly competitive but is mostly dominated by Real Madrid and Barcelona. La Liga has two professional divisions and a series of amateur divisons. Unlike other national leagues, the reserve sides of the major clubs play in the lower divisions, not in a separate reserves league. Real Madrid and Barcelona remain La Liga's most wealthy and successful clubs, with 60 league titles between them.

ENGLISH PREMIER LEAGUE

In the early 1990s, England's first division clubs broke away from league control to form the Premier League. Money has flooded into the top clubs' coffers and a wide gap has opened up between established sides and newly promoted teams who may find it hard to stay up. Manchester United won 13 of the first 21 titles. Their battle for supremacy was fought initially against clubs like Arsenal and Chelsea, before Manchester City, with five recent titles up to 2021, and Liverpool joined the fray. Currently featuring many of the world's most elite players, such as Kevin de Bruyne and Mo Salah, its matches attract massive worldwide TV audiences.

◀ James Milner of Liverpool (left) and Man City's Phil Foden in 2021.

▼ The USA's National Women's Soccer League has been home to many of the world's very best female players, including high profile US internationals such as Megan Rapinoe and Alex Morgan. Below, Orlando Pride's Meggie Dougherty Howard holds off Caprice Dydasco of NJ/NY Gotham City FC.

LIGUE 1

Despite having produced some of the world's greatest players, the French league has traditionally not been as well funded as others in Europe. Its home-grown stars, such as Paul Pogba and Karim Benzema, usually move abroad. Bolstered by PSG's extreme spending, this is now changing, with French teams highly competitive in Europe and home to some of the world's most exciting players. AS Saint-Étienne and Marseille have each won the league ten times, but more recently Lyon (Olympique Lyonnais), Lille and PSG – who won seven titles between 2013 and 2020 – have triumphed.

ASIAN LEAGUES

The first professional league in Asia was South Korea's K-League, which began with just five teams in 1983 and now features 22 sides split over two divisions. The league's most successful side is Seongnam Ilhwa Chunma, with seven titles. Japan's J.League kicked off in 1993 and now has two divisions. Kashima Antlers are the most successful side with eight titles, whilst the league was won in both 2020 and 2021 by Kawasaki Frontale. The Chinese Super League has been won by Guangzhou Evergrande eight times since it began in 2004.

MAJOR LEAGUE SOCCER (MLS)

An unusual league system with two parallel conferences, Eastern and Western, and no promotion or relegation, the MLS kicked off in 1996 with ten teams. It is now expanding to three times that size, with the likes of Austin and Charlotte joining recently, and St Louis and Sacramento arriving in 2023. The league mixes home-grown players with foreign stars, which in the past included David Beckham and Thierry Henry, and currently features Javier Hernandez, Blaise Matuidi and Carles Gil. The LA Galaxy, with five championships and D.C. United with four, are the MLS's most successful sides.

FACTFILE

In the 1998 Swedish league championship, AIK Solna scored fewer goals than any of their 13 opponents (just 25 in 26 matches), yet still managed to win the title.

CLUB CUP COMPETITIONS

In 1872, Wanderers beat Royal Engineers by one goal to nil to win the first FA Cup – the oldest surviving major cup competition. Since that time, hundreds of cup competitions have been introduced all over the world. Some, such as the UEFA Super Cup and the African Super Cup, are contested between the winners of other cup competitions.

COPA LIBERTADORES

South America's first international club competition was staged by Chilean club Colo Colo in 1948 and won by Brazil's Vasco da Gama. However, it was not until 1960 that a regular competition, the Copa Libertadores, was set up. Peñarol of Uruguay won the first two contests, but were defeated in the final of the third by Santos, courtesy of two goals from Pelé. Today, the Copa Libertadores begins with nine groups of four teams and culminates in knockout rounds ending, since 2019, in a single-match final. It is open to the highest-placed sides of each South American nation and between 1960 and 1987, the previous winner received a bye until the semi-finals of the competition. The Copa Libertadores has always outshone the national team competition – the Copa América – and other South American cups in popularity and passion.

Clubs from Argentina (25 times), Brazil (21 times) and Uruguay (8 times) have won the most Copas, with Independiente the leading winners with seven titles. There have been eight occasions when the champions came from elsewhere. In 2016, Colombia's Atlético Nacional triumphed, beating Independiente del Valle of Ecuador in the final. Two years later, another Colombian side, Atlético Huila, won the women's version of the competition, the Copa Libertadores Femenina, which has been held since 2009 and has been mostly won by Brazilian teams.

◀ The 2021 Copa Libertadores final was contested by Palmeiras and Flamengo.

▼ Tamires (left) and Victória of Corinthians with the Copa Libertadores Femenina trophy in 2021.

AROUND THE WORLD

The Copa Libertadores and the UEFA Champions League (see pages 133–134) are the most famous continental club competitions. The winners of these two events used to play each other in the Intercontinental Cup (later, the World Club Cup) but in 2000, a new competition, the FIFA Club World Cup, ran and eventually took over. It features the winners of each continent's leading club competition. The 2021 competition, held in the United Arab Emirates, featured seven teams and was won by Chelsea for the first time.

Africa's most prestigious competition is the African Champions League. In recent years, Tunisian, Moroccan and Egyptian clubs have dominated, with Al-Ahly winning ten times, including the 2020 and 2021 competitions. The last sub-Saharan winners, Mamelodi Sundowns (2016), also hold the record for the biggest victory, an 11-1 thrashing of Côte d'Or FC from the Seychelles in 2019.

The Asian Champions League is highly competitive, with 24 different winners so far, from Thai Farmers Bank to Saudi Arabian club Al-Hilal – the leading winners with four titles.

▲ Al-Ahly's Aliou Dieng (left) is tackled by Mosa Lebusa of Mamelodi Sundowns in a 2021 African Champions League tie.

CUPS IN EUROPE

All European nations have at least one cup competition for clubs in addition to their leagues. Among the most famous are the Copa del Rey in Spain, first held in 1903, and the Coupe de France, which was first contested in 1917. The oldest surviving cup competition in the world is England's FA Cup, which celebrated its 150th birthday in 2021. Arsenal have reached the final the most times (21), winning on a record 14 occasions.

Between 1960 and 1999, national cup winners took part in a European-wide Cup-Winners' Cup, won most often by Barcelona although their 1969 final loss to Slovan Bratislava (now of Slovakia) gave Eastern Europe its first major continental cup winner. From 1999, cup winners in Europe's strongest countries, as well as teams with high league finishes, gained automatic entry into the UEFA Cup – a large competition founded in 1971 to replace the Inter-Cities Fairs Cup. In 2009, the UEFA Cup was reformatted as the Europa League, with preliminary stages followed by 12 mini-leagues, each containing four teams, then a 32-team knockout competition. With multiple entrants from the bigger nations, it is no surprise that ten UEFA Cup or Europa League finals have been contested by teams from the same country. Spanish clubs have won the most titles (13). Sevilla are the most successful team with six victories, the latest in 2020.

▶ Villareal striker Paco Alcácer kisses the UEFA Europa League trophy after his side won the competition for the first time in 2021.

EUROPEAN CHAMPIONS

European club competitions date back to 1927, when the Mitropa Cup was first contested by the leading clubs of central Europe. Sparta Prague were its first winners. The last Mitropa Cup was won by Yugoslav side Borac Banja Luka in 1992, but by then the glamour of the Mitropa had long been eclipsed by the mighty European Cup, a competition that is now known as the UEFA Champions League.

▲ Inter celebrate their win in 1964, a 3-1 victory over Real Madrid.

▼ The two greatest players of the Champions League era, Lionel Messi and Cristiano Ronaldo, compete in 2008.

EARLY DAYS

The European Champion Clubs' Cup, usually known as the European Cup, developed out of a meeting set up by Frenchman Gabriel Hanot. Italian, Spanish, French and Portuguese club sides were keen to take part, as were teams from many other nations. The first European Cup, held in 1955–56, featured major names such as Real Madrid, Sporting Lisbon, Anderlecht and AC Milan. Clubs that are less well known today also entered – Århus GF and FC Saarbrucken, for example. English league champions Chelsea, however, were forbidden from entering, but Scottish club Hibernian reached the semi-final. The first winners of the trophy were Real Madrid.

CHANGING CHAMPIONS

Real won the first five European Cups, before the tournament hit a golden age of competition in the 1960s, with Benfica, Internazionale and AC Milan all winning the trophy. The 1970s saw both Ajax and Bayern Munich crowned champions three years in a row. English clubs won six European Cups in succession from 1977, but were banned from European competition for five years after the 1985 Heysel Stadium disaster (see page 103). There have been 18 Spanish winners, and 13 English and 12 Italian champions.

As the European Cup grew in intensity, it became harder to successfully defend the title. No team managed to retain their crown between AC Milan's win in 1990 and Real Madrid's in 2017. The first year that the final went into extra time was 1958, while the first penalty shootout in the final was in 1984. The two finals won by Eastern European sides, Steaua Bucharest (1986) and Red Star Belgrade (1991), both went to nail-biting penalty shootouts.

FACTFILE
Swedish striker Zlatan Ibrahimovic is the only player to have scored in Champions League games for six teams: Ajax, Juventus, Internazionale, Barcelona, AC Milan and Paris Saint-Germain.

EUROPEAN CUP / CHAMPIONS LEAGUE WINNERS

Year	Winner	Year	Winner	Year	Winner
1956	Real Madrid	1980	Nottingham Forest	2004	Porto
1957	Real Madrid	1981	Liverpool	2005	Liverpool
1958	Real Madrid	1982	Aston Villa	2006	Barcelona
1959	Real Madrid	1983	Hamburg	2007	AC Milan
1960	Real Madrid	1984	Liverpool	2008	Manchester United
1961	Benfica	1985	Juventus	2009	Barcelona
1962	Benfica	1986	Steaua Bucharest	2010	Internazionale
1963	AC Milan	1987	Porto	2011	Barcelona
1964	Internazionale	1988	PSV Eindhoven	2012	Chelsea
1965	Internazionale	1989	AC Milan	2013	Bayern Munich
1966	Real Madrid	1990	AC Milan	2014	Real Madrid
1967	Celtic	1991	Red Star Belgrade	2015	Barcelona
1968	Manchester United	1992	Barcelona	2016	Real Madrid
1969	AC Milan	1993	Marseille	2017	Real Madrid
1970	Feyenoord	1994	AC Milan	2018	Real Madrid
1971	Ajax	1995	Ajax	2019	Liverpool
1972	Ajax	1996	Juventus	2020	Bayern Munich
1973	Ajax	1997	Borussia Dortmund	2021	Chelsea
1974	Bayern Munich	1998	Real Madrid		
1975	Bayern Munich	1999	Manchester United		
1976	Bayern Munich	2000	Real Madrid		
1977	Liverpool	2001	Bayern Munich		
1978	Liverpool	2002	Real Madrid		
1979	Nottingham Forest	2003	AC Milan		

▶ Manchester United's Teddy Sheringham (left) and David Beckham. Sheringham scored the first of two injury-time goals to win the 1999 final.

▲ Gareth Bale scores a spectacular bicycle kick goal for Real Madrid against Liverpool in the 2018 final. He scored a second goal 20 minutes later and was made man of the match.

EXPANSION AND DOMINATION

The format of the European Cup remained almost unchanged for its first 35 years. Teams competed in knockout rounds, playing one match at home and one away. If the scores were tied after the two games, the team with more away goals would go through. For many years, the competition was open only to the league champions of each country. Today, as many as four sides from each top league take part.

In 1992, everything changed. The competition was revamped as the UEFA Champions League. Group stages were introduced, guaranteeing qualifying teams a series of games and vast sums of television money. With a prize pot now in excess of two billion euros per season and more than 85 million euros guaranteed for winning, participating in the competition is essential for the financial health of Europe's top teams. Failure to qualify can be a financial disaster. The format has been tweaked and expanded on a number of occasions, with major changes planned for the 2024-25 season: the abandonment of groups in favour of one 36-club league with teams each playing one match against ten different opponents and the top 16 progressing to the later stages.

MAGIC MOMENTS

Now the most-watched club competition in the world, the UEFA Champions League has provided fans with many astonishing games and moments. These have occurred at the group stage – such as in 1994 when Werder Bremen, down 3-0 after 65 minutes, roared back to triumph 5-3 against Anderlecht. They can also occur in the final, such as in 2005 when AC Milan entered the second half comfortable 3-0 leaders only for their opponents, Liverpool, to stage a remarkable comeback victory. In the same year, Inter Milan's Dejan Stanković produced one of the best goals of the competition, striking a volley from just past the halfway line which sailed over Manuel Neuer into the Schalke net. Another German side, Bayer Leverkusen, were on the receiving end of a Lionel Messi masterclass in 2012 as Barcelona's maestro scored five goals in a 7-1 rout. Messi has scored a staggering 125 goals so far in Champions League games, plus 41 goal assists. He is eclipsed only by his rival Cristiano Ronaldo, who has notched 140 goals and 48 assists in 182 matches, the most appearances of any player. He has won the competition five times. Since Inter Milan's 2010 triumph, all the winners have come from Germany, Spain or England.

FACTFILE

19-year-old Erling Haaland scored a hat-trick in the first half of his debut in the competition for Red Bull Salzburg versus Genk in 2018. For Borussia Dortmund, he was the 2020-21 Champions League top scorer with ten goals.

▲▲ Goalkeeper Georgios Athanasiadis of minnows FC Sheriff celebrates his side's stunning Group D victory over 13-time champions Real Madrid in 2021.

▲ Sebastian Haller scores for four-times champions Ajax against Besiktas in 2021.

◀ Robert Lewandowski with the trophy after Bayern Munich's 2020 triumph.

FACTFILE

Eintracht Frankfurt have conceded the fastest goal in a women's final – scored by Marta after 12 seconds for Umeå in 2008 – and scored the latest goal in a final – by Birgit Prinz after 93 minutes in 2006.

WOMEN'S CHAMPIONS LEAGUE

In 2001, UEFA founded the Women's Cup for leading women's clubs in Europe. Thirty-three clubs entered the competition, which saw Eintracht Frankfurt beat Swedish club Umeå IK 2-0 in the final. In early competitions, mismatches saw some one-sided scorelines – Armenia's CSC Yerevan conceding 18 goals in a 2001-02 group game, for example. At the elite end, competition was hotting up with German, Swedish and French sides to the fore and Russian, English and Spanish sides not far behind.

The competition was rebadged as the UEFA Women's Champions League in 2009 and 53 clubs entered, with Potsdam defeating Lyon 7-6 on penalties in the final. The 2018 final again featured Lyon in the middle of an unprecedented run of five titles. After 90 tense minutes against Vfl Wolfsburg it was 0-0. By the end of extra time however, it was 4-1 to the French champions. One of their goals was scored by Ada Hegerberg, who notched 15 during the campaign – still a competition record. Lyon looked unstoppable season-after-season until they faced PSG in the 2021 quarter-finals and went out on away goals. PSG were then narrowly defeated by Barcelona who routed Chelsea 4-0 in the final to record the first Spanish victory in the competition.

WOMEN'S CUP / WOMEN'S CHAMPIONS LEAGUE WINNERS

2002	Eintracht Frankfurt
2003	Umeå IK
2004	Umeå IK
2005	Turbine Potsdam
2006	Eintracht Frankfurt
2007	Arsenal
2008	Eintracht Frankfurt
2009	FCR 2001 Duisburg
2010	Turbine Potsdam
2011	Lyon
2012	Lyon
2013	Vfl Wolfsburg
2014	Vfl Wolfsburg
2015	Eintracht Frankfurt
2016	Lyon
2017	Lyon
2018	Lyon
2019	Lyon
2020	Lyon
2021	Barcelona

▲ Lieke Martens (top) celebrates after scoring for Barcelona in the second leg of the Champions League semi-final in 2021.

▶ Lyon's Ada Hegerberg with the trophy in 2019. The win over Barcelona was the French club's sixth Champions League title.

BRITISH FOOTBALL

Britain is thought of as the birthplace of football – in the late 19th century, pioneering league and cup competitions were set up in England and Scotland. Many of them survive to this day.

CHANGING DIVISIONS

The English league kicked off in 1888, with 12 teams playing in a single division. It was expanded to two divisions of 18 clubs in 1898 and to four divisions containing 92 teams in 1950. Despite several changes in structure – including the creation in 1992 of a Premier League for the top 22 clubs (reduced to 20 teams in 1994) and the rebranding of the football league as the Championship, League One and League Two – the figure of 92 clubs linked by promotion and relegation between the divisions remains in place. In 2013, Cardiff City were promoted to the Premier League, joining Swansea City as the two Welsh clubs in the top four English divisions, while one England-based club, Berwick Rangers, plays in the Scottish league (formed in 1891).

Many clubs have moved to new grounds, but only one has moved towns – in 2004, Wimbledon became Milton Keynes Dons. In protest, Wimbledon supporters set up their own amateur club, AFC Wimbledon, which began the long climb up the English league pyramid and entered the Football League in 2011. Five years later, they met Milton Keynes Dons in the league for the first time.

CUP DREAMS

Despite the growing influence of European competitions, the FA Cup and Scottish Cup retain their appeal for clubs and fans alike. A staggering 736 clubs entered the 2020–21 FA Cup, most starting in the extra-preliminary rounds. It is the dream of every non-league and lower league club to reach the third round and have the chance of giving one of the huge teams a run for their money. The histories of the two cups are littered with notable giant-killing acts – as a non-league side, Yeovil Town (now in the English league) beat league opposition 20 times. Despite the gulf in finance and quality of players, teams from lower divisions do still beat higher-placed opponents. The 2021–22 FA Cup saw giant-killing triumphs such as League One side Cambridge United humbling Newcastle United, Nottingham Forest knocking out Arsenal and National League side Boreham Wood defeating Bournemouth.

At the start of the season, the winners of the FA Cup and the Premier League meet in the Community Shield (formerly the Charity Shield). The first Charity Shield match, in 1908, was between amateur side Queens Park Rangers (the Southern League champions) and Manchester United (the professional league champions). The 2015 game between Arsenal and Chelsea was the first since 2006 not to feature Manchester United or City.

FOREIGN IMPORTS

In the past 30 years, foreign players from all over the world have played in the Scottish and English leagues. Rangers and Chelsea were the first top-flight teams to field sides containing no British players in a league match, while 121 footballers at the 2018 World Cup played their club football in the English Premier League. Foreign managers were far less common until the mid-1990s. Since then, Pep Guardiola (at Manchester City), Jürgen Klopp (at Liverpool) and Arsène Wenger (at Arsenal) have all enjoyed major success. The reigns of foreign coaches of British national teams, such as Fabio Capello and Berti Vogts, were less smooth, however.

NATIONAL TEAMS

At international level, the national teams have suffered mixed fortunes. Under Gareth Southgate, England reached the semi-finals of the 2018 World Cup and the final of EURO 2020. Apart from defeat on penalties in that final, the side went unbeaten throughout 2021. Scotland and Wales both qualified for EURO 2020, with Wales reaching the Round of 16 stage. Both sides finished second in their 2022 World Cup qualifying groups and entered the play-offs for a spot in the finals. Northern Ireland women's team were able to celebrate their EURO debut in 2022, alongside the hosts, England.

WEBSITES

thefa.com
Information on the England national teams, clubs and league tables, plus a section on the FA Cup.

kickitout.org
Learn more about initiatives to kick racism out of football.

shekicks.net
The home of She Kicks magazine, devoted to news and features on women's football.

theguardian.com/football/series/the-100-best-footballers-in-the-world
Profiles of the 100 best players in the world, updated each year.

football-lineups.com
Diagrams and comments on the formations used by teams in thousands of matches.

stadiumguide.com
Information on stadiums around the world.

FACTS AND FIGURES

ENGLISH LEAGUE CHAMPIONS

Clubs from the Midlands and the north dominated the start of the English league, and it was not until 1931 that a southern club, Arsenal, won the title. Manchester United and Liverpool have won the most league titles. Below are the post-war records.

2021 Manchester City
2020 Liverpool
2019 Manchester City
2018 Manchester City
2017 Chelsea
2016 Leicester City
2015 Chelsea
2014 Manchester City
2013 Manchester United
2012 Manchester City
2011 Manchester United
2010 Chelsea
2009 Manchester United
2008 Manchester United
2007 Manchester United
2006 Chelsea
2005 Chelsea
2004 Arsenal
2003 Manchester United
2002 Arsenal
2001 Manchester United
2000 Manchester United
1999 Manchester United
1998 Arsenal
1997 Manchester United
1996 Manchester United
1995 Blackburn Rovers
1994 Manchester United
1993 Manchester United
1992 Leeds United
1991 Arsenal
1990 Liverpool
1989 Arsenal
1988 Liverpool
1987 Everton
1986 Liverpool
1985 Everton
1984 Liverpool
1983 Liverpool
1982 Liverpool
1981 Aston Villa
1980 Liverpool
1979 Liverpool
1978 Nottingham Forest
1977 Liverpool
1976 Liverpool
1975 Derby County
1974 Leeds United
1973 Liverpool
1972 Derby County
1971 Arsenal
1970 Everton
1969 Leeds United
1968 Manchester City
1967 Manchester United
1966 Liverpool
1965 Manchester United
1964 Liverpool
1963 Everton
1962 Ipswich Town
1961 Tottenham Hotspur
1960 Burnley
1959 Wolverhampton Wanderers
1958 Wolverhampton Wanderers
1957 Manchester United
1956 Manchester United
1955 Chelsea
1954 Wolverhampton Wanderers
1953 Arsenal
1952 Manchester United
1951 Tottenham Hotspur
1950 Portsmouth
1949 Portsmouth

SCOTTISH LEAGUE CHAMPIONS

Rangers and Celtic have dominated the Scottish league. In its first year, 1891, Rangers shared the title with Dumbarton; Celtic claimed their first title in 1893. In 2013, the top division was rebadged the Scottish Premiership.

2021 Rangers
2020 Celtic
2019 Celtic
2018 Celtic
2017 Celtic
2016 Celtic
2015 Celtic
2014 Celtic
2013 Celtic
2012 Celtic
2011 Rangers
2010 Rangers
2009 Rangers
2008 Celtic
2007 Celtic
2006 Celtic
2005 Rangers
2004 Celtic
2003 Rangers
2002 Celtic
2001 Celtic
2000 Rangers
1999 Rangers
1998 Celtic
1997 Rangers
1996 Rangers
1995 Rangers
1994 Rangers
1993 Rangers
1992 Rangers
1991 Rangers
1990 Rangers
1989 Rangers
1988 Celtic
1987 Rangers
1986 Celtic
1985 Aberdeen
1984 Aberdeen
1983 Dundee United
1982 Celtic
1981 Celtic
1980 Aberdeen
1979 Celtic
1978 Rangers
1977 Celtic
1976 Rangers
1975 Rangers
1974 Celtic
1973 Celtic
1972 Celtic
1971 Celtic
1970 Celtic
1969 Celtic
1968 Celtic
1967 Celtic
1966 Celtic
1965 Kilmarnock
1964 Rangers
1963 Rangers
1962 Dundee
1961 Rangers
1960 Heart of Midlothian
1959 Rangers
1958 Heart of Midlothian
1957 Rangers
1956 Rangers
1955 Aberdeen
1954 Celtic
1953 Rangers
1952 Hibernian
1951 Hibernian
1950 Rangers
1949 Rangers

FA CUP

The FA Cup is the world's longest-running knockout competition. Arsenal are the most successful side, while Preston North End hold the record for the biggest win, pummelling Hyde United 26-0 in 1887–88. Below are the FA Cup post-war winners and runners-up. An asterisk denotes that extra time was played.

2021 Leicester City 1 Chelsea 0
2020 Arsenal 2 Chelsea 1
2019 Manchester City 6 Watford 0
2018 Chelsea 1 Manchester United 0
2017 Arsenal 2 Chelsea 1
2016 Manchester United 2 Crystal Palace 1*
2015 Arsenal 4 Aston Villa 0
2014 Arsenal 3 Hull City 2*
2013 Wigan 1 Manchester City 0
2012 Chelsea 2 Liverpool 1
2011 Manchester City 1 Stoke City 0
2010 Chelsea 1 Portsmouth 0
2009 Chelsea 2 Everton 1
2008 Portsmouth 1 Cardiff City 0
2007 Chelsea 1 Manchester United 0*
2006 Liverpool 3 West Ham United 3 (3-1 penalties)
2005 Arsenal 0 Manchester United 0* (5-4 penalties)
2004 Manchester United 3 Millwall 0
2003 Arsenal 1 Southampton 0
2002 Arsenal 2 Chelsea 0
2001 Liverpool 2 Arsenal 1
2000 Chelsea 1 Aston Villa 0
1999 Manchester United 2 Newcastle United 0
1998 Arsenal 2 Newcastle United 0
1997 Chelsea 2 Middlesbrough 0
1996 Manchester United 1 Liverpool 0
1995 Everton 1 Manchester United 0
1994 Manchester United 4 Chelsea 0
1993 Arsenal 2 Sheffield Wednesday 1 (replay)
1992 Liverpool 2 Sunderland 0

1991 Tottenham Hotspur 2
Nottingham Forest 1*
1990 Manchester United 1
Crystal Palace 0
(replay after 3-3)
1989 Liverpool 3 Everton 2*
1988 Wimbledon 1 Liverpool 0
1987 Coventry City 3
Tottenham Hotspur 2*
1986 Liverpool 3 Everton 1
1985 Manchester United 1
Everton 0*
1984 Everton 2 Watford 0
1983 Manchester United 4
Brighton and Hove Albion 0
(replay after 2-2)
1982 Tottenham Hotspur 1
QPR 0 (replay after 1-1)
1981 Tottenham Hotspur 3
Manchester City 2
(replay after 1-1)
1980 West Ham United 1
Arsenal 0
1979 Arsenal 3
Manchester United 2
1978 Ipswich Town 1 Arsenal 0
1977 Manchester United 2
Liverpool 1
1976 Southampton 1
Manchester United 0
1975 West Ham United 2
Fulham 0
1974 Liverpool 3
Newcastle United 0
1973 Sunderland 1
Leeds United 0
1972 Leeds United 1 Arsenal 0
1971 Arsenal 2 Liverpool 1
1970 Chelsea 2 Leeds United 1
(replay after 2-2)
1969 Manchester City 1
Leicester City 0
1968 West Bromwich Albion 1
Everton 0*
1967 Tottenham Hotspur 2
Chelsea 1
1966 Everton 3
Sheffield Wednesday 2
1965 Liverpool 2 Leeds United 1*
1964 West Ham United 3
Preston North End 2
1963 Manchester United 3
Leicester City 1
1962 Tottenham Hotspur 3
Burnley 1
1961 Tottenham Hotspur 2
Leicester City 0
1960 Wolverhampton
Wanderers 3
Blackburn Rovers 0

1959 Nottingham Forest 2
Luton Town 1
1958 Bolton Wanderers 2
Manchester United 0
1957 Aston Villa 2
Manchester United 1
1956 Manchester City 3
Birmingham City 1
1955 Newcastle United 3
Manchester City 1
1954 West Bromwich Albion 3
Preston North End 2
1953 Blackpool 4
Bolton Wanderers 3
1952 Newcastle United 1
Arsenal 0
1951 Newcastle United 2
Blackpool 0
1950 Arsenal 2 Liverpool 0
1949 Wolverhampton
Wanderers 3 Leicester City 1
1948 Manchester United 4
Blackpool 2
1947 Charlton Athletic 1 Burnley 0*

SCOTTISH CUP

The Scottish Cup began in 1873 and for half a century was won by a wide range of teams. Arbroath have never won the cup, but in 1885 they thrashed Bon Accord 36-0, the biggest win in British football.

2021 St Johnstone
2020 Celtic
2019 Celtic
2018 Celtic
2017 Celtic
2016 Hibernian
2015 Inverness Caledonian Thistle
2014 St Johnstone
2013 Celtic
2012 Heart of Midlothian
2011 Celtic
2010 Dundee United
2009 Rangers
2008 Celtic
2007 Celtic
2006 Heart of Midlothian
2005 Celtic
2004 Celtic
2003 Rangers
2002 Rangers
2001 Celtic
2000 Rangers
1999 Rangers
1998 Heart of Midlothian
1997 Kilmarnock
1996 Rangers
1995 Celtic

1994 Dundee United
1993 Rangers
1992 Rangers
1991 Motherwell
1990 Aberdeen
1989 Celtic
1988 Celtic
1987 St Mirren
1986 Aberdeen
1985 Celtic
1984 Aberdeen
1983 Aberdeen
1982 Aberdeen
1981 Rangers
1980 Celtic
1979 Rangers
1978 Rangers
1977 Celtic
1976 Rangers
1975 Celtic
1974 Celtic
1973 Rangers
1972 Celtic
1971 Celtic
1970 Aberdeen
1969 Celtic
1968 Dunfermline Athletic
1967 Celtic
1966 Rangers
1965 Celtic
1964 Rangers
1963 Rangers
1962 Rangers
1961 Dunfermline Athletic
1960 Rangers
1959 St Mirren
1958 Clyde
1957 Falkirk
1956 Heart of Midlothian
1955 Clyde
1954 Celtic
1953 Rangers
1952 Motherwell
1951 Celtic
1950 Rangers
1949 Rangers
1948 Rangers
1947 Aberdeen

THE LEAGUE CUP

The League Cup began in 1960 and is open only to the 92 English league clubs. Recently, it has been known as the Carabao Cup. It awards a UEFA Europa Conference League place to the winners.

Number of wins
9 – Liverpool
8 – Manchester City

5 – Aston Villa, Chelsea,
Manchester United
4 – Nottingham Forest,
Tottenham Hotspur
3 – Leicester City

IN EUROPE

Below is a list of the British clubs that have made the final of a major European cup competition.

2021 Chelsea, Champions League,
winners
2021 Manchester City, Champions
League, runners-up
2020 Manchester United, Europa
League, runners-up
2019 Liverpool, Champions
League, winners
2019 Tottenham Hotspur,
Champions League,
runners-up
2019 Chelsea, Europa League,
winners
2019 Arsenal, Europa League,
runners-up
2018 Liverpool, Champions
League, runners-up
2017 Manchester United, Europa
League, winners
2016 Liverpool, Europa League,
runners-up
2013 Chelsea, Europa League,
winners
2012 Chelsea, Champions League,
winners
2011 Manchester United,
Champions League,
runners-up
2010 Fulham, Europa League,
runners-up
2009 Manchester United,
Champions League,
runners-up
2008 Manchester United,
Champions League, winners
2008 Chelsea, Champions League,
runners-up
2008 Glasgow Rangers, UEFA Cup,
runners-up
2007 Liverpool, Champions
League, runners-up
2006 Arsenal, Champions League,
runners-up
2006 Middlesborough, UEFA Cup,
runners-up
2005 Liverpool, Champions
League, winners
2003 Celtic, UEFA Cup,
runners-up

2001 Liverpool, UEFA Cup, winners

2000 Arsenal, UEFA Cup, runners-up

1999 Manchester United, Champions League, winners

1995 Arsenal, Cup-Winners' Cup, runners-up

1994 Arsenal, Cup-Winners' Cup, winners

1991 Manchester United, Cup-Winners' Cup, winners

1987 Dundee United, UEFA Cup, runners-up

1985 Everton, Cup-Winners' Cup, winners

1985 Liverpool, European Cup, runners-up

1984 Liverpool, European Cup, winners

1984 Tottenham Hotspur, UEFA Cup, winners

1983 Aberdeen, Cup-Winners' Cup, winners

1982 Aston Villa, European Cup, winners

1981 Liverpool, European Cup, winners

1981 Ipswich Town, UEFA Cup, winners

1980 Nottingham Forest, European Cup, winners

1980 Arsenal, Cup-Winners' Cup, runners-up

1979 Nottingham Forest, European Cup, winners

1978 Liverpool, European Cup, winners

1977 Liverpool, European Cup, winners

1976 Liverpool, UEFA Cup, winners

1976 West Ham United, Cup-Winners' Cup, runners-up

1975 Leeds United, European Cup, runners-up

1974 Tottenham Hotspur, UEFA Cup, runners-up

1973 Liverpool, UEFA Cup, winners

1973 Leeds United, Cup-Winners' Cup, runners-up

1972 Tottenham Hotspur, UEFA Cup, winners

1972 Rangers, Cup-Winners' Cup, winners

1972 Wolv. Wanderers, UEFA Cup, runners-up

1971 Leeds United, UEFA Cup, winners

1971 Chelsea, Cup-Winners' Cup, winners

1970 Manchester City, Cup-Winners' Cup, winners

1970 Arsenal, Inter-Cities Fairs Cup, winners

1970 Celtic, European Cup, runners-up

1969 Newcastle United, Inter-Cities Fairs Cup, winners

1968 Manchester United, European Cup, winners

1968 Leeds United, Inter-Cities Fairs Cup, winners

1967 Celtic, European Cup, winners

1967 Rangers, Cup-Winners' Cup, runners-up

1967 Leeds United, Inter-Cities Fairs Cup, runners-up

1966 Liverpool, Cup-Winners' Cup, runners-up

1965 West Ham United, Cup-Winners' Cup, winners

1963 Tottenham Hotspur, Cup-Winners' Cup, winners

1961 Rangers, Cup-Winners' Cup, runners-up

1961 Birmingham City, Inter-Cities Fairs Cup, runners-up

APPEARANCE RECORDS

MOST LEAGUE APPEARANCES
1005 – Peter Shilton (1966–97)

MOST LEAGUE APPEARANCES AT ONE CLUB
770 – John Trollope, Swindon Town (1960–80)

MOST APPEARANCES IN CONSECUTIVE GAMES
401 – Harold Bell, Tranmere Rovers (1946–55)

MOST INTERNATIONAL CAPS
ENGLAND
125 Peter Shilton (1970–90)
120 Wayne Rooney (2003–18)
115 David Beckham (1996–2009)
114 Steven Gerrard (2000–14)

SCOTLAND
102 Kenny Dalglish (1972–87)
91 Jim Leighton (1983–99)
80 Darren Fletcher (2003–17)
77 Alex McLeish (1980–93)

WALES
106 Chris Gunter (2007–)
100 Gareth Bale (2006–)
98 Chris Gunter (2007–)
92 Neville Southall (1982–98)
86 Ashley Williams (2008–19)
85 Gary Speed (1990–2004)

NORTHERN IRELAND
132 Steven Davis (2005–)
119 Pat Jennings (1964–86)
112 Aaron Hughes (1998–2018)
95 David Healy (2000–13)

YOUNGEST INTERNATIONAL CAPS
England – Theo Walcott (17 years, 75 days)
Scotland – John Lambie (17 years, 91 days)
Wales – Harry Wilson (16 years, 207 days)
Northern Ireland – Norman Whiteside (17 years, 41 days)

GOAL RECORDS

MOST GOALS IN A CAREER
550 – Jimmy McGrory (Celtic, Clydebank and Scotland)
464 – Arthur Rowley (West Bromwich Albion, Fulham, Leicester City, Shrewsbury Town)

MOST PREMIER LEAGUE GOALS
260 – Alan Shearer (1992–2005)

MOST GOALS IN A SEASON
60 – Dixie Dean, Everton (1927–28)

MOST GOALS IN A GAME
13 – John Petrie for Arbroath v Bon Accord, 1885

LEADING INTERNATIONAL GOALSCORERS
ENGLAND
53 Wayne Rooney (2003–18)
49 Bobby Charlton (1958–70)
48 Harry Kane (2015–)
48 Gary Lineker (1984–92)
44 Jimmy Greaves (1959–67)

SCOTLAND
30 Kenny Dalglish (1972–87)
30 Denis Law (1959–74)
24 Hugh Gallacher (1924–35)

WALES
36 Gareth Bale (2006–)
28 Ian Rush (1980–96)
23 Ivor Allchurch (1951–66)

NORTHERN IRELAND
36 David Healy (2000–13)
20 Kyle Lafferty (2006–16)
13 Colin Clarke (1986–93)
13 Billy Gillespie (1913–32)

GLOSSARY

Advantage rule A rule that allows the referee to let play continue after a foul if it is to the advantage of the team that has been fouled against.

AFC The Asian Football Confederation, responsible for running football in Asia.

Agent A person who represents footballers and negotiates contracts and transfer moves.

Anchor A midfielder positioned just in front of, and who protects, the defence. An anchor player may allow other midfielders to push further forwards.

Assist A pass that releases a player to score a goal. An assist can be a pass on the ground, a flick or a cross from which a headed goal is scored.

Away goals rule A rule used in some cup competitions. If the scores are equal over two legs, the team that has scored more goals away from home wins.

Backpass rule A law stating that a deliberate pass backwards by a player to his or her goalkeeper cannot be handled by the keeper.

CAF The *Confédération Africaine de Football*, which runs football in Africa.

Cap Recognition given to a player for each appearance in an international game for his or her country.

Catenaccio A defensive tactical system in which a sweeper plays behind a solid defence.

Caution Another word for a yellow card (a warning from the referee to a player for a foul or infringement). A player who receives two yellow cards in a match is automatically shown a red card and sent off.

Central defender The defender who plays in the middle of the last line of defence.

Chip A pass lofted into the air from a player to a team-mate or as a shot on goal.

CONCACAF The Confederation of North, Central American and Caribbean Association Football, which runs football in North and Central America.

CONMEBOL The *Confederación Sudamericana de Fútbol*, which runs football in South America.

Counter-attack A quick attack by a team after it regains possession of the ball.

Cross To send the ball from a wide position towards the centre of the pitch, often into the opposition penalty area.

Cushioning Using a part of the body to slow down a ball in order to bring it under control.

Derby A match between two rival sides, often located in the same town or city.

Direct free kick A kick awarded to a team because of a serious foul committed by an opponent. A goal may be scored directly from the kick.

Dissent When a player uses words or actions to disagree with the referee's decision.

Distribution The way the ball is released by a goalkeeper or is moved around the pitch by a team.

Dribbling Moving the ball under close control with a series of short kicks or taps.

Drop ball A way of restarting play in which the referee releases the ball to a player of the team that last touched the ball. All other players must be at least 4 metres away.

Extra time A way of deciding a drawn match. It involves two periods of additional play, usually lasting 15 minutes each.

FA (Football Association) The national football federation of England.

Feinting Using fake moves of the head, shoulders and legs to deceive an opponent and put him or her off balance.

FIFA The *Fédération Internationale de Football Association*, the international governing body of soccer.

Formation The way in which a team lines up on the pitch in terms of the numbers of defenders, midfielders and forwards.

Foul An action committed intentionally by a defender to stop an opponent who h as a clear run on goal.

Fourth official An additional match official responsible for displaying added-on time, checking substitutions and aiding the referee and his or her two assistants.

Futsal A type of five-a-side football, supported and promoted by FIFA.

Golden Boot An award given to the player who scores the most goals at a World Cup. It is also an annual award given to the top goalscorer in European club football.

Handball The illegal use of the hand or arm by a player.

Hat-trick Three goals scored by a player in a single match.

Indirect free kick A kick awarded to a team because of a minor foul committed by an opponent. A goal cannot be scored from the kick unless the ball is first touched by a player other than the kicker.

Instep The part of a player's foot where his or her bootlaces lie.

Interception When a player gains possession of the ball by latching onto a pass made by the opposition.

Jockeying A defensive technique of delaying an attacker who has the ball.

Laws of the game The 17 main rules of football, established and updated by FIFA.

Libero *See sweeper.*

Man-to-man marking A system of marking in which a defender stays close to and goalside of a single opposition player.

Marking Guarding a player to prevent him or her from advancing the ball towards the goal, making an easy pass or receiving the ball from a team-mate.

MLS Major League Soccer, the American professional male league.

Narrowing the angle A technique in which a goalkeeper moves towards an attacker who has the ball in order to cut down the amount of goal the attacker can aim a shot at.

NWSL National Women's Soccer League, the American professional female league.

Obstruction When a player, instead of trying to win the ball, uses his or her body to prevent an opponent from playing it.

OFC The Oceania Football Confederation, which runs football in Oceania.

Offside A player is offside if he or she is closer to the other team's goal than both the ball and the second-to-last opponent at the moment that the ball is played forwards.

Offside trap A defensive tactic used to trick opposition attackers by leaving them offside. Defenders who play the offside trap usually move upfield together, in a straight line, when the ball is played towards their goal.

Overlap To run outside and beyond a team-mate down the side of the pitch in order to create space and a possible passing opportunity.

Overload When an attacking team has more players in the opposition's half or penalty area than the defending side. An overload often leads to a scoring chance.

Penalty shootout A method of deciding a drawn match by a series of penalties, all taken at one end of the pitch.

Playmaker A skilful midfielder or deep-lying attacker who co-ordinates the attacking movement of a team.

Play-off A match, pair or series of matches used to decide a final placing. In the World Cup, the two losing semi-finalists contest a single play-off game for third place. In many leagues, play-off matches are used to decide relegation and promotion issues.

Referee's assistant An official who assists the referee during the game by signalling for fouls, infringements and offsides.

Reserve team A team made up of players who are not in the first team at a club or national side.

Scout A person employed by a football club who attends games and training sessions to look for up-and-coming players.

Set piece A planned play or move that a team uses when a game is restarted with a free kick, penalty kick, corner kick, goal kick, throw-in or kick-off.

Shielding A technique used by the player with the ball to protect it from a defender who is closely marking them. The player in possession keeps his or her body between the ball and the defender.

Simulation Pretending to be fouled or feigning injury in order to fool the referee. A player found guilty of simulation by the referee receives a yellow card.

Stoppage time Time added to the end of any period of a game to make up for time lost during a major halt in play. Also known as added time or injury time.

Substitution Changing the team line-up on the pitch by replacing one player with another from the substitutes' bench.

Sweeper A defender who can play closest to his or her goal, behind the rest of the defenders, or in a more attacking role with responsibility for bringing the ball forwards.

Tactics Methods of play used in an attempt to outwit and beat an opposition team.

Target man A tall striker, usually the player furthest upfield, at whom team-mates aim their forward passes.

Through ball or pass A pass to a team-mate that puts him or her beyond the opposition's defence and through on goal.

Total football A style of football in which players switch positions all over the pitch. It was made famous by the Dutch national side and Dutch clubs such as Ajax.

UEFA The Union of European Football Associations, which organizes football in Europe.

VAR Short for video assistant referee, this official can be instructed by a referee to review a major incident, such as a penalty or direct red card, on video screens to ensure the right decision is made.

Volley Any ball kicked by a player when it is off the ground.

Wall pass A quick, short pair of passes between two players that sends the ball past a defender. Also known as a one-two pass.

Wing-back A defender on the sides of the pitch who, when the opportunity occurs, makes wide runs forwards in attack.

WUSA The world's first professional football league for women, based in the USA.

Zonal marking A defensive system in which defenders mark opponents who enter their area of the pitch.

INDEX

Page numbers in **bold** refer to main entries.

ACKNOWLEDGEMENTS

The publisher would like to thank the following for permission to reproduce their material.
Top = t, bottom = b, centre = c, left = l, right = r

Prelims and chapter 1
Page 1 LLUIS GENE/AFP/Gettyimages; 2 Matt McNulty—Manchester City/Gettyimages; 4bl Marcio Machado/Gettyimages; 4-5 Alex Pantling/Gettyimages; 5tr Daniel Beloumou Olomo/Gettyimages; 5br Kyodo News/Gettyimages; 6t Popperfoto/Gettyimages; 6bl Stray Toki/Shutterstock; 7t Laurence Griffiths/Gettyimages; 7br Reinhold Thiele/Gettyimages; 8l Alex Caparros—FIFA/Gettyimages; 8t Oli Scarff/Gettyimages; 8cl above Evgeniya Telennaya/Shutterstock; 8br Pressinphoto/Gettyimages; 9tr J. A. Hampton/Stringer/Gettyimages; 9cl below VANDERLEI ALMEIDA/AFP/Gettyimages; 9c Paris Saint-Germain Football/Gettyimages; 10t Central Press/Stringer/Gettyimages; 10b MB Media/Gettyimages; 11l Darren Walsh/Gettyimages; 11r J.LEAGUE/Gettyimages; 12-13 Eric Alonso/Gettyimages.

Chapter 2
14r David Rogers/Gettyimages; 14l; Simon Stacpoole/Offside/Gettyimages; 15tr Kyle Ross/Icon Sportswire/Gettyimages; 15c The Asahi Shimbun/Gettyimages; 15bl Ivica Drusany/Shutterstock; 15br Manuel Queimadelos/Quality Sport Images/Gettyimages; 16t Tim Nwachukwu/Gettyimages; 16b Matt McNulty—Manchester City/Manchester City FC/Gettyimages; 17t PA Images / Alamy Stock Photo; 17c Angel Martinez - FIFA/FIFA/Gettyimages; 18c Matthias Hangst/Gettyimages; 18 bl TT News Agency / Alamy Stock Photo; 18br Silvia Lore/Gettyimages; 19cl OSCAR DEL POZO/AFP/Gettyimages; 19bl LOIC VENANCE/AFP/Gettyimages; 19br Clive Mason/Gettyimages; 20tr ANP Sport/Gettyimages; 20bl Hector Vivas/Stringer/Gettyimages; 21t Andrew Powell/Liverpool FC/Gettyimages; 21l Hector Vivas—FIFA/Gettyimages; 22tr Angel Martinez/Stringer/Gettyimages; 22c ANDREAS SOLARO/AFP/Gettyimages; 22bl Denis Doyle/Stringer/Gettyimages; 22br Harry Langer/DeFodi Images/Gettyimages; 23tr Jose Breton—Pics Action/Shutterstock; 23c Randy Litzinger/Icon Sportswire/Gettyimages; 23bl Andrew Powell/Liverpool FC/Gettyimages; 24t Paul Ellis—Pool/Gettyimages; 24c Randy Litzinger/Icon Sportswire/Gettyimages; 24b Pieter Stam De Jonge/ANP Sport/Gettyimages; 25c Fred Kfoury III/Icon Sportswire/Gettyimages; 25b Buda Mendes/Gettyimages; 26bl Naomi Baker/Gettyimages; 26br Stu Forster/Gettyimages; 27t FRANCK FIFE/AFP/Gettyimages; 27c Alex Livesey—FIFA/Gettyimages; 27b JUSTIN TALLIS/AFP/Gettyimages; 28t Alex Livesey/Stringer/Gettyimages; 28c Michael Regan/Gettyimages; 28b CLIVE BRUNSKILL/POOL/AFP/Gettyimages; 29t LOIC VENANCE/AFP/Gettyimages; 29c FERENC ISZA/AFP/Gettyimages; 30-31 Paul Ellis/Gettyimages.

Chapter 3
32t Ed Lacey/Popperfoto/Gettyimages; 32bl ROMEO GACAD/Staff/Gettyimages; 32br Helios de la Rubia/Real Madrid/Gettyimages; 33t Quality Sport Images/Gettyimages; 33c Central Press/Stringer/Gettyimages; 33b Visionhaus/Gettyimages; 34t Jonathan Moscrop/Gettyimages; 34b Shaun Botterill—UEFA/Gettyimages; 35t Mike Finn-Kelcey/Gettyimages; 35br James Gill-Danehouse/Gettyimages; 35bl Laurence Griffiths/Gettyimages; 36tl Marco Luzzani/Stringer/Gettyimages; 36tr Popperfoto/Gettyimages; 36b Bob Thomas/Gettyimages; 37cl Popperfoto/Gettyimages; 37r Marc Atkins/Gettyimages; 37b Michel Barrault/Onze/Icon Sport/Gettyimages; 38r Ezra O. Shaw/Allsport/Gettyimages; 38tl Popperfoto/Gettyimages; 38b GES-Sportfoto/Gettyimages; 39t Matt McNulty—Manchester City/Gettyimages; 39br Pedro Ugarte/AFP/Gettyimages; 39bl Andrew Dieb/Icon Sportswire/Gettyimages; 40bl Simon

Stacpoole/Offside/Gettyimages; 40c Pressefoto Ulmer/ullstein bild/Gettyimages; 40br Shaun Botterill/Allsport/Gettyimages; 41tl Bob Thomas/Gettyimages; 41cr Popperfoto/Gettyimages; 41bl Alejandro Rios/DeFodi Images/Gettyimages; 42c MICHAEL URBAN/Staff/Gettyimages; 42br Pedro Fiúza/NurPhoto/Gettyimages; 43tl Valerio Pennicino/Corbis/Gettyimages; 43tr Christian Liewig/TempSport/Corbis/Gettyimages; 43bl JEFF PACHOUD/AFP/Gettyimages; 43br Maddie Meyer - FIFA/Gettyimages; 44r John Powell/Liverpool FC/Gettyimages; 44bl Jan Kruger—UEFA/Gettyimages; 45tl Bob Thomas/Gettyimages; 45tr Hulton-Deutsch/CORBIS/Gettyimages; 45b Rafal Oleksiewicz/PressFocus/MB Media/Gettyimages; 46tl Alexandre Schneider/Gettyimages; 46tr Jamie McDonald/Staff/Gettyimages; 46tl Alexandre Schneider/Gettyimages; 47tl Alexander Hassenstein/Staff/Gettyimages; 47tr Ben Radford/Staff/Gettyimages; 47b Bride Lane Library/Popperfoto/Gettyimages; 48bl Mateo Villalba/Quality Sport Images/Gettyimages; 48tr Rolls Press/Popperfoto/Gettyimages; 48br Mark Kolbe/Staff/Gettyimages; 49t Professional Sport/Popperfoto/Gettyimages; 49bl Alessandro Sabattini/Gettyimages; 49br REPORTERS ASSOCIES/Gamma-Rapho/Gettyimages; 50t Alessandro Sabattini/Gettyimages; 50bl David Price/Arsenal FC/Gettyimages; 50br Bob Thomas/Gettyimages; 51t Alex Livesey—FIFA/Gettyimages; 51c Jed Jacobsohn/Gettyimages; 51bl Robyn Beck/AFP/Gettyimages; 51br Baptiste Fernandez/Icon Sport/Gettyimages; 52t Alessandro Sabattini/Gettyimages; 52bl Lars Baron/Gettyimages; 52r Marc Atkins/Gettyimages; 53l Matthias Hangst/Gettyimages; 53b Leo Mason/Popperfoto/Gettyimages; 54 Bob Thomas/Gettyimages; 55 Bob Thomas/Gettyimages.

Chapter 4
56l Dale MacMillan/Soccrates Images/Gettyimages; 56br David Cannon/ALLSPORT/Gettyimages; 57cl TF-Images/Gettyimages; 57bl Yusuf Ozcan/Anadolu Agency/Gettyimages; 57br Matthew Peters/Manchester United/Gettyimages; 58t Stu Forster/Staff/Gettyimages; 58b Adam Pretty/Staff/Gettyimages; 59t Mateo Villalba/Quality Sport Images/Gettyimages; 59cl Brad Smith/ISI Photos/Gettyimages; 60t David Ramos/Staff/Gettyimages; 60b Denis Doyle/Gettyimages; 61t Alexander Hassenstein/POOL/AFP/Gettyimages; 62l Jimmy Bolcina/Photonews/Gettyimages; 62br Jean Catuffe/Gettyimages; 63tl Mike Hewitt/Gettyimages; 63tr Johnny Fidelin/Icon Sport/Gettyimages; 63ct Review News/Shutterstock; 63br VCG/Gettyimages; 64tr VI Images/Gettyimages; 64bl Michael Regan/Staff/Gettyimages; 64br PA Images / Alamy Stock Photo; 65tl Alex Livesey/Staff/Gettyimages; 65c PAUL ELLIS/AFP/Gettyimages; 65b Tottenham Hotspur FC/Gettyimages; 65br Alex Livesey—Danehouse/Gettyimages; 66-67 Richard Heathcote/Gettyimages.

Chapter 5
68bl Popperfoto/Gettyimages; 68br Jamie Sabau/Stringer/Gettyimages; 69l Tony Duffy/Allsport/Gettyimages; 69br Alex Pantling/Gettyimages; 70tr Brad Smith/ISI Photos/Gettyimages; 70br Shaun Botterill/Gettyimages; 71tr Alex Grimm/Gettyimages; 71bl STAFF/AFP/Gettyimages; 72t Rolls Press/Popperfoto/Gettyimages; 72br David Cannon/Allsport/Gettyimages; 73tr Eric Verhoeven/Soccrates Images/Gettyimages; 73cl Paul Popper/Popperfoto/Gettyimages; 73br Julian Finney/Gettyimages; 74tr Rolls Press/Popperfoto/Gettyimages; 74cr Popperfoto/Gettyimages; 74bl Visionhaus/Corbis/Gettyimages; 75bl Allsport/Gettyimages; 75t Alex Grimm/Gettyimages; 76b LLUIS GENE/AFP/Gettyimages; 76tr KHALED DESOUKI/AFP/Gettyimages; 77tr Buda Mendes/Gettyimages; 77bc Popperfoto/Gettyimages; 77bl Clive

Brunskill/Gettyimages; 78tl Jonathan Moscrop/Gettyimages; 78bl Plumb Images/Leicester City FC/Gettyimages; 78/79t RICARDO MORAES/POOL/AFP/Gettyimages; 78/79b Marcelo Endelli/Stringer/Gettyimages; 79cr Gircke/ullstein bild Dtl./Gettyimages; 80tr Laurence Griffiths/Gettyimages; 80br Agustin Marcarian - Pool/Gettyimages; 81tr PHILL MAGAKOE/AFP/Gettyimages; 81bl John Berry/Gettyimages; 82tr Buda Mendes/Gettyimages; 82br Marc Atkins/Gettyimages; 83tr Juan Ignacio Roncoroni—Pool/Gettyimages; 83tr FABRICE COFFRINI/AFP/Gettyimages; 83cl Daniele Badolato—Juventus FC/Gettyimages; 84tr Laurence Griffiths—UEFA/Gettyimages; 84cr Rolls Press/Popperfoto/Gettyimages; 85tr Herman Dingler/BSR Agency/Gettyimages; 85bl Meg Oliphant /Stringer /Gettyimages; 85br Lars Baron/Gettyimages; 86tl Alejandro Rios/DeFodi Images/Gettyimages; 86c KARIM JAAFAR/AFP/Gettyimages; 86br Alexandre Schneider/Stringer/Gettyimages; 87cr Visionhaus/Gettyimages; 87bl Gerrit van Keulen/BSR Agency/Gettyimages; 88tl DRAGOMIR YANKOVIC/PHOTOSPORT/AFP/Gettyimages; 88bl Shaun Botterill/Gettyimages; 88br Ian MacNicol / Stringer/Gettyimages; 89tl Andrey Lukatsky/BSR Agency/Gettyimages; 89br FAYEZ NURELDINE/AFP/Gettyimages; 90-91 Shaun Botterill/Gettyimages.

Chapter 6
92l Andy Bao/Gettyimages; 92br Trond Tandberg/Gettyimages; 93l Pressinphoto/Icon Sport/Gettyimages; 93r The Asahi Shimbun/Gettyimages; 94l Francesco Pecoraro/Stringer/Gettyimages; 94r Urbanandsport/NurPhoto/Gettyimages; 95tl Aurelien Meunier/Stringer/Gettyimages; 95tr Tom Purslow/Manchester United/Visionhaus/Gettyimages; 95bl Joe Prior/Visionhaus/Gettyimages; 95b Wolverhampton Wanderers FC/Gettyimages; 96r (above) Chris Ricco—UEFA/Gettyimages; 96r (below) Alexander Hassenstein—UEFA/Gettyimages; 96b Ali Atmaca/Anadolu Agency/Gettyimages; 97t Ross Kinnaird/Staff/Gettyimages; 97br FRANCOIS XAVIER MARIT/Staff/Gettyimages; 98t Matthias Hangst/Staff/Gettyimages; 98b Simon Stacpoole/Offside/Gettyimages; 99t Marianna Massey—FIFA/Gettyimages; 99l JOHN THYS/AFP/Gettyimages; 99b Marcio Machado/Gettyimages; 100bl DENIS CHARLET/AFP/Gettyimages; 100br Dignity 100/Shutterstock; 101tl Art Konovalov/Shutterstock; 101r Visionhaus/Gettyimages; 101bl OLI SCARFF/AFP/Gettyimages; 102bl David Cannon/Gettyimages; 102br Stuart Franklin/Staff/Gettyimages; 103t STR/Stringer/Gettyimages; 103b Visionhaus/Gettyimages; 104-105 Buda Mendes/Gettyimages.

Chapter 7
106tr Keystone-France/Gamma-Keystone/Gettyimages; 106bl Popperfoto/Gettyimages; 107tl Keystone/Gettyimages; 107t Popperfoto/Gettyimages; 107br ullstein bild/Gettyimages; 108tr ullstein bild/Gettyimages; 108bl Keystone-France/Gettyimages; 109tr Popperfoto/Gettyimages; 109bl Popperfoto/Gettyimages; 110tr STAFF/AFP/Gettyimages; 110bl Alessandro Sabattini/Gettyimages; 111b Bob Thomas/Gettyimages; 112bl Paul Popper/Popperfoto/Gettyimages; 113t Photo by Eric Renard/Onze/Icon Sport/Gettyimages; 113br Bob Thomas/Gettyimages; 114t Lars Baron/Gettyimages; 114bl Laurence Griffiths/Gettyimages; 115t Clive Rose/Gettyimages; 115bl KELLY AYODI/AFP/Gettyimages; 115br Joerg-Drescher/Shutterstock; 116t David Madison/Gettyimages; 116b Bob Thomas/Gettyimages; 117tr Steven Kingsman/Icon Sportswire/Corbis/Gettyimages; 117bl DANIEL ROLAND/AFP/Gettyimages; 117br Baptiste Fernandez/Icon Sport/Gettyimages; 118bl Shaun Botterill/Staff/Gettyimages; 118bc Alex Grimm/Gettyimages; 118br Matthias Hangst/Staff/Gettyimages; 119t Catherine Ivill/Gettyimages; 119b TF-Images/Gettyimages; 120l Gary Prior/Visionhaus/Gettyimages; 120r

Tommy Hindley/Professional Sport/Popperfoto/Gettyimages; 121t Zhizhao Wu/Gettyimages; 121b Alexander Hassenstein/Gettyimages; 122b LatinContent/Stringer/Gettyimages; 122t MB Media/Gettyimages; 123b Visionhaus/Gettyimages; 123t KENZO TRIBOUILLARD/AFP/Gettyimages; 124t Masashi Hara/Gettyimages; 124b KIM JAE-HWAN/AFP/Gettyimages; 125c Nick Tre. Smith/Icon Sportswire/Gettyimages; 125b Anthony Au-Yeung/Stringer/Gettyimages; 126t Baptiste Fernandez/Icon Sport/Gettyimages; 126b Nico Paetzel/TF-Images/Gettyimages; 127l Philippe Crochet/Photo News/Gettyimages; 127r Islam Safwat/NurPhoto/Gettyimages; 127b Steph Chambers/Staff/Gettyimages; 128t Gabriele Maltinti/Stringer/Gettyimages; 128c Alexandre Simoes/Borussia Dortmund/Gettyimages; 128b LLUIS GENE/AFP/Gettyimages; 129t Michael Regan/Staff/Gettyimages; 129b Roy K. Miller/ISI Photos/Gettyimages; 130l Agencia Gamba/Stringer/Gettyimages; 130r EITAN ABRAMOVICH/AFP/Gettyimages; 131t PHILL MAGAKOE/AFP/Gettyimages; 131b Boris Streubel—UEFA/Gettyimages; 132tr Popperfoto/Gettyimages; 132r Jasper Juinen/Staff/Gettyimages; 133r PATRICK HERTZOG/AFP/Gettyimages; 133l David Ramos/Gettyimages; 134tr Diego Souto/Quality Sport Images/Gettyimages; 134cr MAURICE VAN STEEN/ANP/Gettyimages; 134b Matt Childs/Pool/Gettyimages; 135l Eric Alonso/Gettyimages; 135b Daniela Porcelli/Gettyimages.

Poster
Tc Alexandre Schneider/Gettyimages; tr Matthias Hangst/Gettyimages; bc Manuel Queimadelos//Quality Sport Images/Gettyimages; br Catherine Ivill/Gettyimages.